Excel® 2013

FOR

DUMMIES®

eLEARNING KIT

by Faithe Wempen

FOR
DUMMIES®
A Wiley Brand

Excel® 2013 eLearning Kit For Dummies®

Published by: **John Wiley & Sons, Inc.,** 111 River Street, Hoboken, NJ 07030-5774, www.wiley.com

Copyright © 2014 by John Wiley & Sons, Inc., Hoboken, New Jersey

Media and software compilation copyright © 2014 by John Wiley & Sons, Inc. All rights reserved.

Published simultaneously in Canada

No part of this publication may be reproduced, stored in a retrieval system or transmitted in any form or by any means, electronic, mechanical, photocopying, recording, scanning or otherwise, except as permitted under Sections 107 or 108 of the 1976 United States Copyright Act, without the prior written permission of the Publisher. Requests to the Publisher for permission should be addressed to the Permissions Department, John Wiley & Sons, Inc., 111 River Street, Hoboken, NJ 07030, (201) 748-6011, fax (201) 748-6008, or online at http://www.wiley.com/go/permissions.

Trademarks: Wiley, For Dummies, the Dummies Man logo, Dummies.com, Making Everything Easier, and related trade dress are trademarks or registered trademarks of John Wiley & Sons, Inc. and may not be used without written permission. Excel is a registered trademark of Microsoft Corporation. All other trademarks are the property of their respective owners. John Wiley & Sons, Inc. is not associated with any product or vendor mentioned in this book.

For general information on our other products and services, please contact our Customer Care Department within the U.S. at 877-762-2974, outside the U.S. at 317-572-3993, or fax 317-572-4002. For technical support, please visit www.wiley.com/techsupport.

Wiley publishes in a variety of print and electronic formats and by print-on-demand. Some material included with standard print versions of this book may not be included in e-books or in print-on-demand. If this book refers to media such as a CD or DVD that is not included in the version you purchased, you may download this material at http://booksupport.wiley.com. For more information about Wiley products, visit www.wiley.com.

Library of Congress Control Number: 2013946295

ISBN 978-1-118-49304-5 (pbk); ISBN 978-1-118-49191-1 (ebk); ISBN 978-1-118-49310-6 (ebk)

Manufactured in the United States of America

10 9 8 7 6 5 4 3 2 1

Contents at a Glance

Table of Contents

Introduction

*I*f you've been thinking about taking a class on the Internet (it is all the rage these days), but you're concerned about getting lost in the electronic fray, worry no longer. *Excel 2013 eLearning Kit For Dummies* is here to help you, providing you with a hands-on learning experience that includes not only the book and CD you hold in your hands, but also an online course at www.dummieselearning.com. Consider this introduction your primer.

About This Kit

Whether you follow along with the book, go online for the courses, or some combination of the two, the 11 lessons in *Excel 2013 eLearning Kit For Dummies* walk you through examples and exercises so that you learn how to do the following:

- ✔ Create basic worksheets and navigate the Excel interface — no previous experience required!

- ✔ Format and print attractive worksheets and easy-to-read graphical charts. You even find out how to create conditional formatting based on specific criteria, such as which cells hold a value that's higher or lower than a number you specify.

- ✔ Write formulas and functions that calculate and summarize data, including powerful specialized functions for financial, statistical, and logical operations.

- ✔ Manage tables and lists that store database data in Excel format, and use analysis tools, such as Goal Seek and Solver, to make sense of the data.

✔ Analyze and summarize data with PivotTables and PivotCharts.

✔ Find and fix common errors in formulas, and prevent future data entry errors with data validation tools.

✔ Protect, secure, and share Excel data, ensuring that authorized people can access it and unauthorized people can't.

Each piece of this kit works in conjunction with the others, although you don't need them all to gain valuable understanding of the key concepts.

This book uses a tutorial approach to explain how to use Excel's features. In each lesson, you'll find the following elements:

✔ **Lesson opener questions:** To get you warmed up and ready for the lesson material, the questions quiz you on particular points of interest. If you don't know the answer, a page number heads you in the right direction to find it.

✔ **Tutorial step-by-step instruction with sample Excel workbooks:** Each lesson introduces an important task you can do in Excel. You then find step-by-step tutorials that walk you through using the feature or combining skills you've learned so far to accomplish a specific goal. Often, you need to download a sample Excel file that goes with the steps. See the "Beyond the Book" section later in this Introduction for details on downloading the sample files.

✔ **Summing Up:** This section appears at the end of each lesson; it briefly reiterates the content you just learned.

✔ **Try-it-yourself lab:** Test your knowledge of the content just covered by performing an activity from scratch — that is, using general steps only and no sample files.

✔ **Know this tech talk:** Each lesson contains a brief glossary of related terms.

A few style conventions help you navigate the book piece of this kit efficiently:

✔ Instructions and names of the files needed to follow along with the step lists are italicized.

✔ Website addresses, or URLs, are shown in a special monofont typeface `like this`.

✔ Numbered steps that you need to follow and characters you need to type are set in **bold.**

Used in conjunction with the tutorial text, the online course that goes with this kit gives you the tools you need for a productive and self-guided eLearning experience. Here's how the course helps you get up-to-speed on Excel:

- ✔ **Multimedia-based instruction:** After each feature is introduced, you'll find plentiful video clips, illustrations, and interactive widgets that show you how a feature or task works. The course is like having a tutor ready and willing to show you how a process works as many times as you need until you're confident in what you've learned. Or if you're pretty comfortable with certain parts of Excel, you can breeze past those parts of the course instead.

- ✔ **Interactive quizzes and activities:** Ample interactive elements enable you to understand how Excel works and check what you've learned. Hands-on activities enable you to try working in Excel yourself and receive feedback on what skills you still need to practice.

- ✔ **Resources:** Throughout the online course, you'll find extra resources relevant to what you're learning. Also, if you're new to Microsoft Office, you'll find a guide to basic tasks common to all Microsoft Office programs, including Excel as well as Word, PowerPoint, and so on.

For details about getting your access code for the online course, see the "Beyond the Book" section later in this Introduction.

Foolish Assumptions

For starters, I assume you know what eLearning is, need to find out how to use Excel (and fast!), and want to get a piece of this academic action the fun and easy way with *Excel 2013 eLearning Kit For Dummies*.

I assume you have basic Windows and computer skills, such as starting the computer and using the mouse.

To get the most out of this kit, you need a Windows computer running Excel 2013. That way, you can experience the benefit of the tutorial steps in the book and the hands-on instruction in the online course.

Icons Used in This Kit

The familiar and helpful *For Dummies* icons point you in the direction of really great information that's sure to help you as you work your way through this kit. Look for these icons throughout the book and the online course:

The Tip icon points out helpful information that's likely to make your job easier.

This icon marks an interesting and useful fact — something that you might want to remember for later.

The Warning icon highlights lurking danger. When you see this icon, you know to pay attention and proceed with caution.

Sometimes I might change things up by directing you to repeat a set of steps but with different parameters. If you're up for the challenge, look for the Practice icon.

In addition to the icons, you also find two friendly study aids that bring your attention to certain pieces of information:

- ✔ **Lingo:** When you see the Lingo box, look for a definition of a key term or concept.

- ✔ **Extra Info:** This box highlights something to pay close attention to in a figure or points out other useful information that's related to the discussion.

Beyond the Book

This kit includes much more than the book and CD you hold in your hand. This section is your handy guide to finding all the content that goes with this kit, which includes the following:

- ✔ **eCourse:** When you want to learn using the eCourse, visit www.dummies elearning.com and use the access code that comes with this book to access the entire Excel course. For help finding your access code, see the Appendix in the back of this book.

- ✔ **Companion files:** You can download the companion files that go with the tutorial steps in this book from the CD or online at www.dummies. com/extras/excel2013elearning. For details about downloading files from the CD, see the "About the CD" Appendix at the end of this book. If you don't have access to a CD drive, or if you're reading this as an e-book, use your web browser of choice to go to http://book support.wiley.com and access the full contents of the CD-ROM.

- ✔ **Online articles and extras:** If you have questions about Excel that you don't find answered in this kit, check out the free online articles at Dummies.com. You'll also find help with evolving features that are related to Excel, but that Microsoft is likely to change independently of Excel, such as Microsoft's cloud storage space (that is, a free service for storing your files online so you can access them from anywhere).

To find these extras related specifically to this kit, point your browser to www.dummies.com/extras/excel2013elearning.

Where to Go from Here

Now that you're primed and ready, time to begin.

Lesson 1

Creating Basic Worksheets

- Selecting ranges enables you to apply a single command to multiple cells at once.

- You can edit the content of a cell either in the cell itself or in the Formula bar.

- Moving and copying data between cells saves data-entry time and effort.

- Dragging the fill handle copies cell content quickly into many cells at once.

- Inserting and deleting rows and columns in a worksheet changes its structure without moving content.

- Renaming a worksheet tab enables you to assign a more meaningful title to a sheet.

- Inserting new worksheets into a workbook enables you to expand a workbook's capacity.

	A	B	C
9			
10	Date	Pmt#	
11	Jan-15	1	
12	Feb-15	2	
13	Mar-15	3	
14	Apr-15	4	
15	May-15	5	
16	Jun-15	6	
17	Jul-15	7	
18	Aug-15	8	
19	Sep-15	9	
20	Oct-15	10	
21	Nov-15	11	
22	Dec-15	12	
23			
24			

Insert ? ✕

Insert
- ⦿ Shift cells right
- ○ Shift cells down
- ○ Entire row
- ○ Entire column

OK   Cancel

Excel has many practical uses. You can use its orderly row-and-column worksheet structure to organize multi-column lists, create business forms, and much more. Excel provides more than just data organization, though; it enables you to write formulas that perform calculations on your data. This feature makes Excel an ideal tool for storing financial information, such as checkbook register and investment portfolio data.

In this lesson, I introduce you to the Excel interface and teach you some of the concepts you need to know. You learn how to move around in Excel, how to type and edit data, and how to manipulate rows, columns, cells, and sheets.

Understanding the Excel Interface

Excel is very much like Word and other Office applications. Excel has a File tab that opens a Backstage view, a Ribbon with multiple tabs that contain commands you can click to execute, a Quick Access toolbar, a status bar, scroll bars, and a Zoom slider. Figure 1-1 provides a quick overview.

The next several sections walk you through the Excel interface, including both the commands and the work area, and show you how to move around. After you get your bearings in Excel, you're ready to start creating worksheets.

Quick Access toolbar

Tabs

Ribbon

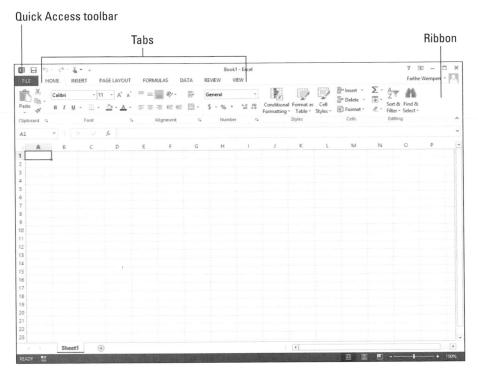

Figure 1-1

Take a tour of the Excel interface

The best way to learn about a new application is to jump in and start exploring. Work through this exercise to see how Excel is set up.

In the following exercise, you start Excel and explore its interface.

Files needed: None

1. **From Windows 8, press the Windows key to display the Start screen, and then click the Excel 2013 tile.**

You may need to scroll the Start screen to the right to find the Excel 2013 title. See Figure 1-2.

Excel 2013 tile on Start screen in Windows 8

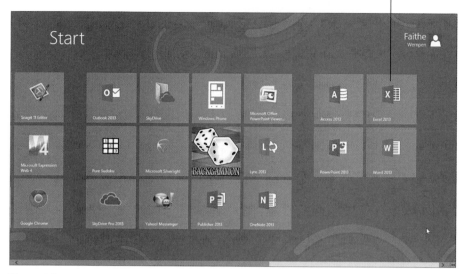

Figure 1-2

You might want to pin the Excel 2013 tile to the taskbar in Windows 8 to save yourself some time in opening it. Right-click the Excel 2013 tile on the Start screen and then click Pin to Taskbar in the command bar that appears at the bottom of the screen. From that point on, you can start Excel by clicking the Excel icon on the taskbar from the desktop.

OR

From Windows 7, choose Start⇨All Programs⇨Microsoft Office⇨ Microsoft Excel 2013.

Excel opens. An opening screen appears, as in Figure 1-3, providing shortcuts to recently used workbook files and thumbnails of some available templates. One of the templates is Blank workbook.

Recently opened files   Blank workbook template

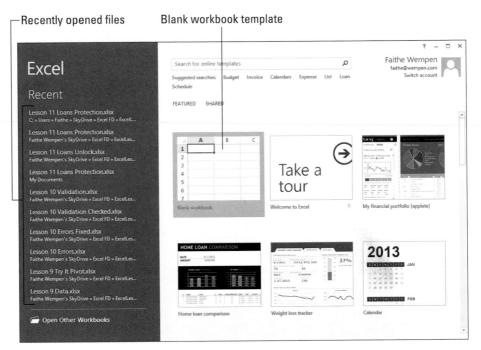

Figure 1-3

2. **Click the Blank Workbook thumbnail image to start a new blank workbook.**

   Alternatively you can also press the Esc key to go to a new blank workbook from the opening screen.

   A new workbook appears, and above it, the Ribbon, which is the main interface from which you select commands in Excel. (Refer to Figure 1-1.)

3. **Click the File tab to open Backstage view and then click Info.**

   Information about the active document appears (see Figure 1-4).

4. **Click the Back arrow, or press the Esc key, to return to the new blank workbook (see Figure 1-5).**

Figure 1-4

Name box shows address of active cell

Active cell (A1) is the cell with the cell cursor around it

View tab

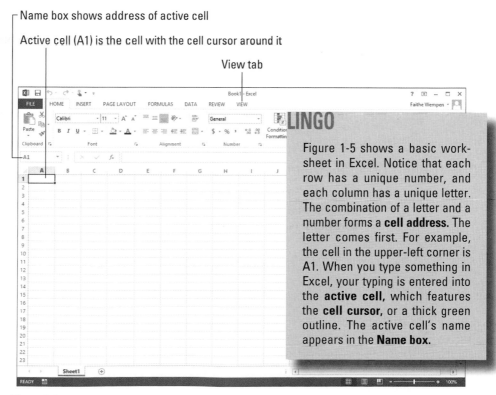

LINGO

Figure 1-5 shows a basic worksheet in Excel. Notice that each row has a unique number, and each column has a unique letter. The combination of a letter and a number forms a **cell address**. The letter comes first. For example, the cell in the upper-left corner is A1. When you type something in Excel, your typing is entered into the **active cell**, which features the **cell cursor**, or a thick green outline. The active cell's name appears in the **Name box**.

Figure 1-5

The Back arrow is the left-pointing arrow in the upper-left corner.

5. **Click the View tab on the Ribbon, and then click the Zoom button so that the Zoom dialog box opens (see Figure 1-6).**

6. **Select 200% and then click OK.**

   The dialog box closes, and the magnification changes to show each cell in a more close-up view.

7. **At the bottom-right corner of the Excel window, drag the Zoom slider left to 100%, changing zoom back to its original setting (see Figure 1-7).**

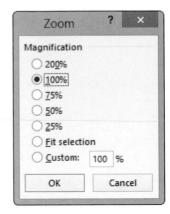

Figure 1-6

Zoom slider

Figure 1-7

Leave the workbook open for the next exercise.

Move the cell cursor

To type in a cell, you must first make it active by moving the cell cursor there. As shown in Figure 1-5, the cell cursor is a thick green outline. You can move the cell cursor by pressing the arrow keys on the keyboard, by clicking the desired cell, or by using one of Excel's keyboard shortcuts. Table 1-1 provides some of the most common keyboard shortcuts for moving the cell cursor.

Table 1-1	Movement Shortcuts
Press This . . .	*To Move . . .*
Arrow keys	One cell in the direction of the arrow
Tab	One cell to the right
Shift+Tab	One cell to the left
Ctrl+arrow key	To the edge of the current data region (the first or last cell that isn't empty) in the direction of the arrow

Press This . . .	To Move . . .
End	To the cell in the lower-right corner of the window*
Ctrl+End	To the last cell in the worksheet, in the lowest used row of the rightmost used column
Home	To the beginning of the row containing the active cell
Ctrl+Home	To the beginning of the worksheet (cell A1)
Page Down	One screen down
Alt+Page Down	One screen to the right
Ctrl+Page Down	To the next sheet in the workbook
Page Up	One screen up
Alt+Page Up	One screen to the left
Ctrl+Page Up	To the previous sheet in the workbook

This works only when the Scroll Lock key has been pressed on your keyboard to turn on the Scroll Lock function.

In the following exercise, you move the cell cursor in a worksheet.

Files needed: None

1. **From any blank worksheet, such as the one from the preceding section, click cell C3 to move the cell cursor there.**

2. **Press the right-arrow key to move to cell D3, and then press the down-arrow key to move to cell D4.**

3. **Press the Home key to move to cell A4.**

   Refer to Table 1-1; pressing Home moves to the beginning of the current row, which in this case, is row 4.

4. **Press the Page Down key.**

The cell cursor moves to a cell that is one screenful down from the preceding position. Depending on the window size and screen resolution, the exact cell varies, but you are still in column A.

5. **Use the vertical scroll bar to scroll the display up so that cell A1 is visible.**

Notice that the cell cursor does not move while you scroll. The Name box still displays the name of the cell you moved to previously.

6. Press Ctrl+Home to move to cell A1.

Leave the workbook open for the next exercise.

Select ranges

Range names are written with the upper-left cell address, a colon, and the lower-right cell address, as in the example A1:F3. Here A1:F3 means the range that begins in the upper-left corner with A1 and ends in the lower-right corner with F3. When a range contains non-contiguous cells, the pieces are separated by commas, like this: B8:C14,D8:G14.

The range name B8:C14,D8:G14 tells Excel to select the range from B8 through C14, plus the range from D8 through G14.

You can select a range by using either the keyboard or the mouse. Table 1-2 provides some of the most common range selection shortcuts.

LINGO

You might sometimes want to select a multi-cell **range** before you issue a command. For example, if you want to format all the text in a range a certain way, select that range and then issue the formatting command. Technically, a range can consist of a single cell; however, a range most commonly consists of multiple cells.

A range is usually **contiguous,** or all the cells are in a single rectangular block, but they don't have to be. You can also select **noncontiguous** cells in a range, by holding down the Ctrl key while you select additional cells.

Table 1-2	Range Selection Shortcuts
Press This . . .	*To Extend the Selection To . . .*
Ctrl+Shift+arrow key	The last nonblank cell in the same column or row as the active cell; or if the next cell is blank, to the next non-blank cell
Ctrl+Shift+End	The last used cell on the worksheet (lower-right corner of the range containing data)
Ctrl+Shift+Home	The beginning of the worksheet (cell A1)
Ctrl+Shift+Page Down	The current and next sheet in the workbook
Ctrl+Shift+Page Up	The current and previous sheet in the workbook
Ctrl+spacebar	The entire column where the active cell is located
Shift+spacebar	The entire row where the active cell is located
Ctrl+A	The entire worksheet

In the following exercise, you practice selecting ranges.

Files needed: None

1. **On any blank worksheet, such as the one from the preceding exercise, click cell B2 to move the cell cursor there.**

2. **While holding down the Shift key, press the right-arrow key twice and the down-arrow key twice, extending the selection to the range B2:D4 (see Figure 1-8).**

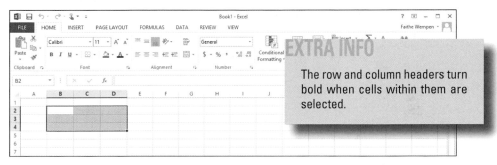

The row and column headers turn bold when cells within them are selected.

Figure 1-8

3. **Hold down the Ctrl key and click cell E2 to add only that cell to the selected range.**

4. **While still holding down the Ctrl key, hold down the left mouse button and drag from cell E2 to cell E8 so that the range is B2:D4,E2:E8, as shown in Figure 1-9.**

5. **Hold down the Ctrl key and click row 10's row header (the number 10 itself, at the left edge of the row) to add that entire row to the selected range.**

6. **Hold down the Ctrl key and click column G's column header (the letter G, at the top of the column) to add that entire column to the selected range.**

   Your selection should look like Figure 1-10 at this point.

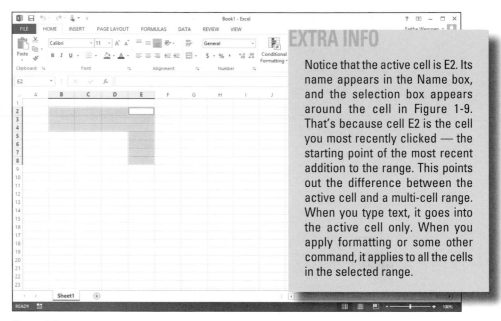

EXTRA INFO

Notice that the active cell is E2. Its name appears in the Name box, and the selection box appears around the cell in Figure 1-9. That's because cell E2 is the cell you most recently clicked — the starting point of the most recent addition to the range. This points out the difference between the active cell and a multi-cell range. When you type text, it goes into the active cell only. When you apply formatting or some other command, it applies to all the cells in the selected range.

Figure 1-9

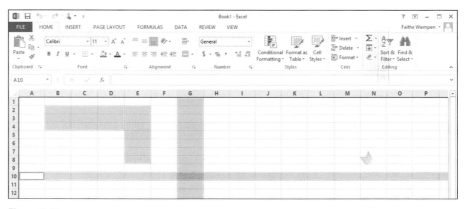

Figure 1-10

7. **Click any cell to cancel the range selection; only that cell you clicked is selected.**

8. Click in cell C4, and then press Ctrl+spacebar to select the entire column and then click any cell to cancel the range selection.

9. Click in cell C4 again, and press Shift+spacebar to select the entire row.

10. Click the Select All button (labeled in Figure 1-11) in the upper-left corner of the spreadsheet grid — where the row numbers and the column letters intersect — to select the entire worksheet, as shown in Figure 1-11.

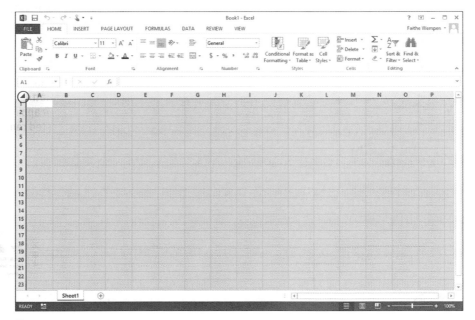

Figure 1-11

Instead of clicking the Select All button, you can press Ctrl+Shift+spacebar.

11. Click any cell to cancel the range selection.

Leave the workbook open for the next exercise.

Typing and Editing Cell Content

Up to this point in the lesson, I've introduced you to some spreadsheet basics. Now it's time to actually do something: Enter some text and numbers into cells.

Type text or numbers into a cell

To type in a cell, simply select the cell and begin typing. When you finish typing, you can leave the cell in any of these ways:

- ✔ **Press Enter:** Moves you to the next cell down.

- ✔ **Press Tab:** Moves you to the next cell to the right.

- ✔ **Press Shift+Tab:** Moves you to the next cell to the left.

- ✔ **Press an arrow key:** Moves you in the direction of the arrow.

- ✔ **Click in another cell:** Moves you to that cell.

If you make a mistake when editing, you can press the Esc key to cancel the edit before you leave the cell. If you need to undo an edit after you leave the cell, press Ctrl+Z or click the Undo button on the Quick Access toolbar.

In the following exercise, you enter text into a worksheet.

Files needed: None

1. **On any blank worksheet, such as the one from the preceding exercise, click cell A1.**

2. **Type** Mortgage Calculator **and press Enter.**

3. **Click cell A1 again to reselect it and notice that the cell's content appears in the Formula bar (see Figure 1-12).**

4. **Click cell A3, type** Loan Amount, **and press Tab so the cell cursor moves to cell B3.**

5. **Type** 250000 **and press Enter so the cell cursor moves to cell A4.**

6. **In cell A4, type** Interest, **and press Tab so the cell cursor moves to cell B4.**

Formula bar

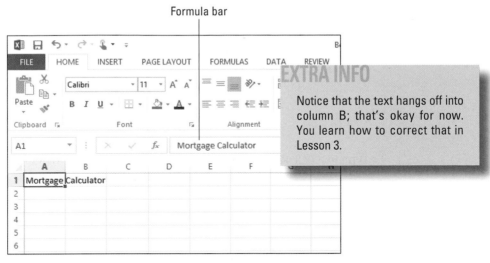

Figure 1-12

7. **Type** .05 **and press Enter so the cell cursor moves to cell A5.**

8. **Type** Periods **and press Tab so the cell cursor moves to cell B5.**

9. **Type** 360 **and press Enter so the cell cursor moves to cell A6.**

10. **Type** Payment **and press Enter so the cell cursor moves to cell A7, and the worksheet looks like Figure 1-13 at this point.**

11. **Save the file as** Lesson 1 Mortgage.xlsx:

   a. *Choose File➪Save.*

   b. *Click Computer.*

   c. *Click Browse. The Save As dialog box opens.*

   d. *Navigate to the location where you want to save the file.*

   e. *In the File Name box, type* **Lesson 1 Mortgage**. *(See Figure 1-14.)*

   f. *Click Save.*

Leave the workbook open for the next exercise.

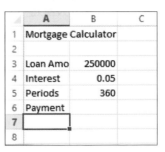

Figure 1-13

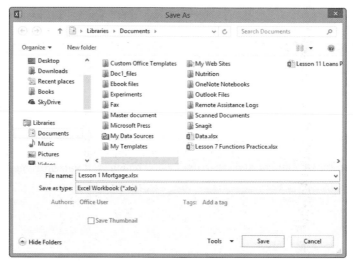

Figure 1-14

Edit cell content

If you need to edit the content in a cell, you can

✔ Click the cell to select it, and then click the cell again to move the insertion point into it. Edit just as you would in any text program.

✔ Click the cell to select it and then type a new entry to replace the old one.

If you decide you don't want the text you typed in a particular cell, you can get rid of it in several ways:

✔ Select the cell; then right-click the cell and choose Clear Contents from the menu that appears.

✔ Select the cell; then choose Home⇨Clear⇨Clear Contents.

✔ Select the cell, press the spacebar, and then press Enter. This technically doesn't clear the cell's content, but replaces it with a space.

✔ Select the cell and press the Delete key.

EXTRA INFO

Don't confuse the Delete key on the keyboard (which issues the Clear command) with the Delete command on the Ribbon. The Delete command doesn't *clear* the cell content; instead, it *removes* the entire cell. You find out more about deleting cells in the upcoming section, "Changing the Worksheet Structure."

And while I'm on the subject, don't confuse Clear with Cut, either. The Cut command works in conjunction with the Clipboard. Cut moves the content to the Clipboard, and you can then paste it somewhere else. Excel, however, differs from other applications in the way this command works: Using Cut doesn't immediately remove the content. Instead, Excel puts a flashing dotted box around the content and waits for you to reposition the cell cursor and issue the Paste command. If you do something else in the interim, the cut-and-paste operation is canceled, and the content that you cut remains in its original location. You learn more about cutting and pasting in the section "Copy and move data between cells" later in this lesson.

In the following exercise, you edit text in a worksheet.

Files needed: Lesson 1 Mortgage.xlsx

1. **In the** `Lesson 1 Mortgage` **file from the preceding exercise, click in cell A3.**

2. **Click in the Formula bar to move the insertion point there, double-click the word *Loan* to select it, press the Delete key, and then press the Delete key again to delete the space before the remaining word *Amount*.**

3. **Press Enter to finalize the edit.**

   The cell cursor moves to cell A4.

4. **Click in B3, type** 300000, **and press Enter.**

   The new value replaces the old one.

5. **Right-click cell B4 and choose Clear Contents. Then type** 0.0635 **and press Enter.**

6. **Click cell B5 to select it, and then double-click in B5 to move the insertion point there. Position the insertion point to the right of the 6, press the Backspace key twice, and type** 18, **changing the value in the cell to 180. Press Enter.**

   The worksheet looks like Figure 1-15.

7. **Click the Save button on the Quick Access toolbar to save the changes to the workbook.**

◢	A	B
1	Mortgage Calculator	
2		
3	Amount	300000
4	Interest	0.0635
5	Periods	180
6	Payment	
7		

Leave the workbook open for the next exercise.

Figure 1-15

Copy and move data between cells

When you're creating a spreadsheet, it's common not to get everything in the right cells on your first try. Fortunately, moving content between cells is easy.

Here are the two methods you can use to move content:

- ✔ **Mouse method:** Point at the dark outline around the selected range and then drag to the new location. If you want to copy rather than move, hold down the Ctrl key while you drag.

- ✔ **Clipboard method:** Choose Home⇨Cut or press Ctrl+X. (If you want to copy rather than simply move, choose Home⇨Copy rather than Cut or press Ctrl+C.) Then click the destination cell and choose Home⇨Paste or press Ctrl+V.

If you're moving or copying a multi-cell range with the Clipboard method, you can either select the same size and shape of range for the destination, or you can select a single cell, in which case the paste occurs with the selected cell in the upper-left corner.

In the following exercise, you move and copy cell content using two methods.

Files needed: Lesson 1 Mortgage.xlsx

1. **In the** `Lesson 1 Mortgage` **file from the preceding exercise, select the range A1:B6.**

    To do so, click A1, hold down the left mouse button, and drag to cell B6. Then release the mouse button.

2. **Point at the border of the selection so the mouse pointer shows a four-headed arrow along with the arrow pointer.**

3. **Drag the selection to C1:D6.**

    An outline shows the selection while you drag the selection, and a ScreenTip shows the cell address of the destination. (See Figure 1-16.)

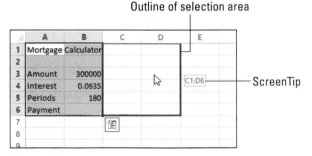

Figure 1-16

4. **Click cell C1 and press Ctrl+X to cut.**

   A dotted outline appears around C1.

5. **Click cell B1 and press Ctrl+V to paste.**

   The text moves from C1 to B1.

6. **Select C3:D6 and then choose Home⇨Cut.**

7. **Click cell B3 and then choose Home⇨Paste.**

   The completed worksheet is shown in Figure 1-17.

◢	A	B	C	D
1		Mortgage Calculator		
2				
3		Amount	300000	
4		Interest	0.0635	
5		Periods	180	
6		Payment		
7				

Figure 1-17

8. **Click the Save button on the Quick Access toolbar to save the changes to the workbook.**

Leave the workbook open for the next exercise.

Use AutoFill to fill cell content

When you have a lot of data to enter and that data consists of some type of repeatable pattern or sequence, you can save time by using AutoFill. To use AutoFill, you select the cell(s) that already contains an example of what you want to fill and then drag the fill handle.

LINGO

The **fill handle** is the little black square in the lower-right corner of the selected cell or range.

Depending on how you use it, AutoFill can either fill the same value into every cell in the target area, or it can fill in a sequence (such as days of the month, days of the week, or a numeric sequence such as 2, 4, 6, 8). Here are the general rules for how it works:

✔ When AutoFill recognizes the selected text as a member of one of its preset lists, such as days of the week or months of the year, it automatically increments those. For example, if the selected cell contains August, AutoFill places September in the next adjacent cell.

✔ When AutoFill does not recognize the selected text, it fills the chosen cell with a duplicate of the selected text.

✔ When AutoFill is used on a single cell containing a number, it fills with a duplicate of the number.

✔ When AutoFill is used on a range of two or more cells containing numbers, AutoFill attempts to determine the interval between them and continues filling using that same pattern. For example, if the two selected cells contain 2 and 4, the next adjacent cell would be filled with 6.

In the following exercise, you autofill cell content using two methods.

Files needed: Lesson 1 Mortgage.xlsx

1. **In the** Lesson 1 Mortgage **file from the preceding exercise, select cell A8 and type** Amortization Table.

2. **Type the following:**

    *a. In cell A10, type **Date**.*

    *b. In cell B10, type **Pmt#**.*

    *c. In cell A11, type **January 2015**. (Note that Excel automatically changes it to Jan-15.)*

    *d. In cell B11, type **1**.*

3. **Click cell A11 and move the mouse pointer over the fill handle.**

    The mouse pointer becomes a black crosshair (see Figure 1-18).

Cross-hair mouse pointer hovering over the fill handle

10	Date		Pmt#	
11	Jan-15			1
12				

4. **Drag the fill handle down to cell A22.**

Figure 1-18

The first year of dates fill in the cells. (See Figure 1-19.)

5. **Click cell B11 and drag the fill handle down to C22. The same number fills all the cells. That's not what you want for this exercise, so press Ctrl+Z to undo the fill.**

6. **Click cell B12, and type** 2. **Select B11:B12 and then drag the fill handle down to cell B22.**

    Figure 1-20 shows the completed series.

Fill handle dragged down to cell A22

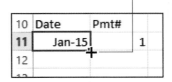

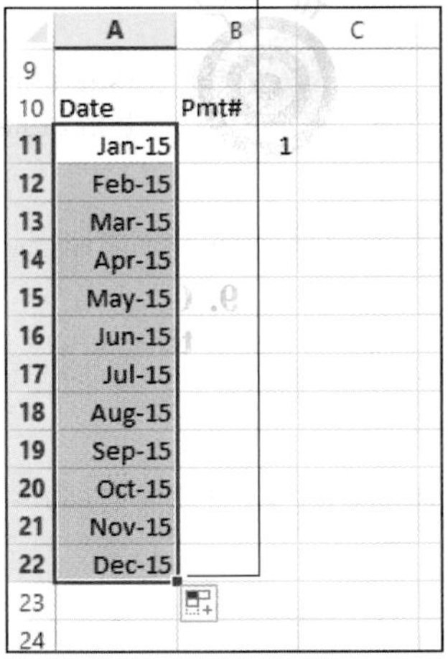

	A	B	C
9			
10	Date	Pmt#	
11	Jan-15		1
12	Feb-15		
13	Mar-15		
14	Apr-15		
15	May-15		
16	Jun-15		
17	Jul-15		
18	Aug-15		
19	Sep-15		
20	Oct-15		
21	Nov-15		
22	Dec-15		
23			
24			

Figure 1-19

Fill handle dragged down to cell B22

	A	B	C
9			
10	Date	Pmt#	
11	Jan-15	1	
12	Feb-15	2	
13	Mar-15	3	
14	Apr-15	4	
15	May-15	5	
16	Jun-15	6	
17	Jul-15	7	
18	Aug-15	8	
19	Sep-15	9	
20	Oct-15	10	
21	Nov-15	11	
22	Dec-15	12	
23			
24			

Figure 1-20

7. Select A22:B22 and drag the fill handle down to B190.

Both series are filled in, down to row 190, where the date is December 2026 and the payment number is 180.

TIP

Here you do Step 7 because the number of periods for this loan is 180 (see cell C5), so the number of payments should be 180 in the amortization table.

8. Press Ctrl+Home to return to the top of the worksheet.

9. Click the Save button on the Quick Access toolbar to save the changes to the workbook.

10. Choose File⇨Close to close the workbook.

Leave Excel open for the next exercise.

Use Flash Fill to Extract Content

New in Excel 2013, the Flash Fill feature enables you to extract data from adjacent columns intelligently by analyzing the patterns in that data. For example, suppose you have a list of e-mail addresses in one column, and you would like the usernames (that is, the text before the @ sign) from each e-mail address to appear in an adjacent column. You would extract the first few yourself by manually typing the entries into the adjacent column, and then use Flash Fill to follow your example to extract the others.

In the following exercise, you use Flash Fill to extract first and last names into separate columns. This exercise also demonstrates how to open files in Excel and save them with different names, a skill you use throughout this book.

Files needed: Lesson 1 Names.xlsx.

1. **Open the** Lesson 1 Names.xlsx **file:**

   a. *Choose File⇨Open.*

   b. *Click Computer, or click SkyDrive, depending on where you have stored the files for this lesson.*

   c. *Click Browse. The Open dialog box opens.*

   d. *Navigate to the location where the data files for this lesson are stored.*

   e. *Click* Lesson 1 Names.xlsx. *(See Figure 1-21.)*

   f. *Click Open.*

Figure 1-21

2. **Save the file as** Lesson 1 Roster.xlsx:

   a. *Choose File⇨Save As.*

   b. *Click Computer, or click SkyDrive, depending on where you want to store your work from this lesson.*

   c. *Click Browse. The Save As dialog box opens.*

   d. *Navigate to the location where you want to save your completed work for this lesson.*

   e. *In the File name box, change the filename to* Lesson 1 Roster. *See Figure 1-22.*

   f. *Click Save.*

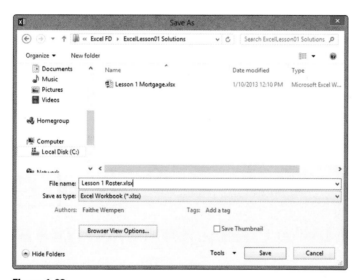

Figure 1-22

3. **In cell B3, type** Tom, **and in cell C3, type** Bailey.

4. **In cell B4 type** Latasha, **and in cell C4 type** Newland.

   See Figure 1-23 for the result.

Figure 1-23

5. **Click cell B5.**

   For Flash Fill to work, the active cell must be in the column that you want to fill.

6. **On the Home tab, in the Editing group, click the Fill button to open a menu.**

7. **Click Flash Fill, as shown in Figure 1-24.**

   The first names fill into column B for the remaining entries on the list.

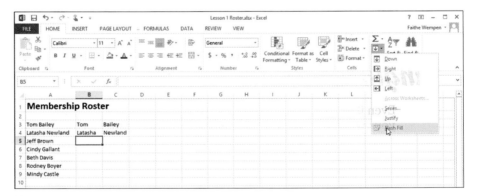

Figure 1-24

8. **Click cell C5.**

9. **On the Home tab, in the Editing group, click the Fill button again, and then click Flash Fill again.**

   The last names fill into column C for the remaining entries on the list. See Figure 1-25.

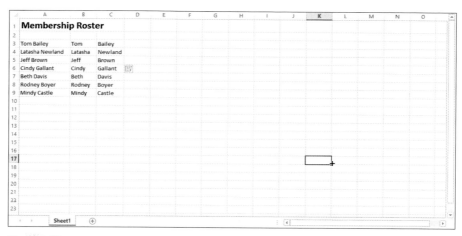

Figure 1-25

10. **Choose File⇨Close to close the workbook. When prompted to save your changes, click Save.**

Leave Excel open for the next exercise.

Changing the Worksheet Structure

Even if you're a careful planner, you'll likely decide that you want to change your worksheet's structure. Maybe you want data in a different column, or certain rows turn out to be unnecessary, Excel makes it easy to insert and delete rows and columns to deal with these kinds of changes.

Insert and delete rows and columns

When you insert a new row or column, the existing ones move to make room for it. You can insert multiple rows or columns at once by selecting multiple ones before issuing the Insert command. (There's no limit on the number you can insert at once!) Similarly, you can delete multiple rows or columns by selecting them before using the Delete command.

In the following exercise, you insert and delete rows and columns.

Files needed: Lesson 1 Mortgage.xlsx

1. **Reopen the** Lesson 1 Mortgage **file you created earlier in the lesson, and click anywhere in column A.**

2. **On the Home tab, click the down arrow on the Insert button and choose Insert Sheet Columns (see Figure 1-26).**

   A new column is placed to the left of the selected column.

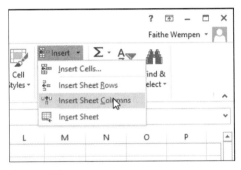

Figure 1-26

3. **Click the column header for column A to select the entire column and then choose Home⇨Delete.**

   The entire column is deleted.

4. **Select rows 7 and 8 by dragging across their row headers and then choose Home⇨Insert.**

   Two new rows are inserted.

5. **Click any cell in row 7; then, from the Home tab, click the down arrow on the Delete button and choose Delete Sheet Rows.**

   Figure 1-27 shows the worksheet after the insertions and deletions.

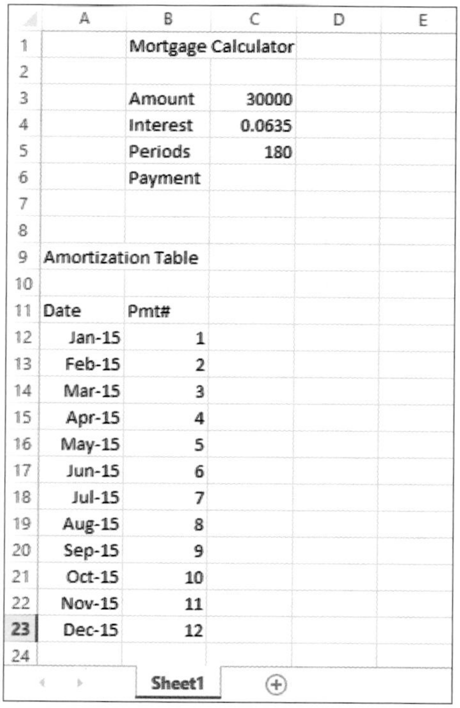

	A	B	C	D	E
1		Mortgage Calculator			
2					
3		Amount	30000		
4		Interest	0.0635		
5		Periods	180		
6		Payment			
7					
8					
9	Amortization Table				
10					
11	Date	Pmt#			
12	Jan-15	1			
13	Feb-15	2			
14	Mar-15	3			
15	Apr-15	4			
16	May-15	5			
17	Jun-15	6			
18	Jul-15	7			
19	Aug-15	8			
20	Sep-15	9			
21	Oct-15	10			
22	Nov-15	11			
23	Dec-15	12			
24					

Sheet1 ⊕

Figure 1-27

Save the changes, and leave the workbook open for the next exercise.

Insert and delete cells and ranges

You can also insert and delete individual cells, or ranges that do not neatly correspond to entire rows or columns. When you do so, the surrounding cells shift. In the case of an insertion, cells move down or to the right of the area where the new cells are being inserted. In the case of a deletion, cells move up or to the left to fill in the voided space.

REMEMBER

Deleting a cell is different from clearing a cell's content, and this becomes apparent when you start working with individual cells and ranges. When you clear the content, the cell itself remains. When you delete the cell itself, the adjacent cells shift.

When shifting cells, Excel is smart enough that it tries to guess which direction you want existing content to move when you insert or delete cells. If you have content immediately to the right of a deleted cell, for example, it shifts it left. If you have content immediately below the deleted cell, it shifts it up. You can still override that, though, as needed.

In the following exercise, you insert and delete cells.

Files needed: Lesson 1 Mortgage.xlsx

1. **In the** Lesson 1 Mortgage **file from the preceding exercise, select A1:A6 and then choose Home⇨Delete.**

   Excel guesses that you want to move the existing content to the left, and it does so.

2. **Click cell A1, and choose Home⇨Insert.**

   Excel guesses that you want to move the existing content down, which is incorrect. The content in column B is off by one row (see Figure 1-28).

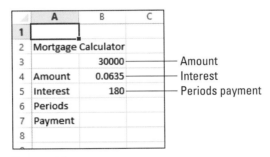

Figure 1-28

3. **Press Ctrl+Z to undo the insertion; then from the Home tab, click the down arrow to the right of the Insert button and choose Insert Cells.**

   The Insert dialog box opens (see Figure 1-29).

4. **Select Shift Cells Right and then click OK.**

   A new cell A1 is inserted, and the previous A1 content moves into B1.

5. **Save the changes to the workbook.**

Leave the workbook open for the next exercise.

Figure 1-29

Working with Worksheets

Each new workbook starts with one sheet — Sheet1. (Not the most interesting name, but you can change it.) You can add or delete worksheets, rearrange the worksheet tabs, and apply different colors to the tabs to help differentiate them from one another, or to create logical groups of tabs.

In the following exercise, you insert, rename, and delete worksheets, and change a tab color.

Files needed: Lesson 1 Mortgage.xlsx

1. **In the** Lesson 1 Mortgage **file from the preceding exercise, double-click the Sheet1 worksheet tab to move the insertion point into it.**

2. **Type** Calculator **and press Enter.**

   The new name replaces the old one.

3. **Right-click the worksheet tab, choose Tab Color, and click the Red standard color.**

   See Figure 1-30.

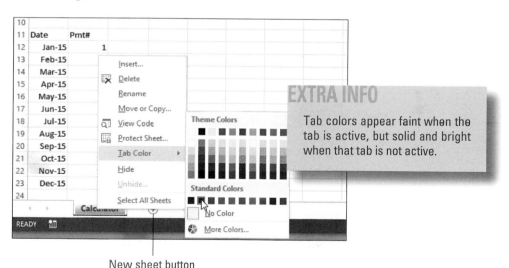

New sheet button

Figure 1-30

4. **Right-click the Calculator tab and choose Insert.**

   The Insert dialog box opens. See Figure 1-31.

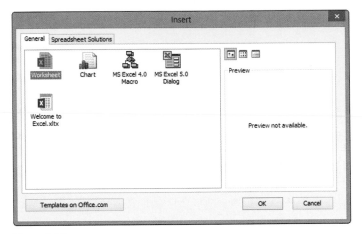

Figure 1-31

5. **Click Worksheet and then click OK.**

   A new sheet named Sheet1 is inserted.

6. **Click the New Sheet button to the right of the existing tabs.**

   The New Sheet button looks like a plus sign inside a circle. Another new sheet named Sheet2 is inserted.

7. **Click the Sheet1 tab, and then right-click it and choose Delete.**

   The sheet is deleted.

8. **Double-click the Sheet2 tab, type** Amortization, **and press Enter.**

9. **Double-click the tab on the Amortization sheet, type** Chart, **and press Enter.**

   The two tabs in the workbook are named and arranged as shown in Figure 1-32.

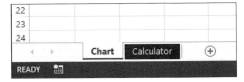

Figure 1-32

10. **Save the changes to the workbook.**

Close the workbook and exit Excel.

Summing Up

Excel is an excellent choice for storing data in rows and columns. In this lesson, you learned how to navigate the Excel interface, including entering and editing content in cells, inserting and deleting cells, and selecting ranges. Here's a quick review:

- ✔ Excel data files are called workbooks. Each workbook can hold multiple worksheets. Each worksheet has a tab at the bottom of the Excel window for quick access to it.

- ✔ Each cell has a cell address consisting of the column letter and row number, such as A1.

- ✔ The active cell is indicated by the cell cursor, a thick green outline. You can move the cell cursor with the mouse or the keyboard arrow keys. When you type text, it is entered into the active cell.

- ✔ A range is a selection that consists of one or more cells. (It's usually more than one.) A contiguous range consists of a single rectangular block of cells.

- ✔ To clear cell contents, select the cell and press the Delete key or choose Home⇨Clear⇨Cell Contents.

- ✔ To move data between cells, drag them, or use the Cut and Paste commands. To copy data, hold down Ctrl and drag the cells, or use the Copy and Paste commands.

- ✔ To fill data from the selected range to adjacent cells, drag the fill handle, which is the green rectangle in the lower-right corner of the selected range.

- ✔ To use Flash Fill to intelligently fill columns, complete a few examples and then use the Home⇨Fill⇨Flash Fill command.

- ✔ To insert a row or column, from the Home tab, open the Insert button's menu and choose either Insert Sheet Rows or Insert Sheet Columns, respectively.

- ✔ When you insert individual cells, the existing content moves over to make room. You can choose which direction it needs to move.

- ✔ To insert a new sheet, right-click an existing sheet and choose Insert. To delete a sheet, right-click its tab and choose Delete.

- ✔ To rename a sheet, double-click its tab name and type a new name.

Try-it-yourself lab

1. **Start Excel, and start a new blank workbook.**

2. **In cell A1, type** Membership List.

3. **In row 3, enter the column headings you would need to store information about the members of an organization you're part of.**

   For example, you might have **First Name**, **Last Name**, and **Phone**.

4. **Starting in row 4, enter the information about the members of the organization.**

   If the organization has many members, you do not have to enter every member in the list.

5. **Insert a new column between two of the existing columns.**

   For example, you could enter a MI column (for Middle Initial) between First and Last.

6. **Change the name of the worksheet tab to** Membership.

7. **Save your workbook as** Lesson 1 Lab.xlsx.

8. **Close your workbook and then close Excel.**

Know this tech talk

active cell: The cell in which new content that you type will be placed.

cell address: The column letter and row number of a cell, such as A1.

cell cursor: The thick green border surrounding the active cell.

cell: The intersection of a row and column in a spreadsheet.

contiguous: A range in which all the selected cells are adjacent to one another, in a rectangular block.

fill handle: The small square handle in the lower-right corner of a selected range.

Flash Fill: A new feature in Excel 2013 that intelligently fills columns with data based on the example of data in adjacent cells.

Formula bar: The bar above the worksheet grid where the formula appears from the selected cell.

Name box: The box to the left of the Formula bar that lists the active cell's cell address.

range: One or more selected cells.

spreadsheet: A grid of rows and columns in which you can store data.

workbook: An Excel data file.

worksheet: The Excel term for a spreadsheet.

worksheet tabs: Tabs at the bottom of a workbook for each worksheet that it contains.

Lesson 2

Creating Formulas and Functions

- Formulas perform math calculations on fixed numbers or on cell contents.

- The order of precedence settles any uncertainties about which math operations execute first.

- Cell references that include sheet names can reference cells on other sheets.

- Relative cell referencing allows cell references to automatically update when copied. Absolute cell referencing keeps a cell reference fixed when copied to other locations.

- Functions perform complex math operations on cell content.

- Named ranges substitute friendly, easy-to-understand words for plain cell and range addresses.

- The new Quick Analysis feature displays formatting, charts, tables, and more to aid analysis.

*M*ath. Excel is really good at it, and it's what makes Excel more than just data storage. Even if you hated math in school, you might still like Excel because it does the math for you.

In Excel, you can write math formulas that perform calculations on the values in various cells, and then, if those values change later, see the formula results update automatically. You can also use built-in functions to handle more complex math activities than you might be able to set up yourself with formulas. That capability makes it possible to build complex worksheets that calculate loan rates and payments, keep track of your bank accounts, and much more.

In this lesson, I show you how to construct formulas and functions in Excel, as well as how to move and copy formulas and functions (there's a trick to it) and how to use functions to create handy financial spreadsheets.

Introducing Formulas

In Excel, formulas are different from regular text in two ways:

- ✔ They begin with an equal sign, like this: =2+2.

- ✔ They don't contain text (except for function names and cell references). They contain only symbols that are allowed in math formulas, such as parentheses, commas, and decimal points.

> ## LINGO
> A **formula** is a math calculation, like 2+2 or 3(4+1), and in Excel, a formula can perform calculations with fixed numbers or cell contents.

Write formulas that calculate

Excel's formulas can do everything that a basic calculator can do, so if you're in a hurry and don't want to pull up the Windows Calculator application, you can enter a formula in Excel to get a quick result. Experimenting with this type of formula is a great way to get accustomed to formulas in general.

Excel also has an advantage over some basic calculators (including the one in Windows): It easily does exponentiation. For example, if you want to calculate 5 to the 8th power, you would write it in Excel as =5^8.

Just as in basic math, formulas are calculated by an order of precedence. Table 2-1 lists the order.

Table 2-1	Order of Precedence in a Formula	
Order	**Item**	**Example**
1	Anything in parentheses	=2*(2+1)
2	Exponentiation	=2^3
3	Multiplication and division	=1+2*2
4	Addition and subtraction	=10−4

In the following exercise, you enter some formulas that perform simple math calculations.

Files needed: None

1. **Start Excel, if needed, and start a new blank workbook. If you already have another workbook open, press Ctrl+N to create a new workbook.**

   You learned about creating a new workbook in Lesson 1.

2. **Click cell A1, type =2+2, and press Enter.**

   The result of the formula appears in cell A1.

3. **Click cell A1 again to move the cell cursor back to it, and then look in the Formula bar.**

   Notice that the formula you entered appears there. (See Figure 2-1.)

4. **Click cell A2, type =2+4*3, and press Enter.**

   The result of the formula appears in cell A2.

   In this case, because of the order of operations (see Table 2-1), the multiplication was done first (4 times 3 equals 12) and then 2 was added, for a total of 14.

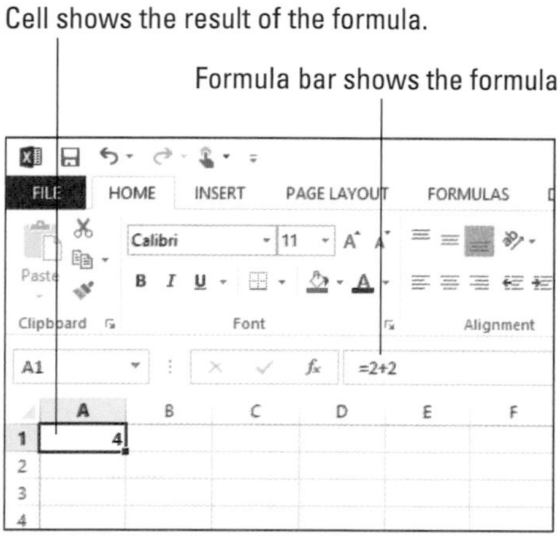

Cell shows the result of the formula.

Formula bar shows the formula.

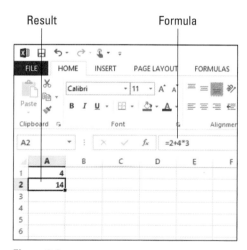

Figure 2-1

> 5. **Press the up-arrow key once to move the cell cursor back to A2, and examine the formula in the Formula bar. (See Figure 2-2.)**

Result   Formula

Figure 2-2

> 6. **In cell A3, type** =(2+4)*3 **and press Enter.**
>
> In this case, the parentheses forced the addition to occur first (2 plus 4 equals 6) and then 3 was multiplied, for a total of 18.
>
> 7. **Press the up-arrow key once to move the cell cursor back to A3 and note the formula shown in Figure 2-3.**

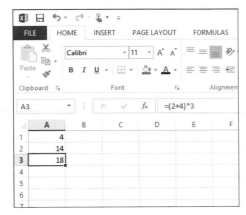

Figure 2-3

8. **Close the workbook without saving changes to it.**

Leave Excel open for the next exercise.

Write formulas that reference cells

One of Excel's best features is that it can reference cells in formulas. When a cell is referenced in a formula, whatever value it contains is used in the formula. When the value changes, the result of the formula changes, too.

In the following exercise, you enter some formulas that contain cell references.

Files needed: Lesson 2 Budget.xlsx

1. **Open** `Lesson 2 Budget.xlsx` **from the data files for this lesson and save it as** Lesson 2 Budget Calculations.

2. **In cell E6, type** =E4.

   The value shown in E4 is repeated in cell E6.

In cell E6, you could have just as easily retyped the value from E4, but this way if the value in E4 changes, the value in E6 also changes.

3. **In cell B7, type** =B4+B5+B6 **so that B7 shows $1,425; in cell B15, type** =B10+B11+B12+B13+B14 **so that B15 shows $975.**

TIP

Typing each cell reference is a lot of work. Later in this lesson in the section "Introducing Functions," you see how to use the SUM function to dramatically cut down on the typing required to sum the values in many cells at once.

4. **In cell B17, type** =B7+B15 **so that B17 shows $2,400; in cell E9, type** =E6–B17 **so that E9 shows –$578 (see Figure 2-4).**

	A	B	C	D	E	F
1	**Budget**					
2						
3	**Fixed Expense**			Income		
4	Rent	$850		Paycheck	$1,822	
5	Car Payment	$325				
6	Student Loan	$250		Total Income	$1,822	
7	**Total Fixed**	$1,425				
8						
9	Variable Expense			Overall	-$578	
10	Utilities	$175				
11	Food	$450		Correction %		
12	Entertainment	$150				
13	Clothes	$100				
14	Miscellaneous	$100				
15	**Total Variable**	$975				
16						
17	Total Expenses	$2,400				
18						
19						
20						
21						

Sheet1   Sheet2   Sheet3   (+)

Figure 2-4

5. **In cell E11, type** =E9/B17.

The value –24% appears in E11.

6. **Save and close the workbook.**

Leave Excel open for the next exercise.

Reference a cell on another sheet

When referring to a cell on the same sheet, you can simply use its column and row: A1, B1, and so on. However, when referring to a cell on a different sheet, you have to include the sheet name in the formula.

The syntax for doing this is to list the sheet name, followed by an exclamation point, followed by the cell reference, like this:

```
=Sheet1!A2
```

In the following exercise, you practice using this notation by creating some multi-sheet formulas.

Files needed: Lesson 2 Sheets.xlsx

1. **Open** Lesson 2 Sheets.xlsx **from the data files for this lesson and save it as** Lesson 2 Budget Sheets.xlsx.

This workbook has the same data that you worked with in the preceding exercise, but the data is split into multiple worksheets.

2. **Click the workbook's Expenses tab, and look at the data there.**

When calculating the overall budget amount, refer to cell B15 there. (See Figure 2-5.)

	A	B	C
1	**Fixed Expense**		
2	Rent	$850	
3	Car Payment	$325	
4	Student Loan	$250	
5	**Total Fixed**	$1,425	
6			
7	**Variable Expense**		
8	Utilities	$175	
9	Food	$450	
10	Entertainment	$150	
11	Clothes	$100	
12	Miscellaneous	$100	
13	**Total Variable**	$975	
14			
15	**Total Expenses**	$2,400	
16			
17			
18			

Figure 2-5

3. **Click the workbook's Income tab and look at the data there. On this sheet, refer to cell B4. (See Figure 2-6.)**

4. **Click the workbook's Overall tab, and in cell B3, type** =Income!B4–Expenses!B15.

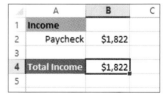

	A	B	C
1	Income		
2	Paycheck	$1,822	
3			
4	Total Income	$1,822	
5			

Figure 2-6

Cell B3 displays –$578.

If you had not looked beforehand at the cells to reference on the other tabs, you might have been at a loss as to what to type when constructing the formula in Step 4. There is another way to refer to cells when writing a formula. The next steps practice that method:

5. **In cell B5, type** =B3/.

6. **Click the Expenses tab, click cell B15 and press Enter.**

The display jumps back to the Overall tab, and completes the formula. (See Figure 2-7.)

7. **Save the changes to the workbook and close it.**

Leave Excel open for the next exercise.

	A	B	C
1	**Budget**		
2			
3	Overall	-$578	
4			
5	Correction %	-24%	
6			
7			
8			

Figure 2-7

Moving and Copying Formulas

In Lesson 1, you learn how to move and copy text and numbers between cells, but when it comes to copying formulas, beware of a few gotchas. The following sections explain relative and absolute referencing in formulas, and how you can use them to get the results you want when you copy.

Copy formulas with relative referencing

When you move or copy a formula, Excel automatically changes the cell references to work with the new location. That's because by default, cell references in formulas are *relative references.* For example, in Figure 2-8, suppose you wanted to copy the formula from B5 into C5. The new formula in C5 should refer to values in column C, not to column B; otherwise the formula wouldn't make much sense. So, when B5's formula is copied to C5, it becomes =C3+C4 there.

Formula in B5 is relative.

The formula copied to C5 becomes =C3+C4.

B5		:	✕	✓	*fx*	=B3+B4

	A	B	C	D	E
1					
2		January	February		
3	South	54	14		
4	North	23	67		
5	Total	77			
6					
7					

Figure 2-8

LINGO

A **relative reference** is a cell reference that changes if copied to another cell.

In this exercise, you copy formulas using relative referencing (the default) and examine the results.

Files needed: Lesson 2 Appliance.xlsx

1. **Open** `Lesson 2 Appliance.xlsx` **from the data files for this lesson and save it as** Lesson 2 Appliance Sales.xlsx.

2. **On Sheet1, click cell B13 and examine the formula in the Formula bar, which contains references to values in column B. (See Figure 2-9.)**

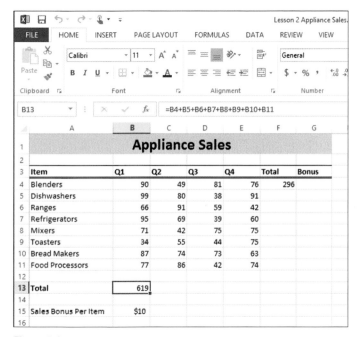

Figure 2-9

3. **Press Ctrl+C to copy the formula to the Clipboard (a dotted outline appears around B13), and then select C13:E13 and press Ctrl+V to paste the formula into those cells.**

4. **Click cell C13 and examine the formula in the Formula bar, which contains references to values in column C. (See Figure 2-10.)**

5. **Click cell F4 and then drag the fill handle down to F11.**

   The formula from F4 is copied into that range, with the row numbers changed to refer to the new positions. (See Figure 2-11.)

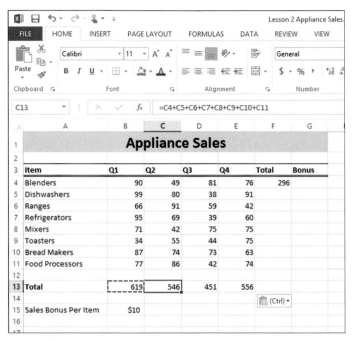

Figure 2-10

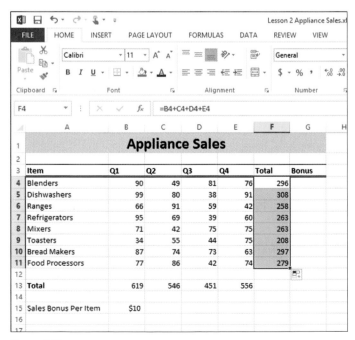

Figure 2-11

6. **Click each of the cells in the F column and examine their formulas in the Formula bar.**

   Note that each one uses the correct row number.

7. **Save the changes to the workbook.**

Leave the workbook open for the next exercise.

Copy formulas with absolute referencing

LINGO

An **absolute reference** is a cell reference that doesn't change when copied to another cell. You can mix relative and absolute references in the same formula. When you do, the result is a **mixed reference**.

You might not always want the cell references in a formula to change when you move or copy it. In other words, you want an *absolute reference* to that cell. To make a reference absolute, you add dollar signs before the column letter and before the row number. So, for example, an absolute reference to cell C1 would be =$C$1.

If you want to "lock down" only one dimension of the cell reference, you can place a dollar sign before only the column, or only the row. For example, =$C1 would make only the column letter fixed, and =C$1 would make only the row number fixed.

In this exercise, you create absolute references and copy formulas that contain them.

Files needed: Lesson 2 Appliance Sales.xlsx from the preceding exercise

1. **In** Lesson 2 Appliance Sales.xlsx, **click cell G4 and type** =F4*$B$15, **which multiplies cell F4 by cell B15, referring to F4 with a relative reference and referring to B15 with an absolute reference.**

2. **Click cell G4 again and then drag the fill handle down to G11, copying the formula to that range.**

3. **Click cell G11 and examine its formula in the Formula bar, as shown in Figure 2-12.**

   Notice that the reference to column F is updated to show cell F11, but the reference to cell B15 has remained fixed.

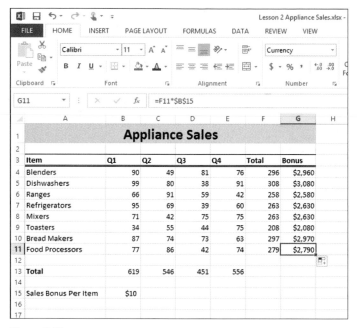

Figure 2-12

4. **Select F11:G11 and then press Ctrl+C to copy; select F13:G13 and then press Ctrl+V to paste.**

5. **Click cell G13 and examine the formula in the Formula bar to confirm it is correct.**

TIP

You could have dragged the fill handle all the way down to cell G13 in Step 2, so you wouldn't have to copy and paste the formula into G13 in Step 4. However, there still would have been another step because you would have had an extraneous function in cell G12 that you would've had to delete.

6. **Save the changes to the workbook.**

Leave the workbook open for the next exercise.

Introducing Functions

Sometimes, as you've seen in earlier exercises in this lesson, it's awkward or lengthy to write a formula to perform a calculation. For example, suppose you want to sum the values in cells A1 through A10. To express that as a formula, you'd have to write each cell reference individually, like this:

```
=A1+A2+A3+A4+A5+A6+
       A7+A8+A9+A10
```

With a function, you can represent a range with the upper-left corner's cell reference, a colon, and the lower-right corner's cell reference. In the case of `A1:A10`, there is only one column, so the upper-left is cell A1 and the lower-right is cell A10.

Range references cannot be used in simple formulas — only in functions. For example, `=A6:A9` would be invalid as a formula because no math operation is specified in it. You can't insert math operators within a range. To use ranges in a calculation, you must use a function.

Each function has one or more arguments, along with its own rules about how many required and optional arguments there are, and what they represent. You don't have to memorize the sequence of arguments (the *syntax*) for each function; Excel asks you for them. Excel can even suggest a function to use for a certain situation if you aren't sure what you need.

Use the SUM function

The SUM function is by far the most popular function; it sums (that is, adds) a data range consisting of one or more cells, like this:

```
=SUM(D12:D15)
```

You don't *have* to use a range in a SUM function; you can specify the individual cell addresses if you want. Separate them by commas, like this:

```
=SUM(D12,D13,D14,D15)
```

LINGO

In Excel, a **function** refers to a certain math calculation. Functions can greatly shortcut the amount of typing you have to do to create a particular result. For example, instead of using the `=A1+A2+A3+A4+A5+A6+A7+A8+A9+A10` formula, you could use the SUM function like this: `=SUM(A1:A10)`.

LINGO

An **argument** is a placeholder for a number, text string, or cell reference. For example, the SUM function requires at least one argument: a range of cells. So, in the preceding example, `A1:A10` is the argument. The arguments for a function are enclosed in a set of parentheses.

LINGO

The **syntax** is the sequence of arguments for a function. When there are multiple arguments in the syntax, they are separated by commas.

If the data range is not a contiguous block, you need to specify the individual cells that are outside the block. The main block is one argument, and each individual other cell is an additional argument, like this:

=SUM(D12:D15,E22)

In this exercise, you replace some formulas with equivalent functions.

Files needed: Lesson 2 Appliance Sales.xlsx from the preceding exercise

1. **In** Lesson 2 Appliance Sales.xlsx, **click cell B13 and type** =SUM(B4:B11) **and press Enter.**

   This function replaces the formula that was previously there. The value in the cell is 619.

2. **Enter a function using another method:**

   a. *Click cell C13 and type* =*SUM(.*

   b. *Drag across the range C4:C11 to select it and then press Enter to enter that range into the function in cell C13.* The value in the cell is 546.

3. **Use the AutoSum button to enter a function:**

   a. *Click cell D13, and then choose Formulas⇨AutoSum. See Figure 2-13.* A dotted outline appears around D4:D12. However, this is not the range you want to sum. You don't want to include D12.

AutoSum button

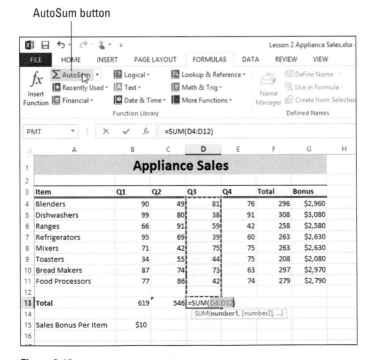

Figure 2-13

b. *Drag across D4:D11 to select that range and then press Enter.* The value in D13 is 451.

c. *Click cell C13 and drag the fill handle to cell F13, copying the function to the adjacent cells.* Figure 2-14 shows the sheet when finished.

Note that the sheet doesn't look any different from before; the functions perform the exact same calculations that the formulas did previously.

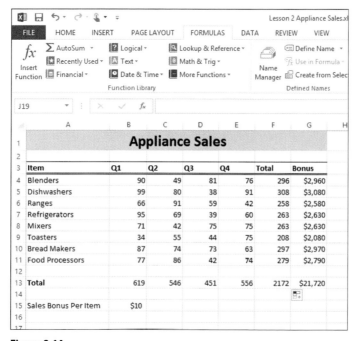

Item	Q1	Q2	Q3	Q4	Total	Bonus
Blenders	90	49	81	76	296	$2,960
Dishwashers	99	80	38	91	308	$3,080
Ranges	66	91	59	42	258	$2,580
Refrigerators	95	69	39	60	263	$2,630
Mixers	71	42	75	75	263	$2,630
Toasters	34	55	44	75	208	$2,080
Bread Makers	87	74	73	63	297	$2,970
Food Processors	77	86	42	74	279	$2,790
Total	619	546	451	556	2172	$21,720
Sales Bonus Per Item	$10					

Figure 2-14

4. **Save the changes to the workbook.**

Leave the workbook open for the next exercise.

Insert a function

Typing a function and its arguments directly into a cell works fine if you happen to know the function you want and its arguments. Many times, though, you may not know these details. In those cases, you can use the Insert Function feature to help you.

Insert Function enables you to pick a function from a list based on descriptive keywords. After you make your selection, it provides fill-in-the-blank prompts for the arguments.

7. **Press Enter or click the Expand Dialog button to return to the Function Arguments dialog box (as shown in Figure 2-18), and then click OK.**

The function enters into cell B16 with the result of 67.875.

Range   Preview of the range's values

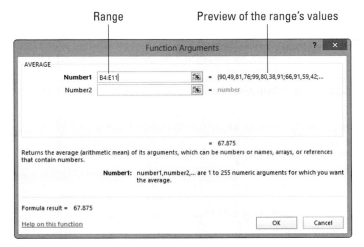

Figure 2-18

8. **Click cell B16 and examine the** =AVERAGE(B4:E11) **function in the Formula bar.**

9. **Save the changes to the workbook.**

Leave the workbook open for the next exercise.

Take a tour of some basic functions

Excel has hundreds of functions, but most of them are very specialized. The basic set that the average user works with is much more manageable.

Start with the simplest functions of them all — those without arguments. Two prime examples are

✔ NOW: Reports the current date and time.

✔ TODAY: Reports the current date.

Even though neither uses any arguments, you still have to include the parentheses, so they look lIke this:

    =NOW()
    =TODAY()

Another basic kind of function performs a single, simple math operation and has a single argument that specifies what cell or range it operates on. Table 2-2 summarizes some important functions that work this way.

Table 2-2	Simple One-Argument Functions	
Function	**What It Does**	**Example**
SUM	Sums the values in a range of cells.	=SUM(A1:A10)
AVERAGE	Averages the values in a range of cells.	=AVERAGE(A1:A10)
MIN	Provides the smallest number in a range of cells.	=MIN(A1:A10)
MAX	Provides the largest number in a range of cells.	=MAX(A1:A10)
COUNT	Counts the number of cells that contain numeric values in the range.	=COUNT(A1:A10)
COUNTA	Counts the number of non-empty cells in the range.	=COUNTA(A1:A10)
COUNTBLANK	Counts the number of empty cells in the range.	=COUNTBLANK(A1:A10)

In this exercise, you add some basic functions to a worksheet.

Files needed: Lesson 2 Appliance Sales.xlsx from the preceding exercise

1. **In** Lesson 2 Appliance Sales.xlsx, **in cell A17, type** Lowest **and in cell A18, type** Highest.

2. **In cell B17, type** =MIN(**and then drag across B4:E11 to select the range. Press Enter to complete the function.**

   You do not need to type the closing parenthesis; Excel fills it in for you. The result is 34.

3. **In cell B18, type** =MAX(B4:E11).

   The result is 99.

4. **In cell H1, type** As of, **and in cell I1, type** =TODAY( ).

   Today's date appears in cell I1. Figure 2-19 shows the completed worksheet.

	A	B	C	D	E	F	G	H	I
1	Appliance Sales							As of	1/10/2013
2									
3	**Item**	**Q1**	**Q2**	**Q3**	**Q4**	**Total**	**Bonus**		
4	Blenders	90	49	81	76	296	$2,960		
5	Dishwashers	99	80	38	91	308	$3,080		
6	Ranges	66	91	59	42	258	$2,580		
7	Refrigerators	95	69	39	60	263	$2,630		
8	Mixers	71	42	75	75	263	$2,630		
9	Toasters	34	55	44	75	208	$2,080		
10	Bread Makers	87	74	73	63	297	$2,970		
11	Food Processors	77	86	42	74	279	$2,790		
12									
13	**Total**	619	546	451	556	2172	$21,720		
14									
15	Sales Bonus Per Item	$10							
16	Average Per Item/Qtr	67.875							
17	Lowest	34							
18	Highest	99							
19									
20									

Figure 2-19

5. **Save the changes to the workbook and then close it.**

Leave Excel open for the next exercise.

Working with Named Ranges

When constructing formulas and functions, naming a range can be helpful because you can refer to that name rather than the cell addresses. Therefore you don't have to remember the exact cell addresses, and you can construct formulas based on meaning.

For example, instead of remembering that the number of employees is stored in cell B3, you could name cell B3 *Employees.* Then in a formula that used B3's value, such as `=B3*2`, you could use the name instead: `=Employees*2`.

Naming a range

You can name a range in three ways, and each has pros and cons:

- **If the default names are okay to use, you may find choosing Formulas⇨Create from Selection useful.** With this method, Excel chooses the name for you based on text labels it finds in adjacent cells (above or to the left of the current cells). This method is very fast and easy, and works well when you have to create a lot of names at once and when the cells are well labeled with adjacent text.

 ✔ **You can select the range and then type a name in the Name box (the area immediately above the column A heading, to the left of the Formula bar).** With this fast and easy method, you get to choose the name yourself. However, you have to do each range separately; you can't do a big batch at a time, the way you can with Formulas⇨Create from Selection.

 ✔ **If you want to more precisely control the options for the name, you can choose Formulas⇨Define Name.** This method opens a dialog box from which you can specify the name, the scope, and any comments you might want to include.

In this exercise, you name several ranges using three methods.

Files needed: Lesson 2 Appliance Sales.xlsx from the preceding exercise

1. **Select cells B3:G11 and then choose Formulas⇨Create from Selection.**

   The Create Names from Selection dialog box opens.

2. **Select the Top Row check box (see Figure 2-20) if it is not already selected, and then click OK.**

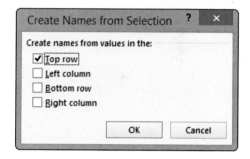

Figure 2-20

   The ranges are assigned names based on the labels in row 3. For example, cells G4:G11 now form a Bonus range because that's the label in G3.

3. **Choose Formulas⇨Name Manager.**

   The Name Manager dialog box opens. The names appear on the list that you just created. (See Figure 2-21.)

4. **Click Close to close the Name Manager dialog box.**

5. **Click cell B15, and in the Name box above column A, type** BonusPer **and press Enter. (See Figure 2-22.)**

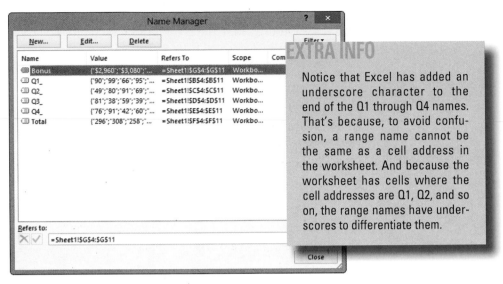

Figure 2-21

EXTRA INFO

Notice that Excel has added an underscore character to the end of the Q1 through Q4 names. That's because, to avoid confusion, a range name cannot be the same as a cell address in the worksheet. And because the worksheet has cells where the cell addresses are Q1, Q2, and so on, the range names have underscores to differentiate them.

Named range (cell B15)

Range name

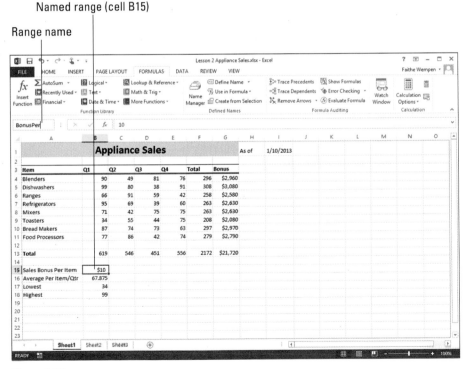

Figure 2-22

6. **Click cell B13 and then choose Formulas⇨Define Name.**

   The New Name dialog box opens.

7. **In the Name text box, type Q1Total, and from the Scope drop-down list, choose Sheet1.**

   Q1Total applies only to this worksheet. (See Figure 2-23.)

8. **Click OK to create the name.**

   The dialog box closes.

9. **Choose Formulas⇨Name Manager.**

   The Name Manager dialog box reopens.

Figure 2-23

10. **Examine the list of all the named ranges you have created, and then click Close to close the dialog box.**

11. **Save the workbook.**

Leave the workbook open for the next exercise.

Using a named range in a formula

The main reason for naming a range is to refer to it in a formula. You can substitute the range name for the cell addresses in any situation where using a range would be appropriate.

When a range contains multiple cells and you use the name in a formula, Excel treats it as if you had specified the range with the starting and ending cell addresses.

In this exercise, you use range names in formulas.

Files needed: Lesson 2 Appliance Sales.xlsx from the preceding exercise

1. **In cells B13, C13, D13, and E13 respectively, enter the following formulas that sum based on the range names (see Figure 2-24):**

   ```
   =SUM(Q1_)
   =SUM(Q2_)
   =SUM(Q3_)
   =SUM(Q4_)
   ```

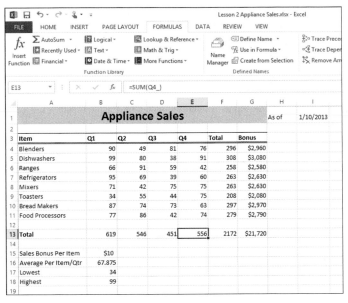

Figure 2-24

2. **In cell G4, edit the formula in the Formula bar as follows:**
=F4*BonusPer.

3. **Select cell G4 and drag the fill handle down to G11, copying the revised formula there.**

TIP

The reference to BonusPer is an absolute reference (as are all named range references), so it copies correctly.

4. **Save the workbook and close it.**

Using Quick Analysis

New in Excel 2013, you can use Quick Analysis to perform common data analysis actions on a range of cells. Choose from five categories of actions. You'll try out each of these categories in the exercise that follows:

EXTRA INFO

Range names that refer to multiple cells may produce an error in a formula where a multi-celled range would not be an appropriate argument. For example, if a Sales range referred to B4:B8, the formula =Sales would result in an error because no math operation is specified. However, =SUM(Sales) would work just fine, as would =SUM(B4:B8).

✔ **Formatting:** Adding data bars, a color scale, icon sets, and other formatting to cells to compare their values to others at a glance. For example, you could make the cells containing the best numbers in the range green and the worst ones red.

✔ **Charts:** Generating charts based on the data in the range. You learn more about charts in Lesson 8, but feel free to experiment with them on your own before then.

✔ **Totals:** Adding functions that summarize the data in the range, such as SUM, AVERAGE, or COUNT.

✔ **Tables:** Converting the range to a table for greater ease of data analysis.

✔ **Sparklines:** Sparklines are mini-charts placed in single cells. They can summarize the trend of the data in adjacent cells.

In this exercise, you use Quick Analysis.

Files needed: Lesson 2 Quick.xlsx

1. **Open** Lesson 2 Quick.xlsx **from the data files for this lesson and save it as** Lesson 2 Sales Analysis.xlsx.

2. **Select the range B3:E11.**

   A Quick Analysis icon appears in the lower-right corner of the selected range.

3. **Click the Quick Analysis icon.**

   A panel of the available actions appears, as shown in Figure 2-25. The five categories of actions appear in all-caps across the top. The first one, FORMATTING, is selected by default, and the available formatting-related actions appear below it.

4. **Click Color Scale.**

   Colors are applied to the cells in the range according to their value, with lower numbers in red and higher numbers in green.

5. **Click away from the selection to clear the selection so you can see the formatting more clearly. (See Figure 2-26.)**

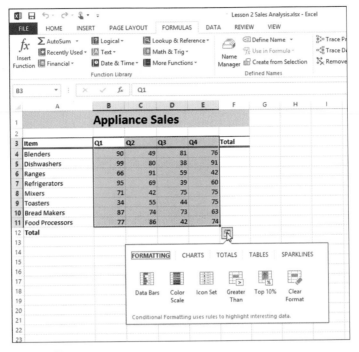

Figure 2-25

Figure 2-26

6. **Press Ctrl+Z to undo the last action, removing the color-scale formatting from the range.**

7. **Select the range A3:E11.**

8. **Click the Quick Analysis icon again, and click CHARTS.**

9. **Point to Stacked Column.**

   A preview appears of a stacked column chart that would be created from the selected data if you chose that action. See Figure 2-27.

Figure 2-27

10. **Click TOTALS.**

    Actions appear for various types of summaries involving functions.

11. **Point to Sum.**

    A boldface Sum row appears below the data in the worksheet, simulating what would appear if you chose this action. (See Figure 2-28.)

12. **Click TABLES.**

    Actions appear for creating a table from the range.

13. **Point to Table.**

    An example appears above the panel, showing what the range would look like if you chose this action to convert it into a table. (See Figure 2-29.)

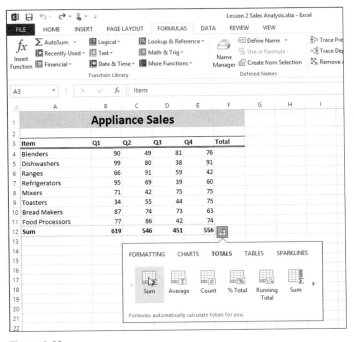

Figure 2-28

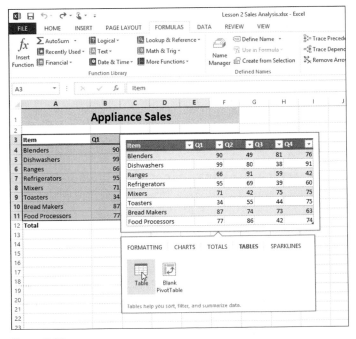

Figure 2-29

14. **Click SPARKLINES**.

Actions appear for adding sparklines for the range.

15. **Point to Line**.

An example appears in column F of sparklines that summarize the data in columns B through E. (See Figure 2-30.)

Figure 2-30

16. **Click away from the panel without making a selection.**

The panel closes.

17. **Close the workbook, saving your changes if prompted, and exit Excel.**

Summing Up

Here are the key points you learned about in this lesson:

- ✔ A formula is a math calculation. Every formula begins with an equal sign.

- ✔ The order of precedence determines the order in which math is processed in a formula: first parentheses, then exponentiation, then multiplication and division, and finally, addition and subtraction.

- ✔ Formulas can contain cell references that substitute the cell's value for the reference when the formula is calculated.

- ✔ When you copy a formula, by default, the cell references in it are relative, so they change based on the new position.

- ✔ Placing dollar signs in a cell reference, such as $A$1, makes it an absolute reference so it does not change when the formula is copied.

- ✔ A function is a word or string of letters that refers to a certain math calculation. A function starts with an equal sign, followed by the function name and a set of parentheses. Arguments for the function go in the parentheses.

- ✔ In functions, you can refer to ranges of cells, such as =SUM(A1:A4).

- ✔ If you don't know which function you want, choose Formulas⇨Insert Function.

- ✔ The NOW function shows the current date and time; the TODAY function shows the current date.

- ✔ SUM sums a range of cells. AVERAGE averages a range of cells.

- ✔ MIN shows the smallest number in a range, and MAX shows the largest number in a range.

- ✔ COUNT counts the number of cells in a range that contains numeric values. Two related functions are COUNTA, which counts the number of non-empty cells, and COUNTBLANK, which counts the number of empty cells.

- ✔ Naming a range enables you to refer to it by a friendly name. Use the commands in the Defined Names group on the Formulas tab.

- ✔ Quick Analysis provides quick access to common tools for analyzing data, including formatting, charting, adding totals, creating tables, and adding sparklines.

Try-it-yourself lab

1. **Start Excel and enter at least six numeric values, along with text labels that explain what each value represents.**

   For example, you might enter the calorie counts of the last six food items you ate, or the prices you paid for the last six books you purchased.

2. **Analyze the data you entered using at least four functions.**

   For example, you could sum, average, and count the data. You could find the minimum and maximum values. You could add text labels that clearly identify what each function's result represents.

3. **Save your work as** Lesson 2 Try It Formulas.xlsx.

Know this tech talk

absolute reference: A cell reference that does not change if copied to another cell.

argument: A placeholder for a number, text string, or cell reference in a function.

AVERAGE: A function that averages a range of values.

COUNT: A function that counts the number of cells that contain numeric values in a range.

COUNTA: A function that counts the number of non-empty cells in the range.

COUNTBLANK: A function that counts the number of empty cells in the range.

formula: A math calculation performed in a cell.

function: A text name that represents a math calculation, such as SUM or AVERAGE.

MAX: A function that provides the largest number in a range of cells.

MIN: A function that provides the smallest number in a range of cells.

mixed reference: A cell reference in which either the row is absolute and the column is relative, or vice versa.

NOW: A function that reports the current date and time.

relative reference: A cell reference that changes if copied to another cell.

sparklines: Mini-charts placed in single cells. They can summarize the trend of the data in adjacent cells.

SUM: A function that sums a range of values.

syntax: The rules that govern how arguments are written in a function.

table: A range of cells that have been specially designated as being part of a related data set. You can perform data-analysis functions on a table that you can't easily perform on non-tabular ranges.

TODAY: A function that reports the current date.

Lesson 3

Formatting and Printing Worksheets

- Resizing rows and columns prevents content from being truncated when an entry is larger than the cell.

- A worksheet background allows a graphic to be used as a backdrop to the worksheet content.

- Headers and footers place repeated information on each page of a printout.

- Customizing a theme enables you to reuse custom font, color, and effect settings easily.

- Formatting a range as a table enables you to apply table styles for quick formatting.

- Creating a new table style enables you to reuse custom table formatting easily.

- Printing a worksheet enables you to share it with others who may not have computer access.

Face it: Plain worksheets aren't that much to look at. A worksheet packed full of rows and columns of numbers is enough to make anyone's eyes glaze over. However, formatting can dramatically improve a worksheet's readability, which in turn enables the reader to understand its meaning much more easily.

You can apply formatting at the whole-worksheet level, or at the individual-cell level. This lesson focuses on formatting entire worksheets — or at least big chunks of them. You learn how to adjust rows and columns, apply worksheet backgrounds, create headers and footers, and format ranges as tables, complete with preset table formatting. You also learn how to print your work in Excel.

Adjusting Rows and Columns

Each column in a worksheet starts with the same width: 8.43 characters (based on the default font and font size), unless you've changed the default setting. That's approximately seven digits and either one large symbol (such as $) or two small ones (such as decimal points and commas).

TIP

You can define the default width setting for new worksheets: Choose Home⇨Format⇨Default Width and then fill in the desired default width.

As you enter the actual data into cells, those column widths may no longer be optimal. Data may overflow out of a cell if the width is too narrow, or there may be excess blank space in a column if its width is too wide. (Blank space is not always a bad thing, but if you're trying to fit all the data on one page, for example, it can be a hindrance.)

In some cases, Excel makes an adjustment for you automatically, as follows:

- ✔ **For column widths:** When you enter numbers in a cell, Excel widens a column as needed to accommodate the longest number in that column, provided you have not manually set a column width for it.

- ✔ **For row heights:** Generally, a row adjusts automatically to fit the largest font used in it. You don't have to adjust row heights manually to allow text to fit. You can change the row height if you want, though, to create special effects, such as extra blank space in the layout.

After you manually resize a row's height or a column's width, it won't change its size automatically for you anymore. That's because manual settings override automatic ones.

The units of measurement are different for rows versus columns, by the way. Column width is measured in characters of the default font size. Row height is measured in points. A point is 1/72 of an inch.

Change a row's height

You can resize rows and columns in several ways. You can auto-fit the cells' sizes to their content, manually drag the widths and heights, or enter a precise value for the widths and heights.

In the following exercise, you adjust row heights in a variety of ways.

Files needed: Lesson 3 Catering.xlsx

1. **Start Excel, if needed, open** `Lesson 3 Catering.xlsx`, **and save it as** Lesson 3 Catering Format.xlsx.

2. **Click the row header for row 4 to select the entire row; then choose Home⇨Format⇨Row Height.**

The Row Height dialog box opens. Note that the row height is currently set to around 18.75. (Yours may be slightly off from that. See Figure 3-1).

The largest font in this row is 14-point, and the additional 4.75 points of height are used for padding. What would happen if you didn't have that extra for padding? The next few steps show this.

Figure 3-1

3. **Type** 14 **in the Row Height box and click OK.**

Notice how the top of the capital letters in row 4 is too close to the cell's upper border now.

4. **Position the mouse pointer between the 4 and 5 row headers, so the pointer turns into a double-headed arrow, and then click and hold the mouse pointer over the divider.**

A ScreenTip appears, showing the current height.

5. **Drag downward until the ScreenTip reads 20.25 points, as shown in Figure 3-2, and then release the mouse button.**

Drag here.

See height setting here.

	A	B	C	D
1	Ralston Catering			
2	No job is too large or too small			
3	Height: 20.25 (27 pixels)			
4	Price List			
5				
6	Item	Per Perso	Min. Persons	
7	Barbecue	9	12	
8	Lemon Ch	8	12	
9	Grilled Ha	12	12	
10	Beef Well	16	12	
11	Ribeye Ste	16	12	
12	Prime Rib	20	24	
13	Surf and T	35	12	

Figure 3-2

EXTRA INFO

You might not be able to drag to an exact amount because the amount has to match with a whole number of pixels. Depending on your screen resolution, the number of pixels that corresponds to a certain number of points may vary. In Figure 3-2, 27 pixels equal 20.25 points, but that might not be so for you. The same goes in Steps 5 and 7; the amounts may be slightly off, depending on your screen resolution.

6. **Position the mouse pointer again over the divider between the row 4 and 5 headers, and double-click.**

The row height auto-resizes to fit.

7. **Click the row 4 header to select the row, and then right-click anywhere in the row and choose Row Height.**

The Row Height dialog box opens again. Notice that its setting is back to somewhere around 18.75.

8. **Click Cancel to close the dialog box.**

Leave the workbook open for the next exercise.

Change a column's width

When content overruns a cell's width, different results occur, depending on the type of data and whether the cell's column width has been adjusted manually.

In the following exercise, you adjust row heights in a variety of ways.

Files needed: Lesson 3 Catering Format.xlsx from the preceding exercise

1. **In** `Lesson 3 Catering Format.xlsx`, **double-click the divider between columns A and B headers.**

   Column A widens enough that the title in cell A1 fits in the cell. (See Figure 3-3.) Although that looks okay, it's not optimal because column A appears too wide.

Double-click here.

	A	B	C	D
1	Ralston Catering			
2	No job is too large or too small			
3				
4	Price List			
5				
6	Item	Per Perso	Min. Persons	
7	Barbecue Chicken	9	12	
8	Lemon Chicken	8	12	
9	Grilled Halibut	12	12	
10	Beef Wellington	16	12	
11	Ribeye Steak	16	12	
12	Prime Rib	20	24	
13	Surf and Turf	35	12	
14				

Figure 3-3

2. **Click and drag the divider between columns A and B headers to the left so that the content of cell A7 fits in the cell with a few characters of space to spare.**

   The content of cell A1 hangs off into cells B1 and C1, but that's okay because they're empty.

3. **Click the column header for column B to select that column, and then choose Home⇨Format⇨AutoFit Column Width.**

   Column B's width increases to accommodate the longest entry (in cell B6).

4. **Click the column header for column C to select it, and then choose Home⇨Format⇨Column Width.**

   The Column Width dialog box opens.

5. **Type 12 in the dialog box, as shown in Figure 3-4, and then click OK.**

   The column width changes to exactly 12 characters.

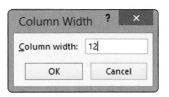

Figure 3-4

Figure 3-5 shows the worksheet after the column-width adjustments.

	A	B	C	D
1	Ralston Catering			
2	No job is too large or too small			
3				
4	Price List			
5				
6	Item	Per Person	Min. Persons	
7	Barbecue Chicken	9	12	
8	Lemon Chicken	8	12	
9	Grilled Halibut	12	12	
10	Beef Wellington	16	12	
11	Ribeye Steak	16	12	
12	Prime Rib	20	24	
13	Surf and Turf	35	12	
14				

Figure 3-5

6. **Save the changes to the workbook and close it.**

Leave Excel open for the next exercise.

Formatting an Entire Worksheet

In addition to formatting individual cells, you can also apply some types of formatting to the entire sheet. For example, you can apply a worksheet background that appears onscreen and can optionally be set to print, and you can control what text appears in a printout's header and footer areas.

Apply a worksheet background

TIP

You can't set a worksheet background to be a solid color with the Background command. However, you can select the entire worksheet by pressing Ctrl+A and then apply a solid color fill to every cell on that worksheet, creating essentially the same effect as applying a solid-color background.

In the following exercise, you apply a worksheet background.

Files needed: Lesson 3 Sheet.xlsx

LINGO

A **worksheet background** is a picture that appears behind the cells. If a cell has no background fill assigned to it, the worksheet background image or color appears as its fill. If the cell already has its own fill, that fill obscures the worksheet background.

1. **Open** Lesson 3 Sheet.xlsx **and then save it as** Lesson 3 Sheet Formatting.xlsx.

2. **Choose Page Layout⇨Background.**

   The Insert Pictures dialog box opens.

3. **In the From a File section, click Browse.**

4. **Navigate to the folder containing the data files for this lesson and click** Lesson 3 Image.jpg.

   See Figure 3-6.

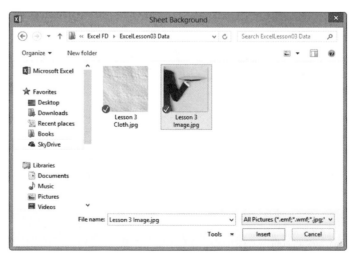

Figure 3-6

5. Click the Insert button.

The image appears as the worksheet background. See Figure 3-7.

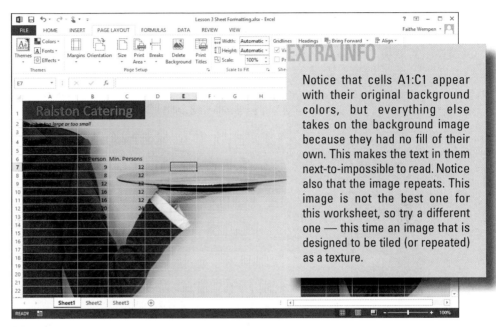

Notice that cells A1:C1 appear with their original background colors, but everything else takes on the background image because they had no fill of their own. This makes the text in them next-to-impossible to read. Notice also that the image repeats. This image is not the best one for this worksheet, so try a different one — this time an image that is designed to be tiled (or repeated) as a texture.

Figure 3-7

6. Choose Page Layout⟹Delete Background, and then choose Page Layout⟹Background.

7. In the From a File section, click Browse.

8. In the folder containing the data files for this lesson, click Lesson 3 Cloth.jpg **and then click the Insert button.**

This image is more suitable for a background because it tiles attractively. See Figure 3-8.

9. Choose File⟹Print and examine the print preview.

Notice that the background will not print.

10. Press Esc to return to normal viewing and save the workbook.

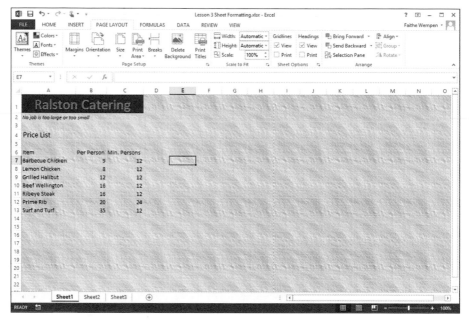

Figure 3-8

Leave the workbook open for the next exercise.

Create a header or footer

In the following exercise, you create a header and footer that prints the company name and a page number.

Files needed: Lesson 3 Sheet Formatting.xlsx from the preceding exercise

1. **In** Lesson 3 Sheet Formatting. xlsx**, choose Insert⇨Header & Footer.**

   The view changes to Page Layout view, so you can see the Header and Footer sections.

   The insertion point moves to the center section of the header.

If your Excel window is not very wide, you might need to click the Text button to open the options in the Text group, and from there click Header & Footer in Step 1.

2. **Type** Ralston Catering Price List **in the center section of the header, as shown in Figure 3-9.**

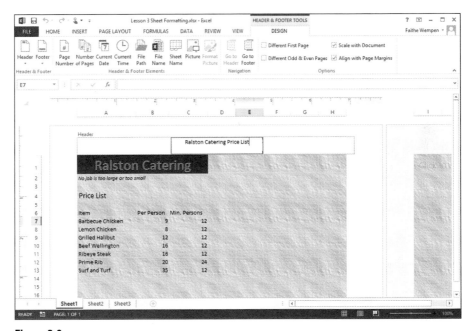

Figure 3-9

3. **Choose Header & Footer Tools Design⇨Go to Footer.**

   The display jumps down to the footer.

4. **Click in the right section of the footer to move the insertion point there.**

5. **Choose Header & Footer Tools Design⇨Page Number.**

   The &[Page] code appears.

6. **Click to place the insertion point to the right of the** &[Page] **code, press the spacebar, type** of, **and press the spacebar again.**

7. **Choose Header & Footer Tools Design⇨Number of Pages.**

   The &[Pages] code appears, as shown in Figure 3-10.

Figure 3-10

8. **Click in the middle section of the footer to move the insertion point away from the page number codes.**

   They change to appear as the actual page numbers: 1 of 1.

9. **Choose Header & Footer Tools Design⇨Go to Header to return to the top of the page and then click in the left section of the header to move the insertion point there.**

10. **Choose Header & Footer Tools Design⇨File Name.**

    The &[File] code appears, as shown in Figure 3-11.

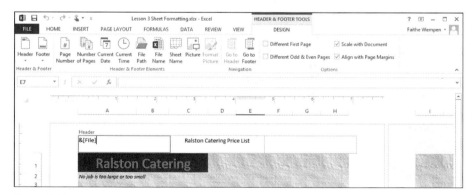

Figure 3-11

11. **Click in the right section of the header to move the insertion point away from the filename code.**

    The actual filename appears in the header.

For more practice, examine the rest of the tools on the Header & Footer Tools Design tab on the Ribbon, and see whether you can determine how each tool might be used. Consult the Help system as needed.

12. **Choose File⟹Print and examine the print preview. Notice that the header and footer appear on the page. Press Esc to leave Backstage view without printing.**

13. **Save your changes and close the workbook.**

Leave Excel open for the next exercise.

Using Theme Formatting

Themes and table styles are two ways of applying formatting to an entire worksheet or data range at once. Each one can be used with preset settings or customized for an individual look. For each one, you can then save your custom formatting to reuse in other workbooks and tables.

Apply a workbook theme

Themes are standard across most Office applications (including Word, Excel, and PowerPoint), so you can standardize your formatting across all the documents you create.

LINGO

Themes are formatting presets that you can apply to entire worksheets.

In the following exercise, you apply a theme and a color theme.

Files needed: Lesson 3 Theme.xlsx

1. **Open** Lesson 3 Theme.xlsx **and save it as** Lesson 3 Theme Formatting.xlsx.

2. **Choose Page Layout⟹Themes.**

A list of themes appears. (See Figure 3-12.)

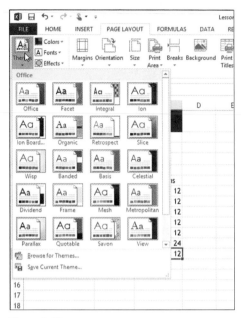

Figure 3-12

3. Choose the Slice theme to apply it.

Notice that the color of the fill behind cells A1:C1 changes, as do the fonts. (See Figure 3-13.)

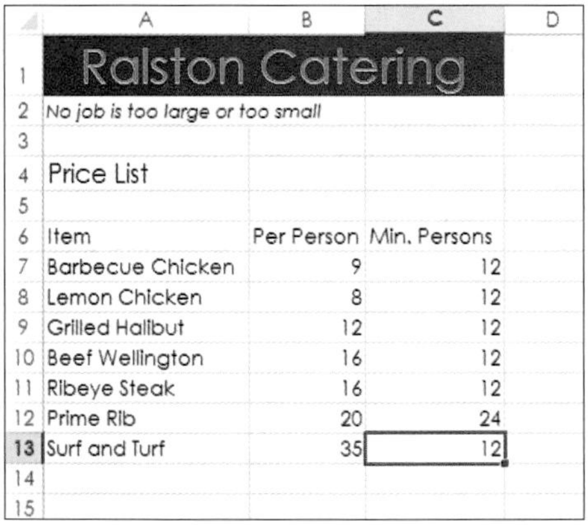

	A	B	C	D
1	Ralston Catering			
2	No job is too large or too small			
3				
4	Price List			
5				
6	Item	Per Person	Min. Persons	
7	Barbecue Chicken	9	12	
8	Lemon Chicken	8	12	
9	Grilled Halibut	12	12	
10	Beef Wellington	16	12	
11	Ribeye Steak	16	12	
12	Prime Rib	20	24	
13	Surf and Turf	35	12	
14				
15				

Figure 3-13

4. Choose Page Layout➪Colors.

A list of color themes appears. (See Figure 3-14.)

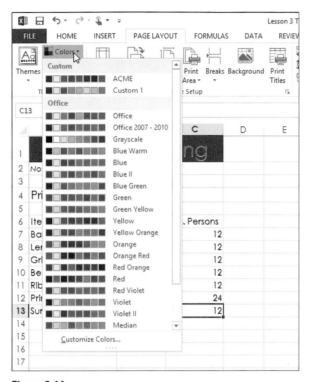

Figure 3-14

5. Choose Red.

The colors change to a black background and yellow letters in cells A1:C1.

6. Save the workbook.

Leave the workbook open for the next exercise.

Customize a theme

If none of the themes suits your needs, you may want to create your own theme. You can do this by choosing the colors, fonts, and effects that you want (from the Page Layout tab) and then saving the unique combination you chose as a new theme.

In this exercise, you create a custom theme.

Files needed: Lesson 3 Theme Formatting.xlsx from preceding exercise

1. **If you did not already change the Color theme to Red in the previous exercise, choose Page Layout➪Colors and then choose Red from the list of color themes that appears.** (Refer to Figure 3-14.)

TIP

You can also create a custom theme by choosing one of the existing themes from the Theme button and then customizing it by selecting a different set of colors, fonts, or effects.

2. **Choose Page Layout➪Fonts and then choose Trebuchet from the list of font themes that appears, as shown in Figure 3-15.**

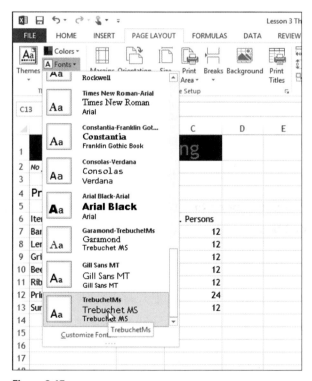

Figure 3-15

3. **Choose Page Layout➪Effects and then choose Glow Edge from the list of effect themes that appears.**

4. **Choose Page Layout➪Themes➪Save Current Theme.**

The Save Current Theme dialog box opens.

5. **In the File Name box, type** Intensity, **as shown in Figure 3-16, and then click Save to save the new theme.**

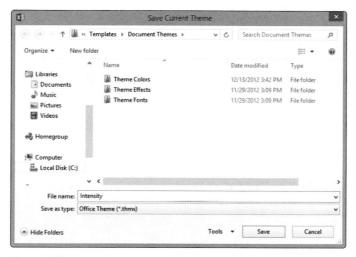

Figure 3-16

TIP

Themes are stored in a common location for all Office applications, so you can reuse your custom theme in Word and PowerPoint.

6. **Choose Page Layout⇨Themes. Notice that your new theme appears at the top of the list.**

7. **Click away from the menu to close it without making a selection.**

8. **Save the workbook.**

Leave the workbook open for the next exercise.

Format a range as a table

You can format certain ranges as tables in Excel, which not only enables you to apply formatting presets more easily, but also gives the range special properties that make it easier to search and sort them. You learn more about working with tables in Lesson 5, but this lesson shows you how to convert a range to a table purely for formatting purposes.

LINGO

A **table,** in the context of an Excel worksheet, is a range that has been marked as a single logical unit for data storage and retrieval.

In this exercise, you convert a range to a table and apply table style formatting.

Files needed: Lesson 3 Theme Formatting.xlsx from the preceding exercise

1. **In** `Lesson 3 Theme Formatting.xlsx`, **select cells A6:C13 and then choose Home⇨Format as Table.**

   A gallery of formatting styles appears. See Figure 3-17.

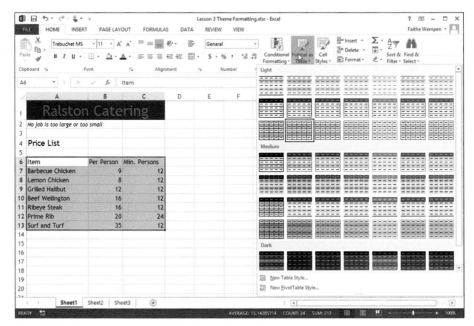

Figure 3-17

2. **Click the Table Style Medium 9 style (**the ninth style in the Medium section).

   The Format as Table dialog box opens, with the range already filled in from the selection you made in Step 1. See Figure 3-18.

3. **Click OK.**

   The range is converted to a table and the style is applied. The Table Tools Design tab becomes active. On this tab are commands for formatting that can be used only on ranges that are defined as tables.

4. **Deselect the Banded Rows check box to see how the alternate-row color banding is removed. Re-select the check box to restore the banding.**

5. **Save the workbook.**

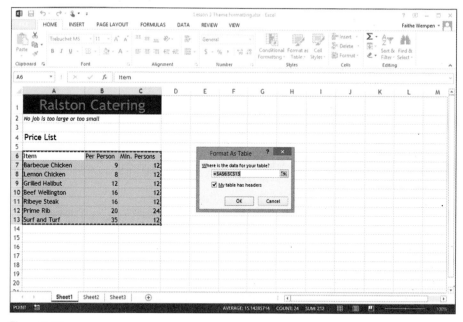

Figure 3-18

Leave the workbook open for the next exercise.

Create a custom table style

You can rely on the standard table styles that Excel provides, or you can customize a table style and then save it as a new style that you can then apply to other ranges.

In this exercise, you create a custom table style.

Files needed: Lesson 3 Theme Formatting.xlsx from the preceding exercise

1. **Choose Home⇨Format as Table⇨New Table Style.**

   The New Table Quick Style dialog box opens.

2. **In the Name box, replace the default name with** Custom Table 1.

3. **In the Table Element list, select Header Row, as shown in Figure 3-19.**

4. **Click the Format button to open the Format Cells dialog box.**

5. **Click the Fill tab and then click the fifth square in the next-to-the-last row of colors, as shown in Figure 3-20.**

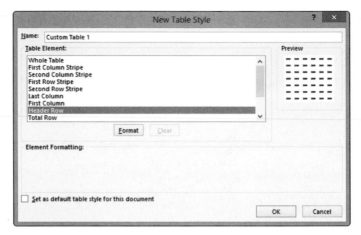

Figure 3-19

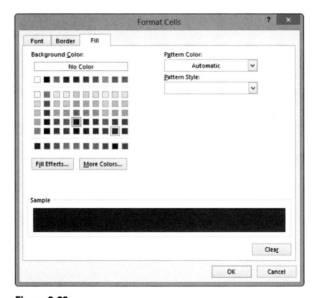

Figure 3-20

6. **Click the Font tab; then open the Color drop-down list and choose the white square in the Theme Colors section, as shown in Figure 3-21.**

7. **Click OK to return to the New Table Style dialog box and then click OK to create the new table style.**

TIP

Creating a new table style does not automatically apply it to the selected range, so you must apply the style.

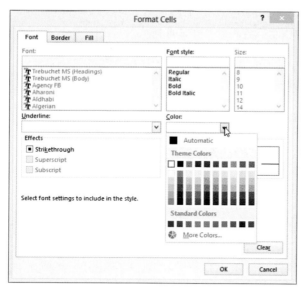

Figure 3-21

8. **Select cells A6:C13 and then choose Home⇨Format as Table; in the Custom section at the top of the menu, select the new style you just created, as shown in Figure 3-22.**

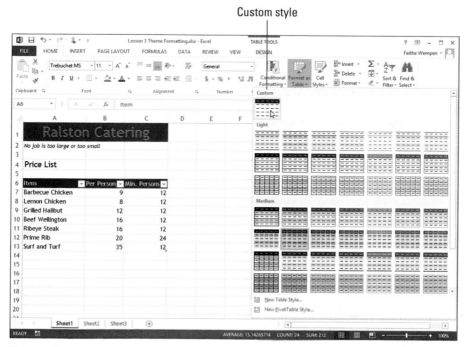

Figure 3-22

9. **Save the workbook.**

Leave the workbook open for the next exercise.

Printing Worksheets

You can print your work in Excel on paper, to share with people who may not have computer access, or to pass out as handouts at meetings and events. You can print the quick-and-easy way with the default settings or customize the settings to fit your needs.

Preview and print the active worksheet

By default, when you print, Excel prints the entire active worksheet — that is, whichever worksheet is displayed or selected at the moment. But Excel also gives you other printing options:

- ✔ **Print multiple worksheets:** If more than one worksheet is selected (for example, if you have more than one worksheet tab selected at the bottom of the Excel window), all selected worksheets are included in the printed version. As an alternative, you can print all the worksheets in the workbook.

- ✔ **Print selected cells or ranges:** You can choose to print only selected cells, or you can define a print range and print only that range (regardless of what cells happen to be selected).

In Excel 2013, Print Preview is built into Backstage view, so you see a preview of the printout at the same place where you change the print settings.

In this exercise, you preview and print a worksheet.

Files needed: Lesson 3 Theme Formatting.xlsx from the preceding exercise

1. **Choose File⇨Print.**

   The Print settings appear, along with a preview of the printout. (See Figure 3-23.)

2. **In the Copies box, click the up-increment arrow to change the value to 2.**

3. **Click the Print button to send the job to the printer.**

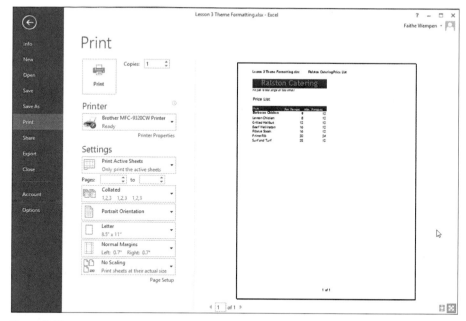

Figure 3-23

Leave the workbook open for the next exercise.

Set and use a print range

There are two ways to print only a certain range of cells on the active worksheet. If you want to select a certain range for a one-time print job, you can just select them and then choose to print only the selection. If you want the same cells (only) to print each time you print this worksheet in the future too, you can select them as a print range, and Excel remembers them.

In this exercise, you print only certain cells, using two methods.

Files needed: Lesson 3 Theme Formatting.xlsx from the preceding exercise

1. **Select the range A6:C13 and then choose File⇨Print.**

2. **Click the Print Active Sheets button, and then choose Print Selection from the menu that appears, as shown in Figure 3-24.**

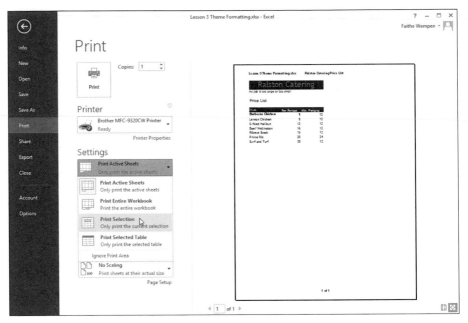

Figure 3-24

3. **Click Print.**

   The copy that prints contains only the range you specified.

4. **Choose Page Layout⇨Print Area ⇨Set Print Area, as shown in Figure 3-25.**

Figure 3-25

5. **Click away from the selected range to deselect it and then choose File⇨Print.**

6. **Examine the preview of the print job, as shown in Figure 3-26.**

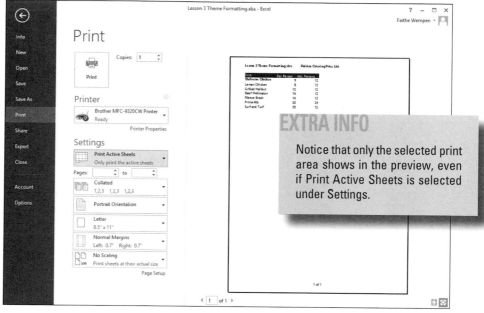

EXTRA INFO

Notice that only the selected print area shows in the preview, even if Print Active Sheets is selected under Settings.

Figure 3-26

7. **Press Esc to close Backstage view.**

8. **Choose Page Layout➪Print Area➪Clear Print Area.**

9. **Save the workbook.**

Leave the workbook open for the next exercise.

Adjust the page size, orientation, and margins while printing

You can set the page size, orientation, and margins at any time from the Page Layout tab. Doing so permanently changes those settings. If you want to change any of those settings only for one particular print job, though, you can change them from Backstage view, as part of the printing options. When you change the settings in Backstage view, they don't "stick." The next time you open and work with the workbook, the settings go back to what they were before.

In this exercise, you change the page size, orientation, and margins for a one-time print job.

Files needed: Lesson 3 Theme Formatting.xlsx from the preceding exercise

1. **Choose Print Area⇨Clear Print Area to make sure there is no print area set from a previous exercise.**

2. **Choose File⇨Print.**

3. **Click the Portrait Orientation button to open a menu and choose Landscape Orientation.**

   As in Figure 3-27, the print preview changes to show the new orientation.

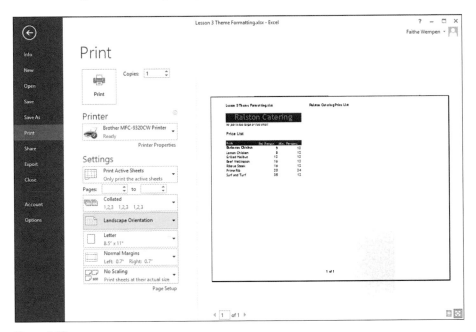

Figure 3-27

4. **Click the Letter 8.5" x 11" button to open a menu and choose B6 4.92" x 6.93".**

   Figure 3-28 shows the menu.

   The paper size changes in the preview to the smaller size. This change, shown in Figure 3-29, bunches up the text in the header so that the text overlaps unattractively.

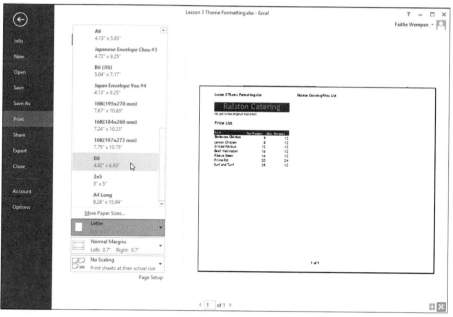

Figure 3-28

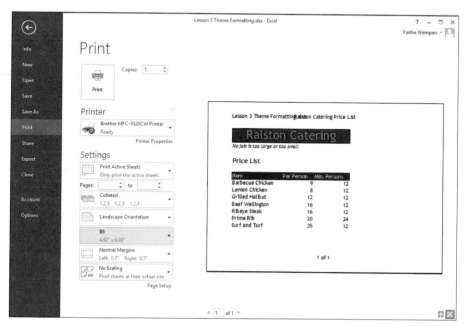

Figure 3-29

5. Click the Page Setup hyperlink.

The Page Setup dialog box opens.

6. Click the Header/Footer tab and then click the Custom Header button.

The Header dialog box opens. (See Figure 3-30.)

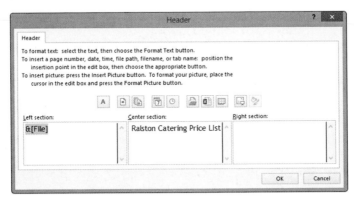

To format text: select the text, then choose the Format Text button.
To insert a page number, date, time, file path, filename, or tab name: position the insertion point in the edit box, then choose the appropriate button.
To insert picture: press the Insert Picture button. To format your picture, place the cursor in the edit box and press the Format Picture button.

Left section: &[File]

Center section: Ralston Catering Price List

Right section:

Figure 3-30

7. Delete the code in the Left Section box, click OK to close the Header dialog box, and then click OK to close the Page Setup dialog box.

8. Click the Normal Margins button and choose Narrow.

9. Click the No Scaling button, and choose Fit Sheet on One Page.

Steps 7 and 8 are not necessary for this worksheet because it fits on one page already, but these techniques will be useful to you in real-life usage.

10. Click Print to print the worksheet.

11. Save the workbook and close it.

Exit Excel.

Summing Up

Here are the key points you learned about in this lesson:

- ✔ You can adjust the sizes of rows and columns by dragging the dividers between row or column headers, or by double-clicking the dividers to auto-size.

- ✔ To add a background to a worksheet, choose Page Layout⇨Background.

- ✔ Choose Insert⇨Header & Footer to create headers and footers that repeat on each page of a printout.

- ✔ Themes standardize the fonts, colors, and effects across multiple workbooks. To apply a theme, choose Page Layout⇨Theme.

- ✔ Formatting a range as a table enables you to apply the table formatting presets from the Home tab. It also has some other benefits, which you learn about in Lesson 5.

- ✔ You can format the text in a cell in much the same way as in Word: Use the controls in the Font group on the Home tab, or on the mini toolbar.

- ✔ When you print from Excel, you can print the active worksheet or select only a range of cells to print by setting the Print Area.

Try-it-yourself lab

1. **Start Excel, open the file** Lesson 3 Try It Table.xlsx, **and save it as** Try It Table Final.xlsx.

2. **Adjust the column widths so that no text is truncated.**

3. **Format cells A10:F12 as a table, using your choice of table styles.**

4. **In the footer of the worksheet, in the center, place the text** Thank You for Your Business. **Then return to Normal view.**

5. **Apply the Organic theme, or another theme of your choice.**

6. **Print one copy of the worksheet in Landscape orientation.**

7. **Save the workbook and close Excel.**

Know this tech talk

footer: Repeated text at the bottom of each page of a printout.

header: Repeated text at the top of each page of a printout.

print range: A defined range of cells that prints whenever the active worksheet is printed, rather than the entire worksheet printing.

table: In Excel, a range that has been marked as a single logical unit for data storage and retrieval.

theme: A formatting preset that you can apply to an entire worksheet, consisting of fonts, colors, and effects.

worksheet background: A picture that appears behind the cells of a worksheet.

Lesson 4
Formatting Data

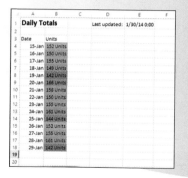

✔ Applying a background fill and outline to a cell makes it stand out.

✔ Formatting the text in a cell makes it more attractive and readable.

✔ Wrapping text in a cell enables a cell's height to expand as needed to accommodate more content.

✔ Aligning text in a cell in ways different from the default allows flexibility in worksheet design.

✔ Applying number formats gives context to a number by presenting it as currency, a percentage, or some other type.

✔ Conditional formatting formats the text in a cell differently, depending on its content.

In this lesson, you learn a variety of techniques for formatting the data in individual cells of a worksheet — and for formatting the cells themselves. You can use these techniques to improve your own worksheets and, when you receive worksheets from someone else, to quickly make plain worksheets more readable. You learn how to change the row and column sizes, how to format the text in cells, and how to apply fill formatting to the cells themselves. You also learn how to create conditional formatting rules that change the way the data is formatted depending on its value.

Formatting Cells

By modifying cell fill and border, you can make a worksheet much easier to read and interpret. For example, you could make the background of a cell that contains a grand total a different color from the rest, and place a thick border around the cell to draw attention to it. Borders can also be used to create dividing lines between certain rows and columns, and alternate-row shading within a dense list of data can help the eye follow a long row across the page.

LINGO

Cells can have formatting assigned to them, independently of the formatting assigned to their content. Each cell has two main formatting properties: its **fill** (that is, its inner color) and its **border** (that is, the outline around it). By default, cell borders are set to No Border.

Apply a fill to a cell or range

A background fill can be any solid color, or a gradient or pattern. You can choose from the theme colors or some fixed standard colors, or open a Color dialog box in which you can select from many other colors or specify a color by number.

In this exercise, you fill cells with theme colors, standard colors, and custom colors.

Files needed: Lesson 4 Catering.xlsx

1. **Open** `Lesson 4 Catering.xlsx` **and save it as** Lesson 4 Catering Final.xlsx.

2. **Select cells A6:C6; then from the Home tab, click the down arrow to the right of the Fill Color button, opening a color palette.**

3. **Click the bright red square under Standard Colors, as shown in Figure 4-1.**

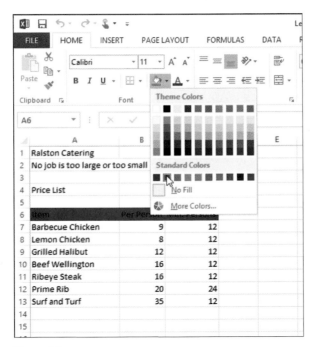

Figure 4-1

For more practice, before you click the red square in Step 3, point at several other colors to preview them on the selected range behind the open palette.

4. **Click the arrow to the right of the Fill Color button again, and in the Theme Colors section, choose Olive Green, Accent 3, Darker 25%. Point to a color to see a ScreenTip showing its name.**

To determine a color's name, point the mouse at it and read the ScreenTip.

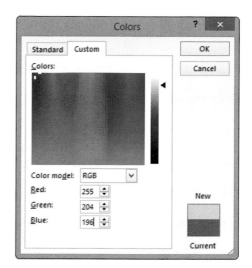

Figure 4-2

5. **Click the arrow to the right of the Fill Color button again, and choose More Colors.**

6. **Click the Custom tab if it's not already selected, and in the Color Model drop-down list, choose RGB if it's not already selected.**

7. **Enter the following values, as shown in Figure 4-2: Red** 255, **Green** 204, **and Blue** 196.

8. **Click OK to accept the new custom color and then save the changes to the workbook.**

Leave the workbook open for the next exercise.

Format a cell's border

Borders are a bit more complex than fills because they have a color as well as a style (such as dotted or dashed) and a weight (or thickness). You can also place a border around individual sides of a cell or range of cells.

In this exercise, you apply several types of borders to cells, using several methods.

Files needed: Lesson 4 Catering Final.xlsx from the preceding exercise

1. **In** Lesson 4 Catering Final.xlsx, **select cells A6:C6.**

2. **From the Home tab, click the down arrow to the right of the Border button and choose Thick Bottom Border, which is one of several presets in the middle of the menu, as shown in Figure 4-3.**

LINGO

Do not confuse borders with gridlines. The **gridlines** are the edges of the cells that you see, by default, onscreen in gray. They don't print. A **border** is an outline that you specifically apply to a cell; it does print. You can turn off the onscreen display of gridlines on the View tab.

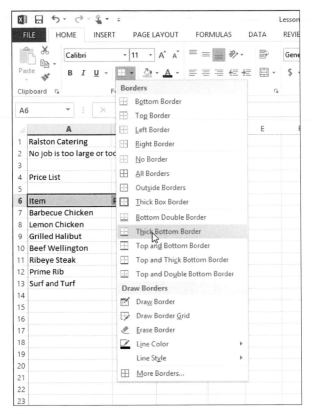

Figure 4-3

3. **Click away from the selection so you can see the new line.**

4. **From the Home tab, click the down arrow to the right of the Border button and choose Line Color to open a color palette.**

5. **Click Dark Red from the Standard Colors section.**

As shown in Figure 4-4, the menu closes and the mouse pointer turns into a pencil symbol.

6. **Click the down arrow to the right of the Border button again, choose Line Style, and choose a dashed line style.**

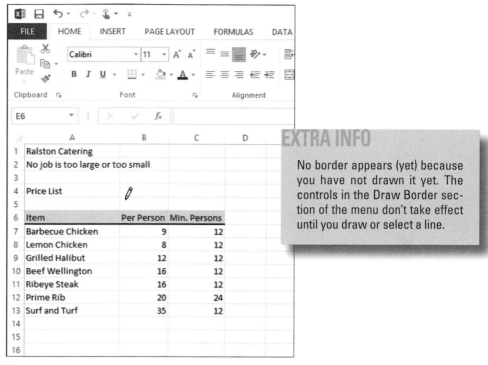

Figure 4-4

EXTRA INFO

No border appears (yet) because you have not drawn it yet. The controls in the Draw Border section of the menu don't take effect until you draw or select a line.

7. **Drag to draw a line under cell A4, and another one above cell A4. Then press the Esc key to turn off the pencil mouse pointer.**

   See Figure 4-5.

8. **Select the range A6:C13, click the down arrow to the right of the Border button, and choose All Borders.**

   The same dashed, dark-red border is applied to all borders of all cells in the selected range.

9. **Press Ctrl+Z to undo the last action.**

	A	B	C	D
1	Ralston Catering			
2	No job is too large or too small			
3				
4	Price List			
5				
6	Item	Per Person	Min. Persons	
7	Barbecue Chicken	9	12	
8	Lemon Chicken	8	12	
9	Grilled Halibut	12	12	
10	Beef Wellington	16	12	
11	Ribeye Steak	16	12	
12	Prime Rib	20	24	
13	Surf and Turf	35	12	
14				

Figure 4-5

10. **Click the down arrow to the right of the Border button and choose More Borders.**

The Format Cells dialog box opens with the Border tab displayed.

11. **In the Style section, click the thinnest solid line (the bottom line in the left column).**

12. **Open the Color drop-down list and click the bright red square under Standard Colors.**

13. **Click the Outline button.**

Borders appear in the preview area around the outside of the selection.

14. **Click the Inside button.**

Borders appear in the preview area around the inner borders of the selection.

Figure 4-6 shows the completed dialog box.

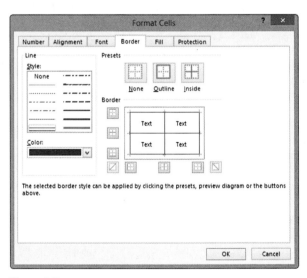

Figure 4-6

15. **Click OK to apply the border to the cells.**

16. **Click the down arrow to the right of the Border button and choose Erase Border.**

The mouse pointer turns into an eraser symbol.

17. **Click the borders above and below cell A4 to erase them.**

18. **Press the Esc key to turn off the eraser cursor on the mouse pointer, and click away from the selection to deselect it.**

Figure 4-7 shows the completed worksheet.

19. **Save the changes to the workbook.**

Leave the workbook open for the next exercise.

⏴	A	B	C	D
1	Ralston Catering			
2	No job is too large or too small			
3				
4	Price List			
5				
6	Item	Per Person	Min. Persons	
7	Barbecue Chicken	9	12	
8	Lemon Chicken	8	12	
9	Grilled Halibut	12	12	
10	Beef Wellington	16	12	
11	Ribeye Steak	16	12	
12	Prime Rib	20	24	
13	Surf and Turf	35	12	
14				
15				

Figure 4-7

Formatting Cell Content

In addition to formatting the cell itself, you can also format its content. This can include applying text formatting (such as font, size, color, and effect) much as you do in Word. You can also wrap text in the cell to multiple lines when it's too long to fit on one row, set the vertical and horizontal alignment within a cell, format numbers in different ways (such as currency or percentage), and apply cell styles that provide different preset combinations of the previously mentioned types of formatting.

When formatting cell contents, in addition to the Ribbon-based methods that the following exercises use, you can also use the mini toolbar. Right-click the selected cell (or cells) to make the mini toolbar appear, and then select commands from the mini toolbar rather than from the Home tab on the Ribbon, if you prefer.

Change font and font size

Font and font size are controlled with their respective drop-down lists on the Home tab, or from the mini toolbar.

If you want to format a worksheet using themes (on the Page Layout tab), as described in Lesson 3, the fonts in the theme will not be applied if you have manually changed to different fonts. To get back to using the defaults so the theme-font changes will apply, choose a font from the Theme Fonts section of the Font drop-down list.

In the following exercise, you improve a worksheet's appearance by changing some fonts and sizes.

Files needed: Lesson 4 Catering Final.xlsx from the preceding exercise

1. **In** Lesson 4 Catering Final.xlsx, **select cell A1. Then, from the Home tab, choose Aharoni from the Font drop-down list.**

   As Figure 4-8 shows, the font is applied to the text in cell A1.

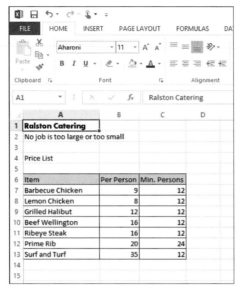

Figure 4-8

For more practice, change the font several more times, each time choosing a different font. You can also try changing it with the mini toolbar: Right-click cell A1 and then open the Font drop-down list from the mini toolbar that appears.

2. **With A1 still selected, from the Home tab, choose 24 from the Font Size drop-down list.**

   See Figure 4-9. The font size changes to 24-point.

3. **Choose Home⇨Increase Font Size.**

   The font goes up one size (2 points). The new size reported in the Font Size box on the Home tab is 26 points.

4. **Click in the Font Size box on the Home tab, moving the insertion point into it, and type** 30, **replacing the current entry. Press Enter to apply the new font size to cell A1.**

   See Figure 4-10.

When you manually type in the font size, as in Step 4, you can use any size you want, with increments as small as $\frac{1}{10}$th of a point.

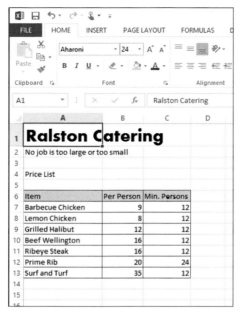

Figure 4-9

EXTRA INFO

Notice that the Font Size drop-down list does not increment by 1 point at the larger sizes. There are some fairly large gaps, such as the one between 28 and 36 points.

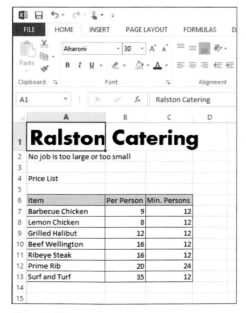

Figure 4-10

5. Save the changes to the workbook.

Leave the workbook open for the next exercise.

Change font color and attributes

Text color and attributes can have an impact on the readability and attractiveness of a worksheet. As with font and size changes, you can apply color and attributes either from the Home tab, or from the mini toolbar that appears when you right-click the selected cell(s). You can also set text formatting from the Font tab of the Format Cells dialog box.

In the following exercise, you improve the look of a worksheet by applying font colors and attributes.

Files needed: Lesson 4 Catering Final.xlsx from the preceding exercise

1. **In** `Lesson 4 Catering Final.xlsx`, **select cell A1. Then from the Home tab, click the down arrow to the right of the Font Color button to open its palette.**

2. **In the Theme Colors section of the palette, click Orange, Accent 6, changing to a theme color.**

   See Figure 4-11. You can point to a color on the palette to see a ScreenTip telling its name.

3. **Right-click cell A4, opening the mini toolbar, as shown in Figure 4-12. On the toolbar, click the down arrow to the right of the Font Color button, and then click Orange, Accent 6, Darker 50%.**

4. **Choose Home⇨Bold to apply bold to the text in cell A4. Choose Home⇨Italic to apply italics to the text in cell A4.**

You can also use keyboard shortcuts for Bold (Ctrl+B), Italic (Ctrl+I), and Underline (Ctrl+U).

Click here.

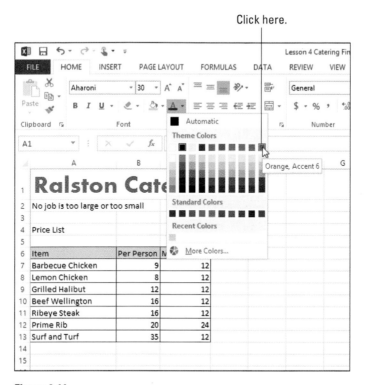

Figure 4-11

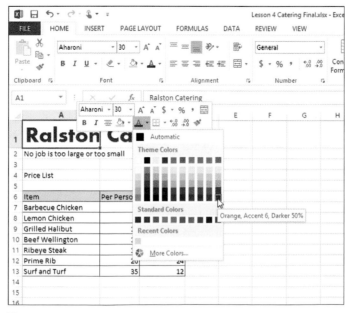

Figure 4-12

5. **Click the dialog box launcher in the Font group, opening the Font tab of the Format Cells dialog box (see Figure 4-13).**

Figure 4-13

6. **Choose Double from the Underline drop-down list and click OK.**

The text in cell A4 is double-underlined.

The Underline button on the Home tab has a drop-down list with different underline styles, so you don't always have to open the Format Cells dialog box when you want a non-standard underline. However, the Underline drop-down list has only two choices: Underline and Double Underline. The drop-down list in the dialog box has some other choices too, such as Single Accounting and Double Accounting.

7. **Save the workbook.**

Leave the workbook open for the next exercise.

Wrap text in a cell

When a cell's entry is too wide for the cell, you can widen the cell, as you learn in Lesson 3. Or you can allow the cell's content to wrap to additional lines in the cell. The cell gets taller (automatically) but retains its width.

EXTRA INFO

You can manually break the text to the next line in a cell by pressing Alt+Enter where you want the break to occur, but it's easier to use the automatic method shown in the following exercise.

In the following exercise, you wrap text in cells so you can decrease column widths without truncating any entries.

Files needed: Lesson 4 Catering Final.xlsx from the preceding exercise

1. **In** `Lesson 4 Catering Final.xlsx`, **select the range B6:C6 and then choose Home➪Wrap Text (see Figure 4-14).**

   Nothing changes in the worksheet because the columns are wide enough that the text in those cells doesn't need to wrap to the next line.

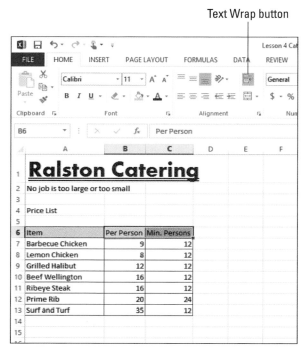

Text Wrap button

Figure 4-14

2. **With B6:C6 still selected, choose Home➪Format➪Column Width.**

   The Column Width dialog box opens (see Figure 4-15).

3. **Type** 8 **and click OK. The column width changes for columns B and C to 8 characters.**

   Because the row height for row 6 has previously been adjusted manually, it no longer automatically adjusts to the new content, so the additional wrapped

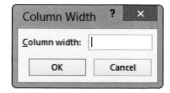

Figure 4-15

lines may be truncated. That makes it necessary to readjust the row height in the next step. You might not have to do that on your own worksheets.

4. **Point to the divider between the headers for rows 6 and 7 and double-click, auto-fitting the row height for row 6 to the wrapped content.**

See Figure 4-16 for the final result.

	A	B	C	D	E
1	**Ralston Catering**				
2	No job is too large or too small				
3					
4	Price List				
5					
6	Item	Per Person	Min. Persons		
7	Barbecue Chicken	9	12		
8	Lemon Chicken	8	12		
9	Grilled Halibut	12	12		
10	Beef Wellington	16	12		
11	Ribeye Steak	16	12		
12	Prime Rib	20	24		
13	Surf and Turf	35	12		
14					
15					

Figure 4-16

For more practice, select cell A2 and click the Wrap Text button to see an example of a cell where the height adjusts automatically when you wrap the text. That's because row 2 had no previous manual adjustment made to its row height. Click Wrap Text again to toggle the text wrapping off when you've finished experimenting with row 2.

5. **Save the workbook.**

Leave the workbook open for the next exercise.

Align text in a cell

By default, text in a cell aligns horizontally to the left and vertically to the bottom. You can see this if you look at Figure 4-16, where the word *Item* is in the bottom-left corner of cell A6. Numbers align horizontally to the right, as you can see in cells B7:C13.

Each cell can have any of the following horizontal alignments. Some of them are available only via the Format Cells dialog box:

✔ **General:** The default setting. Left-aligns text, and right-aligns numbers.

✔ **Left (Indent):** Aligns the content to the left, regardless of its type. You can optionally specify an amount of indentation from the left side.

✔ **Center:** Centers the entry evenly between the left and right sides of the cell.

✔ **Right (Indent):** Aligns the content to the right, regardless of its type. You can optionally specify an amount of indentation from the right side.

✔ **Fill:** Repeats the value in the cell so that the cell is completely filled. For example, if you enter **X**, the cell is filled with as many Xs as it takes to stretch the width of the column.

✔ **Justify:** Applicable only in a cell that uses Text Wrap. On every line except the last one, adds space between words as needed so the entry stretches across the entire width of the column. The last line is left-aligned.

✔ **Center Across Selection:** Applicable only when you select multiple cells before you apply it, this setting centers the content of the top-left cell in the selected range across the selection.

✔ **Distributed (Indent):** Adds space between words as needed so the entry stretches across the entire width of the column. This is different from Justify in that it applies to all lines, so its effect can be seen on cells that are not word-wrapped. You can optionally specify an amount of indent.

Vertical alignment is simpler; it can only be set to Top, Middle, Bottom, Justify, or Distributed. Justify and Distributed both spread out a multi-line entry to align at both the bottom and top of a cell. The difference between them is that, when applied to a single-line entry, Justify top-aligns the content, whereas Distributed center-aligns the content.

In the following exercise, you set the vertical and horizontal alignment for content in cells.

Files needed: Lesson 4 Catering Final.xlsx from the preceding exercise

1. **In** `Lesson 4 Catering Final.xlsx`**, select cell A6.**

2. **Choose Home⇨Center to center the text horizontally. Choose Home⇨ Middle Align to center the text vertically. See Figure 4-17.**

3. **Select the range A7:A13 and from the Home tab, click the Alignment group's dialog box launcher.**

   The Format Cells dialog box opens with the Alignment tab displayed.

Figure 4-17

4. **Choose Left (Indent) from the Horizontal drop-down list.**

5. **In the Indent box, click the up-increment arrow once to add a one-character indentation.**

6. **Choose Center from the Vertical drop-down list.**

Figure 4-18 shows the completed dialog box.

7. **Click OK.**

The alignments are applied, but you don't really notice a difference in the vertical alignments because the cell heights are auto-fitted. Vertical alignment becomes apparent only in cells with extra vertical space, such as cell A6.

For even more practice, set cell A2 to Wrap Text, and then apply the various horizontal and vertical Justify and Distribute settings to the cell to experiment with their differences.

8. **Select the range A1:D1, and choose Home⇨Merge & Center.**

This command simultaneously merges the selected cells into one unit, places the text from the leftmost cell in the range (cell A1) in that unit, and sets the horizontal alignment to Center Across Selection. (See Figure 4-19.)

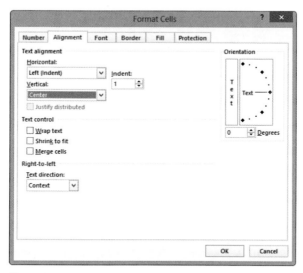

Figure 4-18

Merge and Center button

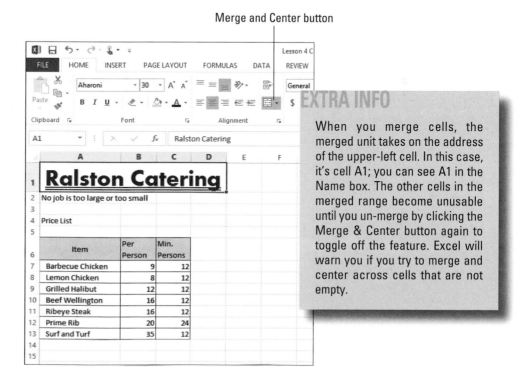

EXTRA INFO

When you merge cells, the merged unit takes on the address of the upper-left cell. In this case, it's cell A1; you can see A1 in the Name box. The other cells in the merged range become unusable until you un-merge by clicking the Merge & Center button again to toggle off the feature. Excel will warn you if you try to merge and center across cells that are not empty.

Figure 4-19

9. **Save the workbook.**

Leave the workbook open for the next exercise.

Apply cell styles

In the following exercise, you apply cell styles, and you create and apply your own custom cell style.

Files needed: Lesson 4 Catering Final.xlsx from the preceding exercise

1. **In** Lesson 4 Catering Final.xlsx, **click cell A4, choose Home⇨Cell Styles to open the gallery of cell-style presets, and click Heading 1, as shown in Figure 4-20.**

LINGO

Cell styles are formatting presets you can apply to cells. You can use any of the default presets that Excel provides, or you can create your own. Creating your own cell styles can help you format a worksheet more quickly when there is a lot of repetitive formatting to be done.

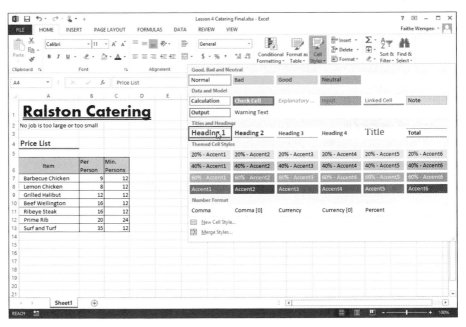

Figure 4-20

2. **Click the Undo button on the Quick Access toolbar, or press Ctrl+Z, to undo the style application.**

3. **Click Home⇨Increase Font Size twice to increase the font size of the text in A4 to 14-point.**

4. **Choose Home⇨Cell Styles⇨New Cell Style to open the Style dialog box.**

REMEMBER

When you create a new cell style, you base it on an example, so you must select a cell that already contains the formatting you want before issuing the command.

5. **In the Style name box, type** Major Heading. **Clear all the check boxes in the dialog box except Font, as shown in Figure 4-21. Then click OK.**

6. **Click in cell A15 and type** Setup Costs **and press Enter.**

7. **Re-select cell A15, and then choose Home⇨Cell Styles⇨Major Heading.**

You find the Major Heading style at the top of the gallery, in the Custom section. The custom style is applied to cell A15.

8. **Save the workbook.**

Leave the workbook open for the next exercise.

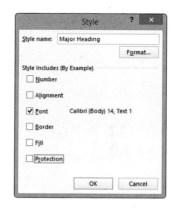

Figure 4-21

Formatting Numbers

You can apply number formats to cells to specify how numeric data will display. The major formatting types that number formats apply are

- The *helper characters* (if any) such as currency symbols, commas, and percentage symbols that a number will have in a cell.

- The number of decimal places that will show.

- The way a cell displays negative numbers: with parentheses, a minus sign, and/or red font.

LINGO

Number formats control how numeric data displays, but they do more than just make a worksheet attractive. They also help the user understand what the data represents. For example, when presenting data that includes both quantities and dollar amounts, applying a Currency number format to the dollar amounts can help distinguish them from the quantities.

Apply number formats

Basic number formatting is easy to apply from the Home tab. You can choose from a variety of number formats from the buttons and drop-down lists in the Number group.

In the following exercise, you apply number formats to cells.

Files needed: Lesson 4 Catering Final.xlsx from the preceding exercise

1. **In** `Lesson 4 Catering Final.xlsx`**, select the range B7:B13.**

2. **Choose Home⇨Accounting Number Format.**

   (That's the button with the $ sign on it.) The numbers in the selected range are formatted with a dollar sign (left-aligned) and two decimal places. (See Figure 4-22.)

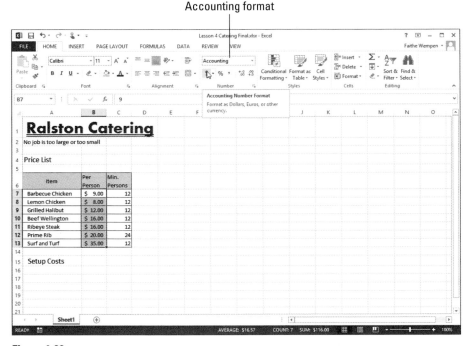

Figure 4-22

3. **Click the arrow to the right of the Accounting Number Format button and choose English (United Kingdom).**

   As Figure 4-23 shows, the currency symbol changes to the British pound sign.

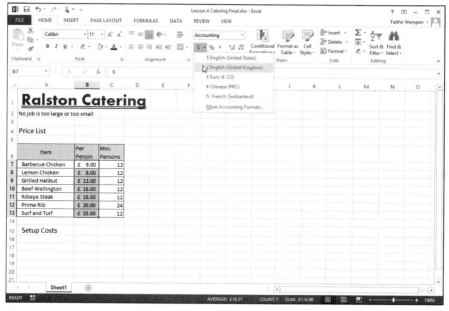

Figure 4-23

4. **From the Number Format drop-down list (which currently shows Accounting), choose Currency.**

The currency changes back to U.S. dollars, and the dollar sign right-aligns. (See Figure 4-24.)

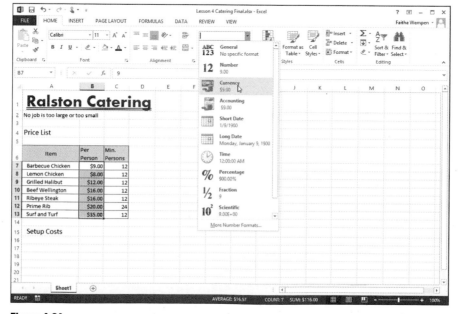

Figure 4-24

5. From the Home tab, click the **Decrease Decimal** button twice to set the amounts to no decimal places, as shown in Figure 4-25.

Decrease Decimal button

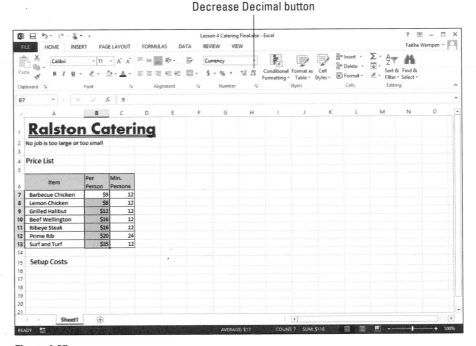

Figure 4-25

6. From the Number Format drop-down list, choose **More Number Formats.**

The Format Cells dialog box opens with the Number tab displayed. Currency is already selected as the category, with 0 decimal places.

7. In the Negative Numbers section, select the **($1,234) entry that appears in red, as shown in Figure 4-26, and click OK.**

No change is apparent in the worksheet because all the numbers are positive.

8. Change the value in cell B13 to –35 to see the effect of the negative number formatting and then change B13 back to 35.

Pressing Ctrl+Z or clicking Undo on the Quick Access toolbar reverses your last action, which is an easy way to change –35 to 35.

9. Save the workbook and close it.

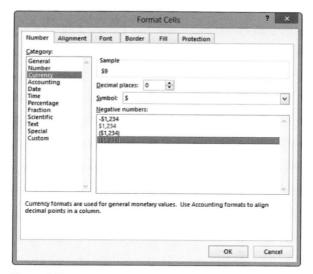

Figure 4-26

Leave Excel open for the next exercise.

Format dates and times

Dates and times are stored in Excel as numbers, but you don't usually see them that way because they have a Date or Time number format applied. A date's *raw number* is the number of days between January 1, 1900 and the date being represented. For example, January 2, 1900 would be stored as 2; in the same way, January 3, 1900 would be stored as 3, and so on.

Times are stored as values following the decimal place in the number. For example, the number 2.5 would be 12:00 noon (halfway through the day) on January 2, 1900.

In this exercise, you apply several date and time formats, and look behind the scenes to see how dates and times appear as raw numbers.

Files needed: Lesson 4 Production.xlsx

1. **Open** Lesson 4 Production.xlsx **and save it as** Lesson 4 Production Formatting.xlsx.

2. **In the Sheet1 worksheet, click in cell E1, type** 1/30/2014, **and press Enter.**

   Notice that the column automatically widens itself to accommodate the entry.

3. **On the Home tab, in the Number group, open the Number Format drop-down list and choose General (see Figure 4-27).**

The number in E1 changes to `41669`. That's the number of days between January 1, 1900 and January 30, 2014.

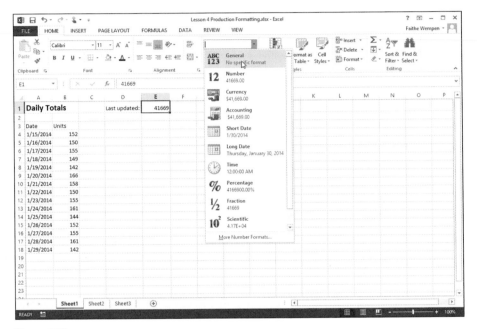

Figure 4-27

4. **With E1 still selected, click the Number group's dialog box launcher.**

The Format Cells dialog box opens with the Number tab displayed.

5. **Select the Date category on the left, and in the Type list, scroll down and select 3/14/12 13:30 (that's just a sample date, not the actual date in the cell).**

Note that the year in your examples might be different from the ones shown in Figure 4-28.

6. **Click OK.**

The format is applied to the number in the cell, and it appears as `1/30/14 0:00`.

7. **Select the range A4:A18.**

8. **In the Number group on the Home tab, open the Number Format drop-down list and choose More Number Formats.**

This is an alternate method to using the dialog box launcher.

The Format Cells dialog box reopens with the Number tab displayed.

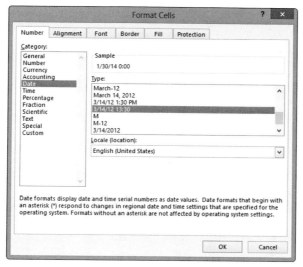

Figure 4-28

9. **Select Date in the Category list (if not already selected). In the Type list, select 14-Mar and click OK. Then click away from the selection to deselect it.**

The dates in cells A4:A18 change to `15-Jan` through `29-Jan`. See Figure 4-29.

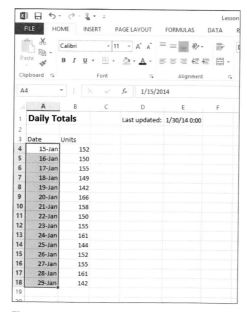

Figure 4-29

For more practice, try some other date formats, including a format with a time.

10. Save the workbook.

Leave the workbook open for the next exercise.

Create custom number formats

If none of the number format types listed in the Format Cells dialog box are exactly what you want, you can create your own type.

A custom number format may have up to four sections. If there are multiple sections, they are separated by a semicolon, in this order:

- ✔ Positive numbers
- ✔ Negative numbers
- ✔ Zero numbers
- ✔ Text

If a particular section is left out, no special formatting is applied. For example

```
0.00
```

contains only one section, and it's assumed that it's for positive numbers.

The code

```
0.00;[Red]0.00
```

contains two sections, and it's assumed that they're for positive and negative numbers. The [Red] code indicates that negative numbers should appear in red.

If you want to omit a section but then use one that's later in the sequence, add an extra semicolon for the blank section. For example, to specify formatting for positive and zero numbers but not negative, use

```
0.00;;[Green]0.00
```

Table 4-1 lists some of the codes used for creating custom number formats.

Table 4-1	Common Custom Number Format Codes	
Code	**Represents**	**Example**
0	Any digit (required)	0.00
#	Any significant digit	#,###
A color name, such as black, green, white, blue, magenta, yellow, cyan, or red, in square brackets	The text in the named color	[Green]#,##0

Many other codes can be used for specific number formats. For example, various combinations of m, d, and y are used to build date formats. For more information, see the Help system.

Certain characters can be included in a custom number format simply by including them in the code string. These are listed in Table 4-2.

Table 4-2	Literal Symbols for Custom Number Format Code
Symbol	**Name**
$	Dollar sign
+	Plus sign
(	Left parenthesis
:	Colon
^	Circumflex accent (caret)
'	Apostrophe
{	Left curly bracket
<	Less-than sign
=	Equal sign
-	Minus sign
/	Slash mark
)	Right parenthesis
!	Exclamation point
&	Ampersand
~	Tilde
}	Right curly bracket
>	Greater-than sign
	Space character

If you want to include any other symbols or text as literal values in a code, you must either put the text characters in double quotation marks, or precede the single character with a backslash (\).

In this exercise, you create a custom number format.

Files needed: Lesson 4 Production Formatting.xlsx from the preceding exercise

1. **Select the range B4:B18, and from the Home tab, click the Number group's dialog box launcher.**

   The Format Cells dialog box opens with the Number tab displayed.

2. **In the Category list, select Custom; in the Type box, delete the entry that is already there (General), and type the following:**

   ```
   #,##0" Units"
   ```

   Make sure you type a space between the opening quotation mark and the word *Units*. You can see how the custom format looks in the Format Cells dialog box in Figure 4-30.

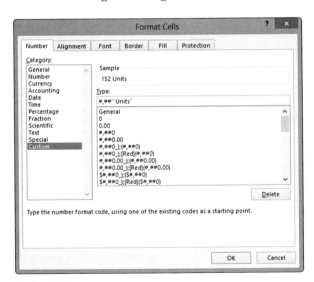

Figure 4-30

3. **Click OK, and then click away from the range to deselect it.**

   The word *Units* appears after each number in B4:B18. See Figure 4-31.

4. **Click the Sheet2 tab, select the range B4:B7, and from the Home tab, click the Number group's dialog box launcher.**

   The Format Cells dialog box opens with the Number tab displayed.

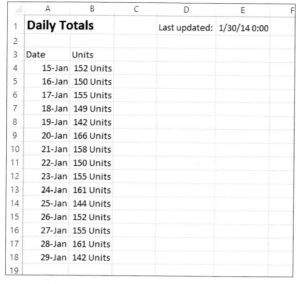

Figure 4-31

5. **In the Category list, select Custom; in the Type box, delete the current entry (General), and type the following:**

   `#,##0;[Red]#,##0;[Green]0`

   This code formats positive numbers with the `#,##0` format in the default color (black), negative numbers the same way but in red, and zero values in green. (See Figure 4-32.)

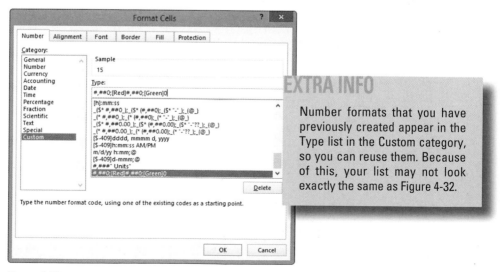

EXTRA INFO

Number formats that you have previously created appear in the Type list in the Custom category, so you can reuse them. Because of this, your list may not look exactly the same as Figure 4-32.

Figure 4-32

6. **Click OK.**

Cells B4 and B5 appear in red, cell B6 in green, and cell B7 in black.

7. **In cell B4, type** 12, **and press Enter.**

Now that the value is positive, it appears in black.

8. **Save the workbook.**

Leave the workbook open for the next exercise.

Using Conditional Formatting

Custom number formatting, as in the preceding section, can provide a rudimentary level of conditional formatting by formatting negative numbers differently. However, you can do much more with conditional formatting, such as specifying multiple formatting conditions and applying icon sets.

Conditionally format data

Excel provides many conditional-formatting presets. For example, you can find the top and bottom values in a list, highlight cells that are greater than or less than certain values, or apply data bars that show gradient fills in proportion to the amounts in the cells.

Each of the conditional formatting presets has its own numeric or percentile settings that work well all by themselves in many situations. However, you can also change the settings in the Conditional Formatting Rules Manager to fine-tune what each formatting type represents. For example, you could choose to have formatting based on a specific number instead of a percentage or average value.

In this exercise, you apply conditional formatting.

Files needed: Lesson 4 Production Formatting.xlsx from the preceding exercise

1. **On the Sheet1 worksheet, select the range B4:B18 and then choose Home⇨Conditional Formatting⇨Highlight Cells Rules⇨Greater Than.**

See Figure 4-33. The Greater Than dialog box opens.

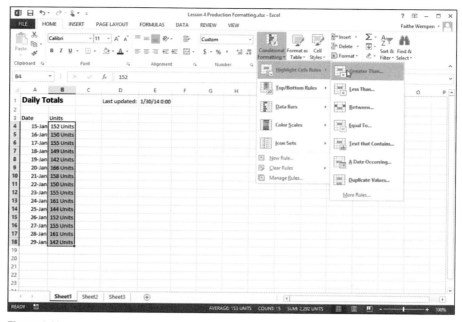

Figure 4-33

2. In the Format Cells That Are GREATER THAN box, type 150 and in the With drop-down list, choose Green Fill with Dark Green Text (see Figure 4-34).

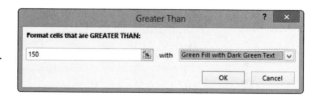

Figure 4-34

3. Click OK, and all values over 150 become green.

4. Click the Undo button on the Quick Access toolbar or press Ctrl+Z to undo the conditional formatting you just applied.

5. With the range B4:B18 still selected, click the Flash Fill icon in the lower right corner of the range.

   The Flash Fill panel appears. The FORMATTING category is already selected. See Figure 4-35.

6. Click Greater Than.

   The Greater Than dialog box opens again. (It's the same feature as before; this is just an alternate way of getting to it.)

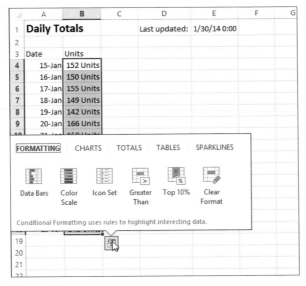

Figure 4-35

7. **Click Cancel to close the Greater Than dialog box.**

8. **Choose Home⇨Conditional Formatting⇨Top/Bottom Rules⇨Below Average.**

   The Below Average dialog box opens. See Figure 4-36.

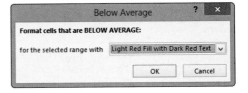

Figure 4-36

9. **Click OK to accept the default formatting (Light Red Fill with Dark Red Text).**

   The values that are below the average of all values appear in red.

10. **Click the Undo button on the Quick Access toolbar or press Ctrl+Z to undo the conditional formatting you just applied.**

11. **With B4:B18 still selected, choose Home⇨Conditional Formatting⇨Color Scales⇨Green-Yellow-Red Color Scale.**

    (That's the first one in the first row.)

    Different colors are applied to the cells based on their values, with higher values in green and lower values in red.

12. **Click away from the selection to deselect it so you can see the colors more clearly, as shown in Figure 4-37.**

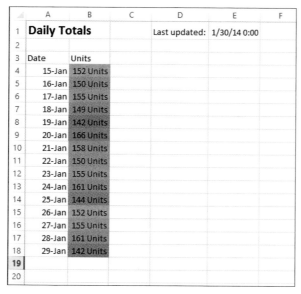

Figure 4-37

13. **Select B4:B18 again and choose Home⇨Conditional Formatting⇨ Manage Rules.**

    The Conditional Formatting Rules Manager dialog box opens. (See Figure 4-38.)

Figure 4-38

14. **Click the Edit Rule button.**

    The Edit Formatting Rule dialog box opens.

15. **In the Edit the Rule Description area, in the Midpoint column, choose Number in the Type drop-down list.**

16. **In the Value box also in the Midpoint column, type** 150 **as shown in Figure 4-39.**

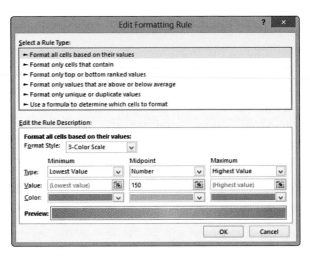

Figure 4-39

17. **Click OK to return to the Conditional Formatting Rules Manager dialog box, and click OK to apply the changes to the rule.**

18. **Click the Undo button on the Quick Access toolbar twice or press Ctrl+Z twice to remove the conditional formatting from the text.**

19. **Save the workbook.**

Leave the workbook open for the next exercise.

Create multiple formatting conditions

You can start with conditional formatting by selecting preset conditional formatting from Home⇨Conditional Formatting. You can then modify the presets as needed and create new conditions.

In this exercise, you apply a formatting condition preset and create a new condition.

Files needed: Lesson 4 Production Formatting.xlsx from the preceding exercise

1. **On the Sheet1 worksheet, select the range B4:B18 and choose Home⇨ Conditional Formatting⇨Highlight Cell Rules⇨Greater Than.**

The Greater Than dialog box opens.

2. **In the Format Cells That Are GREATER THAN box, type** 150 **and in the With drop-down list, choose Green Fill with Dark Green Text.**

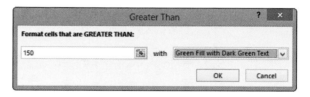

Figure 4-40

See Figure 4-40.

3. **Click OK and then choose Home⇨Conditional Formatting⇨Manage Rules.**

The Conditional Formatting Rules Manager dialog box opens. (See Figure 4-41.)

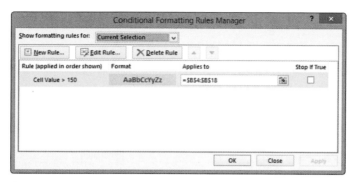

Figure 4-41

4. **Click the New Rule button.**

The New Formatting Rule dialog box opens.

5. **In the Select a Rule Type area, select Format Only Cells That Contain.**

6. **In the Format Only Cells With area, leave the first drop-down list set to its default of Cell Value. Leave the second drop-down list set to its default of Between. In the third box, type** 145. **In the fourth box, type** 149.

See Figure 4-42.

7. **Click the Format button to open the Format Cells dialog box.**

8. **Click the Fill tab and then click a pale blue color square (the fourth color in the second row), as shown in Figure 4-43.**

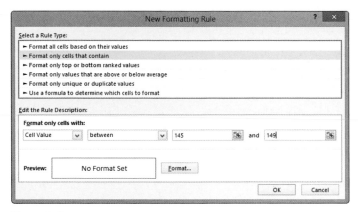

Figure 4-42

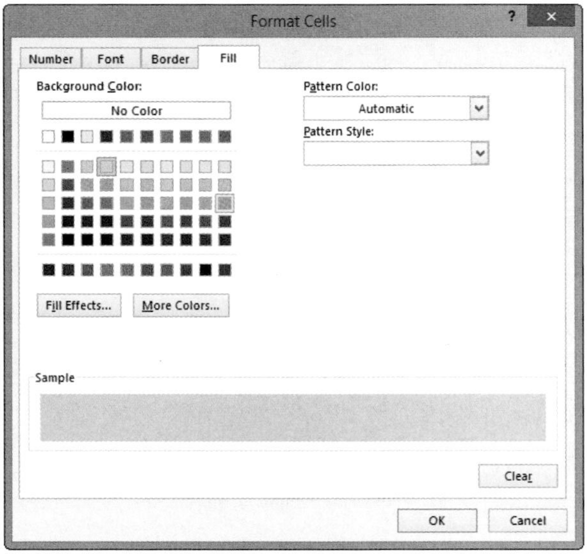

Figure 4-43

9. **Click the Font tab; from the Color drop-down list, choose a dark blue square (the fourth color in the first row), and click OK.**

10. **Back in the New Formatting Rule dialog box, click OK to finalize the rule.**

Both rules appear in the Conditional Formatting Rules Manager dialog box, shown in Figure 4-44.

Figure 4-44

11. **Click OK. Then click away from the selection to deselect it.**

   Cell B7 appears in blue because its value falls within the range specified by the new rule.

12. **Click cell B17, type** 148, **and press Enter.**

   The formatting changes in B17 to reflect the new conditional format. See Figure 4-45.

	A	B	C	D	E	F
1	**Daily Totals**			Last updated:	1/30/14 0:00	
2						
3	Date	Units				
4	15-Jan	152 Units				
5	16-Jan	150 Units				
6	17-Jan	155 Units				
7	18-Jan	149 Units				
8	19-Jan	142 Units				
9	20-Jan	166 Units				
10	21-Jan	158 Units				
11	22-Jan	150 Units				
12	23-Jan	155 Units				
13	24-Jan	161 Units				
14	25-Jan	144 Units				
15	26-Jan	152 Units				
16	27-Jan	155 Units				
17	28-Jan	148 Units				
18	29-Jan	142 Units				
19						
20						

Figure 4-45

PRACTICE

For more practice, set up an additional rule that colors values that are less than 145 with a pink background and dark red text.

13. **Select the range B4:B18 again and choose Home⇨Conditional Formatting⇨Manage Rules.**

    The Conditional Formatting Rules Manager dialog box opens (refer to Figure 4-44).

14. **Select the first rule and click the Delete Rule button; select the next rule and click the Delete Rule button again. (If there are any other rules, delete them also.)**

15. **Click OK.**

    The conditional formatting is removed.

16. **Save the workbook.**

Leave the workbook open for the next exercise.

Apply icon sets

In this exercise, you apply and customize an icon set.

Files needed: Lesson 4 Production Formatting. xlsx from the preceding exercise

1. **On the Sheet1 tab, select the range B4:B18 and choose Home⇨Conditional Formatting⇨Icon Sets.**

2. **In the Indicators section of the menu, click the set that contains a green check mark, yellow exclamation point, and red X, as shown in Figure 4-46.**

LINGO

Icon sets are a form of conditional formatting that adds icons next to entries in cells depending on the cells' content. For example, you could place check marks next to values that are higher than a certain amount.

TIP

When you apply the icon set, the values in column B change to hash marks ####. This happens because the column is no longer wide enough to accommodate the content.

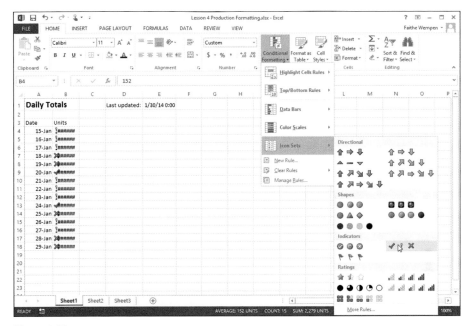

Figure 4-46

3. **Double-click between the B and C column headings to widen column B so the content is once again visible.**

TIP

Only two entries have green check marks. Next, you modify the criteria for the icon set so that more entries have green check marks.

4. **Choose Home⇨Conditional Formatting⇨Manage Rules.**

The Conditional Formatting Rules Manager dialog box opens, with the Icon Set rule in it. (See Figure 4-47.)

5. **Click the Icon Set rule and then click the Edit Rule button.**

The Edit Formatting Rule dialog box opens.

6. **In the Type column at the bottom of the dialog box, open each of the drop-down lists (which currently show Percent) and choose Number.**

REMEMBER

When you switch between Percent and Number, as in Step 6, any previously entered values are erased. Make sure you choose the desired setting (Percent or Number) before you enter the values to be used; otherwise you have to re-enter them.

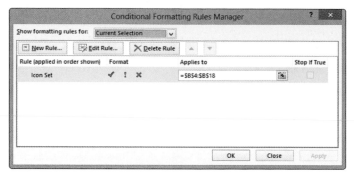

Figure 4-47

7. In the Value column, on the first line (for the green check mark), enter 150 and on the second line (for the yellow exclamation point), enter 145, as shown in Figure 4-48.

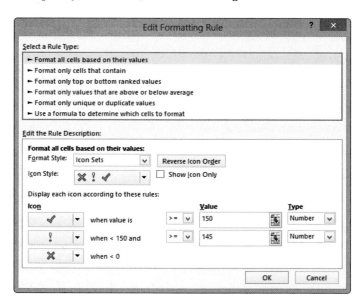

Figure 4-48

8. Click OK to close the Edit Formatting Rule dialog box. Click OK to close the Conditional Formatting Rules Manager dialog box and apply the rule.

9. Click away from the selection to deselect it so you can see the icons more clearly, as shown in Figure 4-49.

10. Save the workbook and close Excel.

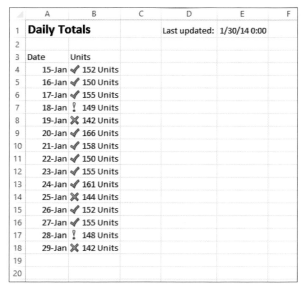

Figure 4-49

 Summing Up

Here are the key points you learned about in this lesson:

- ✔ Each cell has a fill (its inner color) and a border (its outline). By default, a cell is set for No Border. The faint outlines that define each cell onscreen are gridlines; they're not the same thing as borders.

- ✔ To apply a cell fill, use the Fill Color button on the Home tab.

- ✔ To apply a cell border, use the Border button on the Home tab. You can define the border of each side of a cell or range independently.

- ✔ You can format the text in a cell in much the same way as in Word: Use the controls in the Font group on the Home tab, or on the mini toolbar.

- ✔ Use the Wrap Text button on the Home tab to allow a cell's content to wrap to additional lines if necessary.

- ✔ Cells have vertical and horizontal alignments that determine where the text will align in the cell when the cell is larger than it needs to be to accommodate that text.

- ✔ Cell styles are formatting presets you can apply to cells. You can create your own cell styles easily via the Cell Styles button on the Home tab.

✔ Number formats help put numbers in context and can be applied from the Number group on the Home tab. Examples include Currency and Percentage.

✔ To create your own custom number formats, choose Custom as the type and then enter the codes from Tables 4-1 and 4-2 to build your own format.

✔ To conditionally format cells, choose Home⇨Conditional Formatting.

Try-it-yourself lab

1. **Start Excel, open the file** Lesson 4 Try It Cells.xlsx, **and save it as** Lesson 4 Try It Cells Final.xlsx.

2. **Using the formatting skills you learn in this lesson, create a packing slip that resembles Figure 4-50 as closely as possible.**

   Skills you need include

   - Adjusting column widths and row heights

   - Changing horizontal and vertical alignments

   - Changing fonts, sizes, colors, and attributes

   - Applying cell borders and fills

   - Applying number formats

   - Merging and centering a heading across multiple cells

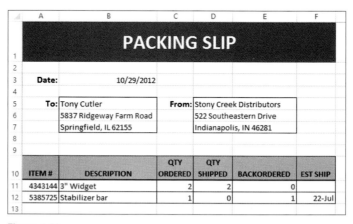

Figure 4-50

Know this tech talk

attributes: Text effects, including bold and italic, underlining, strike-through, superscript, and subscript.

border: The color and style of the outside of a cell.

cell style: A formatting preset that you can apply to a cell.

conditional formatting: Formatting that is applied only when the content of the cell meets specified criteria.

fill: The color of the inside of a cell.

gridlines: The edges of the cells that you see by default onscreen.

horizontal alignment: The horizontal position of data in a cell, such as Left, Right, or Center.

icon sets: A form of conditional formatting that adds icons next to entries in cells depending on the cells' content.

number format: A format applied to a cell that makes numbers in it appear with certain characteristics, such as commas, dollar signs, or percentage symbols.

vertical alignment: The vertical position of data in a cell, such as Top, Middle, or Bottom.

Storing and Managing Tables and Lists

- ✔ Sorting data arranges records in a different order to more easily find the records you want.

- ✔ Filtering data hides records that don't match your specs.

- ✔ Table styles quickly apply professional-looking formatting to an entire table.

- ✔ A Total row provides an easy way to add summary statistics to a table.

- ✔ Converting a table to a range returns the data to a regular Excel range, without table features.

- ✔ Merging data from two cells into one concatenates data.

- ✔ Splitting data from one column into two or more columns enables you to extract individual values from a combined entry.

$\mathcal{B}$esides its calculation capabilities, Excel also has some great features for managing databases. You can store, search, sort, and filter large lists of information with ease in Excel. And by converting a range to a table in Excel, you can access certain sorting and filtering commands even more easily.

In this lesson, you learn some database concepts, and find out how to create and manage tables in a workbook. You also learn how to merge and split data, so you can combine values from two or more fields into a single one or split a single field into multiple pieces.

Understanding Databases

In Excel, the word *table* has a special meaning: a contiguous range of cells that you have specially designated as a database. When you designate a certain range as a table, you can perform actions on it such as searching, sorting, totaling, and other activities more easily than you can on a regular range.

Figure 5-1 points out the key elements in a simple database table. In this lesson, you learn how to create and manipulate a single-table database in Excel.

Columns are fields.

Rows are records.

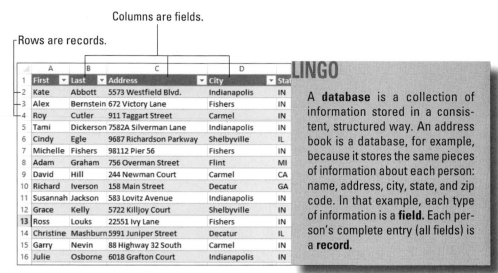

Figure 5-1

LINGO

A **database** is a collection of information stored in a consistent, structured way. An address book is a database, for example, because it stores the same pieces of information about each person: name, address, city, state, and zip code. In that example, each type of information is a **field.** Each person's complete entry (all fields) is a **record.**

Working with Tables in Excel

You can store database data in simple ranges in Excel, but for full access to Excel's data management features, it's often better to convert the range to a table. Tables have several advantages over ranges:

EXTRA INFO

When most people think about databases, they think about complex, multi-table databases in which each table is related to another one in some way. Such databases are **relational databases**. You can use Microsoft Access to create such databases. (Access is included with some versions of Microsoft Office but isn't covered in this book.)

- ✔ You can filter by columns using an easy drop-down list.
- ✔ You can add a Total row that adds summary calculations without manually entering the formula for it.
- ✔ You can apply table formatting presets.
- ✔ You can publish a table to a SharePoint server.

Convert a data range to a table

Before you convert a range to a table, make sure you have properly prepared the range. Specifically, you need to do the following:

✔ Make sure that the first row contains the field names you want to use. The entries in the first row become column headings.

✔ Make sure that each row contains one record.

✔ Make sure that no blank rows appear between rows containing records.

When the data is cleaned up and ready to go, choose Insert⇨Table to convert the range to a table. Alternatively, you can choose Home⇨Format as Table, which applies a format of your choice and makes the range into a table in a single step. You see that method in Lesson 3.

In the following exercise, you convert a data range to a table.

Files needed: Lesson 5 Addresses.xlsx.

1. **Start Excel, if needed, open** Lesson 5 Addresses.xlsx, **and save it as** Lesson 5 Address Book.xlsx.

2. **Select the range A1:F16 and then choose Insert⇨Table.**

   The Create Table dialog box opens with the selected range already filled in, as shown in Figure 5-2.

Figure 5-2

3. **Click OK.**

   The range is converted to a table, and default table formatting is applied to it. This formatting consists of banded blue and white rows and blue column headings, as well as a Filter arrow next to each field name at the top of each column, as shown in Figure 5-1.

4. **Save the workbook.**

Leave the workbook open for the next exercise.

Sort table data

You can sort a table's data by a single field or by multiple fields. When you sort by a single field, Excel rearranges the records in A to Z (ascending) or Z to A (descending) order based on the field you specify. When you sort by multiple fields, Excel does a single sort by the first field you specify; in the event of a tie for that field, you specify additional field(s) to break the tie. For example, if you sort first by City and then by State, Decatur, GA comes before Decatur, IL.

In the following exercise, you sort table data.

Files needed: Lesson 5 Address Book.xlsx from the preceding exercise

1. **In** `Lesson 5 Address Book.xlsx`**, click in any cell in the State column and choose Data⇨Sort A to Z.**

   The records are reordered by state. A small arrow appears on the Filter arrow button (the up arrow to the right of the State field) to indicate that field is sorted. (See Figure 5-3.)

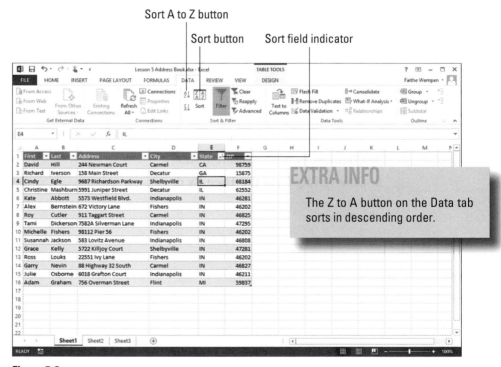

Figure 5-3

2. **Click the Filter arrow button to the right of the ZIP field to open a Filter menu, as shown in Figure 5-4, and then choose Sort Smallest to Largest.**

   The table is sorted by ZIP, and not by State.

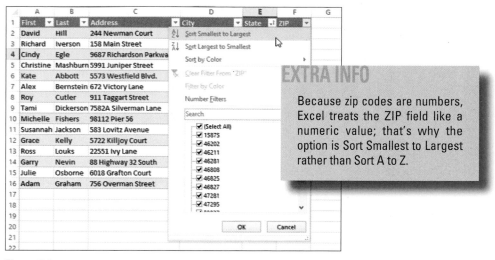

Figure 5-4

3. **Choose Data⇨Clear to remove the sort and then choose Data⇨Sort to open the Sort dialog box.**

4. **Choose State from the Sort By drop-down list.**

   This sets the primary sort as the State field.

5. **Click the Add Level button. Another line is added to the dialog box.**

6. **Choose City from the Then By drop-down list.**

   This sets the secondary sort as the City field, as shown in Figure 5-5.

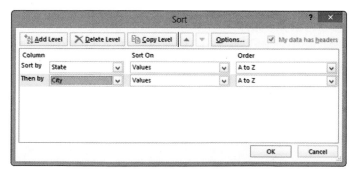

Figure 5-5

7. **Click OK to apply the sort.**

   Notice that both the City and State fields' Filter arrow buttons have a Sort symbol on them.

8. **Starting in cell A17, type the following to create a new record:** Brooke Sanner, 124 South Street, Decatur, IL 62558

   Excel automatically extends the table to include the new record.

9. **Click anywhere in the table, and then choose Data⇨Reapply.**

   The table is re-sorted to place the new record in the appropriate order.

10. **Save the workbook.**

Leave the workbook open for the next exercise.

Filter data in a table

Excel gives you several ways to specify filter criteria so that you see only the database records you want to see. You can use the Filter menu for a particular field (from the Filter down arrow to the right of each field name) to choose certain values to include and to omit others. Depending on the content of the field (text, date, number, and so on), you can also use logical filter statements for that type of data. When a field's content is text, your options for logical filter statements include Begins With, Ends With, or Contains. For numbers, the options include Greater Than, Less Than, or Between.

LINGO

Filtering data hides certain records and displays only the ones that match criteria you specify. Perhaps the easiest method is to **filter by selection,** which hides all records in which the specified field does not contain a sample value you select.

In the following exercise, you filter table data using a variety of methods.

Files needed: Lesson 5 Address Book.xlsx from the preceding exercise

1. **In** `Lesson 5 Address Book.xlsx`**, click the Filter arrow to the right of the State field to open its Filter menu (see Figure 5-6).**

   Notice that each check box for the entries in that column is selected, indicating that nothing is filtered.

2. **Deselect the check boxes for all states except IL and IN, and then click OK.**

   The list is filtered to show only those two states.

3. **Choose Data⇨Clear to remove the filtering and any previously applied sort.**

4. **Right-click in any cell in the State column that contains IL and choose Filter⇨Filter by Selected Cell's Value, as shown in Figure 5-7.**

   The table filters to show only Illinois (IL) records.

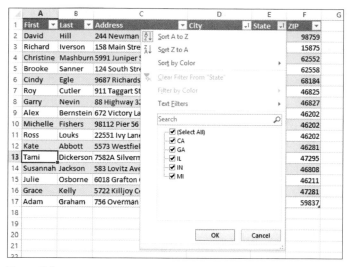

Figure 5-6

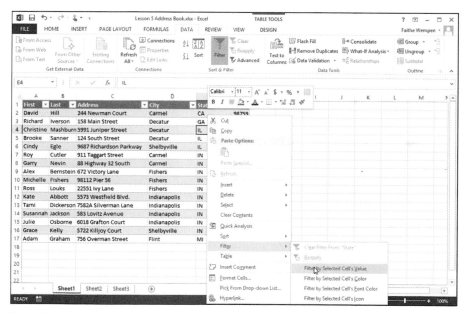

Figure 5-7

5. **Click the Filter arrow to the right of the State field's column heading and choose Clear Filter from "State."**

   The filter is removed.

6. **Click the Filter arrow to the right of the ZIP field's column heading and choose Number Filters⇨Between.**

The Custom AutoFilter dialog
box opens.

7. **In the first text box on the right,
type** 40000. **In the second text
box on the right, type** 70000, **as
shown in Figure 5-8.**

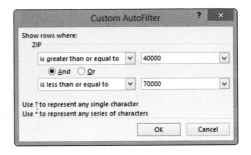

For more practice, try some of
the other number filters, such as
Less Than or Greater Than. Still
want more practice? Filter by
last name using a Begins With
filter to find only names that
begin with a certain letter.

Figure 5-8

8. **Click OK.**

The list filters to show zip codes between the limits you specified.
Notice that the list is not sorted by zip code but only filtered by it.

9. **Choose Data⇨Clear to clear the filter and then save the workbook.**

Leave the workbook open for the next exercise.

Format a table

In Lesson 3, you learn how to apply table formatting to a range, and the pro-
cedure is the same with an existing table. Excel offers a variety of table styles
for quickly formatting a table; you can access these styles either from the
Table Tools Design tab or by choosing Home⇨Format as Table. (The style
choices are the same no matter which method you use.)

You can also specify which table style options will take effect by selecting
or deselecting check boxes on the Table Tools Design tab in the Table Style
Options group.

In the following exercise, you apply table formatting.

Files needed: Lesson 5 Address Book.xlsx from the preceding exercise

1. **In** Lesson 5 Address Book.xlsx, **click anywhere in the table, and
then from the Table Tools Design tab, click the More button in the
Table Styles group to open a palette of table styles.**

2. **In the Dark section (scroll down if needed), choose Table Style Dark
3 (the one with the black column headings and red striped rows), as
shown in Figure 5-9.**

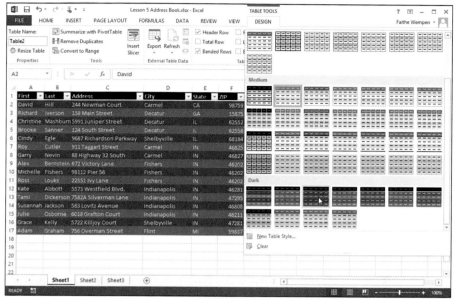

Figure 5-9

For more practice, try some of the other table styles.

3. In the Table Style Options group, deselect the Banded Rows check box and select the Banded Columns check box, as shown in Figure 5-10.

For more practice, select and deselect each of the check boxes in the Table Style Options group to see what they do. First Column and Last Column formatting would be useful if those columns contained something special; you learn about the Total Row option in the next exercise.

4. Choose Home⇨Format as Table⇨Table Style Medium 10.

(It's one of the red styles in the Medium section. You can point to a style to see a ScreenTip that shows its name.) Notice that the options you set in Step 3 still apply.

5. On the Table Tools Design tab, deselect the Banded Columns check box and select the Banded Rows check box.

6. Save the workbook.

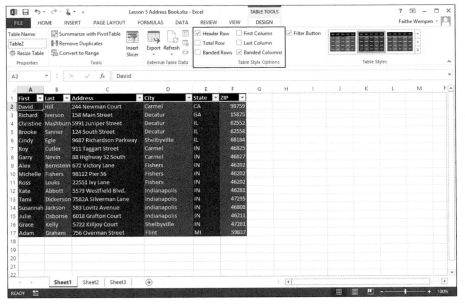

Figure 5-10

Leave the workbook open for the next exercise.

Add a Total row to a table

One of the advantages of making a data range into a table is the ability to show a Total row as part of the table. As you probably expect, more options for calculating totals are available when working with a numeric field, but even text fields have some totals they can display, such as a count of the number of records. You can use any function in Excel for figuring totals, but the most common ones — such as Sum, Average, and Count — are available from a menu for easy access.

In the following exercise, you add a Total row to a table.

Files needed: Lesson 5 Address Book.xlsx from the preceding exercise

1. **In** Lesson 5 Address Book.xlsx, **click anywhere in the table and then choose Table Tools Design⇨Total Row to turn on the Total row for the table.**

The Total row appears at the bottom of the table. Excel considers only the ZIP field in the table as numeric, so it automatically applies a SUM function to that field. (That's not very useful, but Excel doesn't know that yet.)

2. **Click cell F18 to select the automatically created total in that cell. Click the down arrow that appears and choose Count, as shown in Figure 5-11.**

   Cell F18 then shows 16, the number of records in the table.

	A	B	C	D	E	F	G
1	First	Last	Address	City	State	ZIP	
2	David	Hill	244 Newman Court	Carmel	CA	98759	
3	Richard	Iverson	158 Main Street	Decatur	GA	15875	
4	Christine	Mashburn	5991 Juniper Street	Decatur	IL	62552	
5	Brooke	Sanner	124 South Street	Decatur	IL	62558	
6	Cindy	Egle	9687 Richardson Parkway	Shelbyville	IL	68184	
7	Roy	Cutler	911 Taggart Street	Carmel	IN	46825	
8	Garry	Nevin	88 Highway 32 South	Carmel	IN	46827	
9	Alex	Bernstein	672 Victory Lane	Fishers	IN	46202	
10	Michelle	Fishers	98112 Pier 56	Fishers	IN	46202	
11	Ross	Louks	22551 Ivy Lane	Fishers	IN	46202	
12	Kate	Abbott	5573 Westfield Blvd.	Indianapolis	IN	46281	
13	Tami	Dickerson	7582A Silverman Lane	Indianapolis	IN	47295	
14	Susannah	Jackson	583 Lovitz Avenue	Indianapolis	IN	46808	
15	Julie	Osborne	6018 Grafton Court	Indianapolis	IN	46211	
16	Grace	Kelly	5722 Killjoy Court	Shelbyville	IN	47281	
17	Adam	Graham	756 Overman Street	Flint	MI	59837	
18	Total					16	
19						None	
20						Average	
21						Count	
22						Count Number	
						Max	
						Min	
	Sheet1	Sheet2	Sheet3	⊕		Sum	
						StdDev	
READY						Var	
						More Function	

Figure 5-11

3. **Click in cell A18 and type** Count, **replacing** *Total.*

   It's important to clearly label each calculation in a worksheet, and this table is no exception.

4. **Save the workbook.**

For more practice, reopen the menu for cell F18 and try some of the other functions on the list. They won't make logical sense when calculated on zip codes, but you still get an idea of how they work.

Leave the workbook open for the next exercise.

Convert a table to a range

Some of Excel's features don't work on cells that are part of a table. If you do something that triggers an error message that says the operation can't be performed on a table or if you just don't want the table anymore, you can convert the table back to a regular range.

When you convert a table to a range, you get to keep the table formatting that you have previously applied to it, but you lose the Filter arrows on each column.

In the following exercise, you convert a table to a range.

Files needed: Lesson 5 Address Book.xlsx from the preceding exercise

1. **In** `Lesson 5 Address Book.xlsx`, **click anywhere in the table and then choose Table Tools Design⇨Convert to Range.**

2. **Click Yes in the confirmation box that appears.**

   All the data and formatting remain, but the Filter arrows disappear from the column headings. The Table Tools Design tab is no longer available.

3. **Click in cell F18.**

   Notice that instead of an available drop-down list, you see a SUBTOTAL function: `=SUBTOTAL(103,Sheet1!$F$2:$F$17)`, as shown in the Formula bar of Figure 5-12.

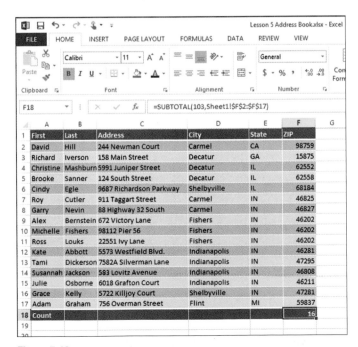

Figure 5-12

4. Save the workbook.

Leave the workbook open for the next exercise.

 TIP

You might have been surprised that cell F18 (in Step 3) contained a SUBTOTAL function and not a COUNT function. That's a remnant of the table's Total row. When you add a Total row to a table, the SUBTOTAL function is used no matter which of the operations you choose from the drop-down list. Each of the available functions has a numeric value. The COUNT function's number happens to be 103, which is why the first argument in the function in F18 is 103. The second argument is the range: F2:F17 (with absolute cell references, hence the dollar signs) on Sheet1. An advantage of the SUBTOTAL function is that it includes only visible cells, so that if any filters are applied to the table, the filtered data's subtotals are accurate.

Merging and Splitting Data

As you build a database in Excel, you may decide that you made some mistakes in how you've broken up your data into fields. Fortunately, you're not stuck, nor do you have to retype all the data. You can use Excel's features that merge and split cell contents based on criteria you specify.

Merge the contents of multiple columns

You can merge the content of two or more cells into a single cell using the CONCATENATE function. For example, if cell A2 contains *David* and B2 contains *Hill,* you could concatenate those values into a new cell that displays *David Hill.* You can then copy that function to an entire column, converting a whole column of data at once.

LINGO

Concatenate means to join together end to end. In Excel, you use the CONCATENATE function to combine cell content and add literal character strings as well, if you want.

You can choose to leave the data in the new concatenated cells, but those cells will always contain a function that relies on the original data being present to refer to. If you want to delete the original cells that contained the concatenated data, you must copy the results of the concatenation formula to a new cell using a Paste Special option, and paste the value rather than the formula.

In the following exercise, you concatenate the first and last names in a data range into a new column, and then delete the original columns.

Files needed: Lesson 5 Address Book.xlsx from the preceding exercise

1. **In** `Lesson 5 Address Book.xlsx`, **drag across the column headers for columns C and D to select those two columns, and then choose Home⇨Insert.**

   Two new columns are inserted, as shown in Figure 5-13.

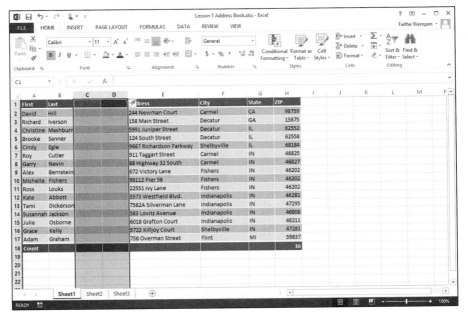

Figure 5-13

2. **In cell C2, type the following:**

   `=CONCATENATE(`

3. **Click cell A2, type the following:**

   `, " ",`

   That's a comma, quotation marks with a space in between, and another comma. Then click cell B2 and press Enter.

4. **Click cell C2, which reads** *David Hill,* **and view the function in the formula bar.**

   The function looks like `=CONCATENATE(A2, " ",B2)`, as shown in Figure 5-14.

5. **Drag the fill handle from cell C2 down to C17, copying the function to the rest of the names.**

6. **Double-click the divider between column headings C and D to widen column C so that the contents fit.**

7. **Select the range C2:C17 and press Ctrl+C to copy them to the Clipboard.**

Concatenate function

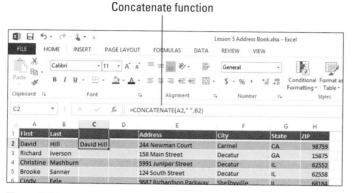

Figure 5-14

8. **Click in cell D2 and from the Home tab, click the down arrow under the Paste button and choose Values (the first icon) from the Paste Values section.**

   Figure 5-15 shows the values from column C pasted into column D.

9. **Double-click the divider between columns D and E to widen column D to fit the contents.**

10. **Drag across the column headers for columns A:C to select those columns.**

11. **Choose Home⇨Delete, and then click in cell A1 and type Name, defining a new column header label.**

   The completed data range appears in Figure 5-16.

12. **Save the workbook.**

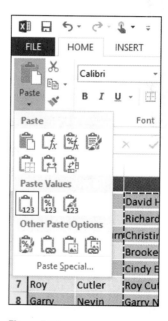

Figure 5-15

	A	B	C	D	E
1	Name	Address	City	State	ZIP
2	David Hill	244 Newman Court	Carmel	CA	98759
3	Richard Iverson	158 Main Street	Decatur	GA	15875
4	Christine Mashburn	5991 Juniper Street	Decatur	IL	62552
5	Brooke Sanner	124 South Street	Decatur	IL	62558
6	Cindy Egle	9687 Richardson Parkway	Shelbyville	IL	68184
7	Roy Cutler	911 Taggart Street	Carmel	IN	46825
8	Garry Nevin	88 Highway 32 South	Carmel	IN	46827
9	Alex Bernstein	672 Victory Lane	Fishers	IN	46202
10	Michelle Fishers	98112 Pier 56	Fishers	IN	46202
11	Ross Louks	22551 Ivy Lane	Fishers	IN	46202
12	Kate Abbott	5573 Westfield Blvd.	Indianapolis	IN	46281
13	Tami Dickerson	7582A Silverman Lane	Indianapolis	IN	47295
14	Susannah Jackson	583 Lovitz Avenue	Indianapolis	IN	46808
15	Julie Osborne	6018 Grafton Court	Indianapolis	IN	46211
16	Grace Kelly	5722 Killjoy Court	Shelbyville	IN	47281
17	Adam Graham	756 Overman Street	Flint	MI	59837
18					16

Figure 5-16

Leave the workbook open for the next exercise.

Split a column's content into multiple columns

If you put more data in a single column than you should have, you can split the data into multiple cells. Text to Columns is the main splitting feature in Excel. New in Excel 2013, you can also use the Flash Fill feature to split the contents of a cell into multiple cells. See the section on using Flash Fill to extract content in Lesson 1 to try that out.

For Text to Columns to work, a consistently used, separator character differentiates the data that should be in one cell from the data that should be in another. For example, if you want to separate first and last names, such as David Hill, the separator character is a space. If some names have three space-separated parts to them, the split won't work right and you'll have to correct those entries manually afterward. However, if most of the data falls into a consistent pattern, you can save some time by allowing Excel to split as many entries as it can.

In the following exercise, you split first and last names into separate cells.

Files needed: Lesson 5 Address Book.xlsx from the preceding exercise

1. **In** `Lesson 5 Address Book.xlsx,` **click the column letter B and then choose Home⇨Insert to insert a new column.**

2. **Select the range A2:A17 and then choose Data⇨Text to Columns.**

The Convert Text to Columns Wizard – Step 1 of 3 dialog box opens. See Figure 5-17.

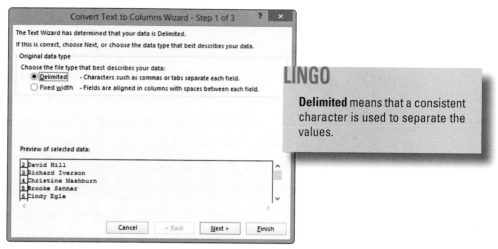

LINGO

Delimited means that a consistent character is used to separate the values.

Figure 5-17

3. **Click Next to select the default Delimited data type and move on to the Convert Text to Columns Wizard – Step 2 of 3 dialog box.**

4. **Select the Space check box, deselect the Tab check box, and confirm that the Treat Consecutive Delimiters as One check box is selected.**

   The Treat Consecutive Delimiters as One option ignores the second delimiter if there are two in a row, and it allows for data-entry errors where an extra space might have been inserted. That doesn't apply to the data being used for this exercise, but it might apply in data you create for yourself later.

5. **Preview the split in the Data Preview area (shown in Figure 5-18), and then click Next.**

   The Convert Text to Columns Wizard – Step 3 of 3 dialog box appears. In this dialog box, you can fine-tune the data types, such as Text or Date.

6. **Select the Text option to set the first column as Text; then click the second column in the Data Preview area and select the Text option to set the second column as Text, as shown in Figure 5-19.**

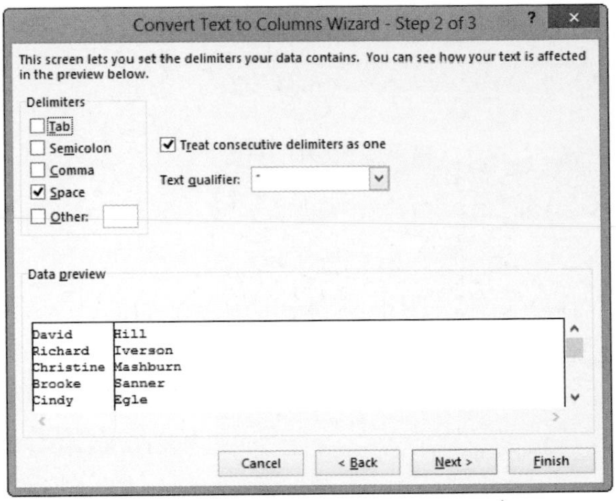

Figure 5-18

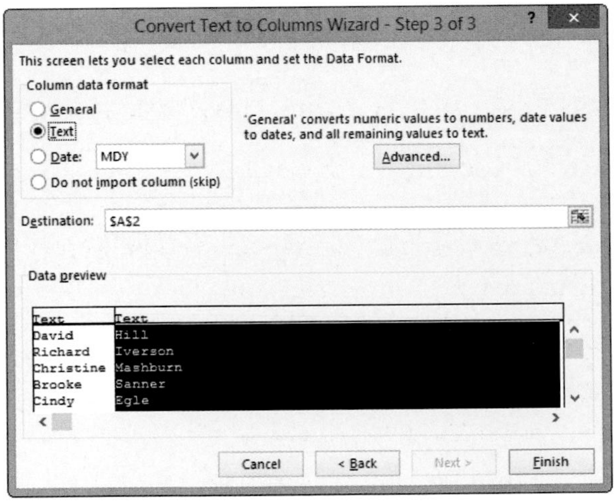

Figure 5-19

7. **Click the Finish button.**

   A dialog box appears asking whether you want to replace the contents of the destination cells.

8. **Click OK, and the last names are placed into column B.**

9. **In cell A1, type** First. **In cell B1, type** Last.

   The names are split into two separately named columns, as shown in Figure 5-20.

	A	B	C	D	E	F
1	First	Last	Address	City	State	ZIP
2	David	Hill	244 Newman Court	Carmel	CA	98759
3	Richard	Iverson	158 Main Street	Decatur	GA	15875
4	Christine	Mashburn	5991 Juniper Street	Decatur	IL	62552
5	Brooke	Sanner	124 South Street	Decatur	IL	62558
6	Cindy	Egle	9687 Richardson Parkway	Shelbyville	IL	68184
7	Roy	Cutler	911 Taggart Street	Carmel	IN	46825
8	Garry	Nevin	88 Highway 32 South	Carmel	IN	46827
9	Alex	Bernstein	672 Victory Lane	Fishers	IN	46202
10	Michelle	Fishers	98112 Pier 56	Fishers	IN	46202
11	Ross	Louks	22551 Ivy Lane	Fishers	IN	46202
12	Kate	Abbott	5573 Westfield Blvd.	Indianapolis	IN	46281
13	Tami	Dickerson	7582A Silverman Lane	Indianapolis	IN	47295
14	Susannah	Jackson	583 Lovitz Avenue	Indianapolis	IN	46808
15	Julie	Osborne	6018 Grafton Court	Indianapolis	IN	46211
16	Grace	Kelly	5722 Killjoy Court	Shelbyville	IN	47281
17	Adam	Graham	756 Overman Street	Flint	MI	59837
18						16

Figure 5-20

10. **Save the workbook and close it. Close Excel.**

Summing Up

Here are the key points you learned about in this lesson:

- ✔ A database is a collection of information stored in a consistent, structured way.
- ✔ Each type of information is a field, and each complete entry for an instance is a record.
- ✔ Excel stores simple databases in tables. You can use ranges, but tables offer additional sorting, filtering, and summarizing capabilities.
- ✔ To convert a range to a table, you can select the data and then choose Insert⇨Table or Home⇨Format as Table.
- ✔ Click the Filter arrow to the right of a field name in a table header to open a menu containing sorting and filtering commands.
- ✔ You can filter data in many ways, including using the Filter menu, right-clicking the data, or using filter commands on the Data tab.
- ✔ You can format a table from the Table Tools Design tab, in the Table Styles group, or by choosing Home⇨Format as Table.
- ✔ To add a Total row to a table, select the Total Row check box on the Table Tools Design tab.
- ✔ To convert a table back to a range, choose Table Tools Design⇨Convert to Range.

✔ To merge data from multiple cells, use the CONCATENATE function.

✔ To split data into multiple cells, choose Data➪Text to Columns. In Excel 2013, the new Flash Fill feature, explained in Lesson 1, may also save you a little time in splitting data.

Try-it-yourself lab

1. **Start Excel, open the file** Lesson 5 Try It.xlsx, **and save it as** Lesson 5 Splits.xlsx.

2. **Using the Text to Columns feature, split the cities, states, and zip codes into separate columns.**

   Hint: Use Comma and Space as the delimiters.

3. **Convert the range containing all the data to a table.**

4. **Rename each of the column headings from the default names (Column1 through Column6) to more appropriate names.**

5. **Save the workbook and close Excel.**

Know this tech talk

CONCATENATE: An Excel function that merges data from two or more cells into one cell.

database: A collection of information stored in a consistent, structured way.

field: A specific type of information, such as cities or zip codes.

filter: To hide data that does not match criteria you specify.

filter by selection: To hide data that does not match a selection.

record: All the stored information about one instance, such as an individual person's name and contact information.

relational database: A multi-table database, such as one created in Microsoft Access.

table: In Excel, a range that has been defined as a database.

Text to Columns: An Excel feature that splits data from one column into multiple columns.

Total row: In a table, an optional row that performs summary operations on one or more fields in the table.

Lesson 6

Exploring Financial Functions and Scenarios

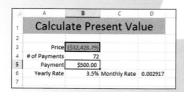

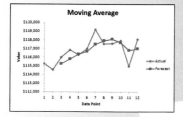

✔ The PV, FV, PMT, RATE, and NPER functions calculate parts of a loan or investment.

✔ Goal Seek helps you set variables for a formula to the exact amounts needed for the formula's result to come out a certain way.

✔ The Analysis ToolPak add-in offers additional features for performing data calculation and analysis.

✔ A moving average is more accurate as an estimator of future performance than a regular average when there are large fluctuations in the data.

✔ The Solver add-in finds optimal answers to complex questions that rely on multiple variables and constraints.

✔ The Scenarios feature lets you create and save multiple scenarios for what-if analysis.

✔ Naming a range makes it easier to refer to the range in formulas and functions.

O ne of the most common uses for Excel is to analyze financial data. Excel offers a huge variety of functions that can help make sense of money, and also a variety of add-ins, wizards, and other advanced features that can help, too.

In this lesson, you learn about a set of related financial functions for calculating loan payments and interest: PV, FV, PMT, RATE, and NPER. You also learn how to load add-ins, such as the Analysis ToolPak and Solver, and how to use them to find the best answers to financial questions. Finally, you learn how to save your what-if possibilities as scenarios, and how to name ranges to make it easier to refer to cells in formulas.

Exploring Financial Functions

Financial functions are some of the most useful tools for home and small business worksheets because they're all about the money: borrowing it, lending it, and monitoring it.

Here's the basic set:

- ✔ PV: Calculates the present value or principal amount. In a loan, it's the amount you're borrowing; in a savings account, it's the initial deposit.

- ✔ FV: The future value. This is the principal plus the interest paid or received.

- ✔ PMT: The payment to be made per period. For example, for a mortgage, it's the monthly payment; in a savings account, it's the amount you save each period. A *period* can be any time period, but it's usually a month.

- ✔ RATE: The interest rate to be charged per period (for a loan), or the percentage of amortization or depreciation per period.

- ✔ NPER: The number of periods. For a loan, it's the total number of payments to be made, or the points in time when interest is earned if you're tracking savings or amortization.

These financial functions are related. Each is an argument in the others; if you're missing one piece of information, you can use all the pieces you *do* know to find the missing one. For example, if you know the loan amount, the rate, and the number of years, you can determine the payment.

To see how these functions are all intertwined with each other, take a look at the syntax for each function. The optional parts are in italics. Notice how one piece of information is an argument in another's function. For example, PV is an argument in the FV, MT, RATE, and NPER functions, and vice-versa:

```
PV(RATE, NPR, PMT, FV, Type)
FV(RATE, NPER, PMT, PV, Type)
PMT(RATE, NPER, PV, FV, Type)
RATE(NPER, PMT, PV, FV, Type)
NPER(RATE, PMT, PV, FV, Type)
```

Here's a closer look at how the PMT function works, so you can see how you can use numeric values or cell values. Say the rate is 0.833 percent per month (that's 10 percent per year) for 60 months, and the amount borrowed is $25,000. The Excel formula looks like this:

```
=PMT(.00833,60,25000)
```

EXTRA INFO

The Type argument specifies when the payment is made: 1 for the beginning of the period, or 0 at the end of the period. Type is not a required argument, and I don't use it in the examples here.

Enter that into a worksheet cell, and you find that the monthly payment is $531.13. You could also enter those values into cells, and then refer to the cells in the function arguments, like this (assuming you entered them into cells B1, B2, and B3):

```
=PMT(B1,B2,B3)
```

The following sections offer hands-on examples that enable you to try working with the PMT, NPER, and PV functions.

Use the PMT function

The PMT function calculates the payment amount on a loan, given the rate, number of periods, and the present value. Use this function to answer the question: "What would my monthly payment be?"

In this exercise, you calculate a loan payment.

Files needed: Lesson 6 Loans.xlsx

1. **Open** Lesson 6 Loans.xlsx **and save it as** Lesson 6 Loans Practice.xlsx.

2. **On the PMT worksheet, select cell B5, and then choose Formulas⇨Insert Function.**

3. **In the Insert Function dialog box that appears, from the Or Select a Category drop-down list, choose Financial.**

4. **Select PMT from the Select a Function list, as shown in Figure 6-1, and then click OK.**

   The Function Arguments dialog box opens.

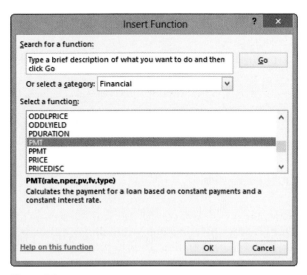

Figure 6-1

5. **Drag the dialog box to the side so you can see columns B through D on the worksheet; in the dialog box, click in the Rate text box and then click cell D6 in the worksheet.**

TIP

   Interest rates on loans are commonly discussed as a yearly rate, but when calculating a payment, you need to use the monthly rate. The amount in cell D6 is the yearly rate (cell B6) divided by 12.

6. **In the dialog box, click in the Nper text box, and then click cell B4 on the worksheet.**

7. **In the dialog box, click in the Pv text box, and then click cell B3 on the worksheet, as shown in Figure 6-2.**

8. **Click OK.**

   The calculated payment $-\$566.14$ appears in cell B5. It is a negative number (and therefore appears in red and in parentheses) because the amount entered in cell B3 is positive.

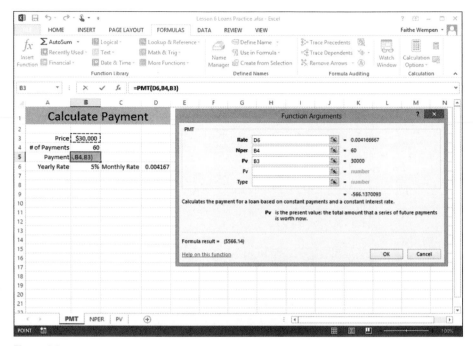

Figure 6-2

If you want the value in cell B5 to appear as a positive number, make the amount in cell B3 negative. If you want them both to appear as positives, enclose the function in B5 in an ABS (absolute value) function. To do this, change the entry in B5 to =ABS(PMT(D6,B4,B3)).

9. Save the changes to the workbook.

Leave the workbook open for the next exercise.

Use the NPER function

The NPER function calculates the number of payments (in other words, the length of the loan), given the rate, the present value, and the payment amount. Use this function to answer the question: "How long will it take to pay this off?"

In this exercise, you calculate the number of periods for a loan.

Files needed: Lesson 6 Loans Practice.xlsx from the preceding exercise

1. **In** Lesson 6 Loans Practice.
   xlsx, **click the NPER worksheet
   tab, click cell B4, and type the
   following:**

   =NPER(

   A ScreenTip appears below the
   cell to prompt you for the arguments. (See Figure 6-3.) The first
   argument, rate, is bold in the
   ScreenTip.

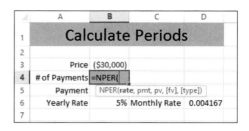

Figure 6-3

2. **Type** D6 **and then type a comma.**

   The ScreenTip makes the next argument prompt (pmt) bold. The formula now looks like this:

   =NPER(D6,

3. **Type** B5 **and then type a comma.**

   The ScreenTip makes the next argument prompt (pv) bold. The formula
   now looks like this:

   =NPER(D6,B5,

4. **Type** B3 **and then press Enter.**

   The function is complete. The number of payments is 69.18744.

You can't have a fractional payment in real life, so you might want to
use the ROUNDUP function to round up the value in cell B4 to the near-
est whole number. To do so, enclose the current function in a ROUNDUP
function like this: =ROUNDUP(NPER(D6,B5,B3),0). The comma and
zero near the end are required; the zero says to use no decimal places.

5. **Click the PMT worksheet tab and note the payment amount calculated
   for a loan of 60 months: $566.14.**

6. **Click the NPER worksheet tab
   and change the value in cell B5
   to $566.14.**

   The number of payments in cell
   B4 changes to 60 (assuming you
   added the ROUNDUP function as
   in the previous note); Figure 6-4
   shows the completed worksheet.

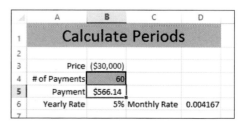

Figure 6-4

7. **Save the changes to the
   workbook.**

Leave the workbook open for the next exercise.

Use the PV function

The PV function calculates the starting value of a loan (assuming it starts in the present moment) given the rate, the number of periods, and the payment amount. Use this function to answer the question: "How much can I borrow?"

In this exercise, you calculate the present value for a loan.

Files needed: Lesson 6 Loans Practice.xlsx from the preceding exercise

1. **In** Lesson 6 Loans Practice.xlsx, **click the PV worksheet tab, and then in cell B3, type the following:**

   =PV(D6,B4,B5)

2. **Press Enter.**

   The function is complete, and the value is ($26,495.35), which is negative. You can tell it's negative because of the parentheses.

3. **Select cell B3 and note the function in the formula bar is**
   =PV(D6,B4,B5).

4. **Change the value in cell B6 from 5% to 3.5%.**

   The amount in B3 changes to ($27,484.99). You can borrow more money if you get an interest rate lower than 5%.

5. **Change the value in cell B4 from 60 to 72.**

   The amount in B3 changes to ($32,428.79). You can borrow more money if you increase the length of the loan. Figure 6-5 shows the completed worksheet.

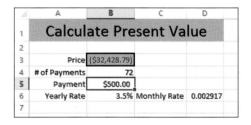

6. **Save the changes to the workbook.**

   Figure 6-5

Leave the workbook open for the next exercise.

Analyzing Data

Besides using functions, you can analyze data in Excel in other ways. In the following sections, you learn about some of these methods, including using Goal Seek, using Solver, and calculating a moving average.

Using Goal Seek to find a value

When you create formulas that rely on values from multiple cells, you can usually experiment with various values to approximate a certain desired value in the formula's result. For example, suppose you have a PMT (payment) function set up and are trying to determine the maximum amount you can spend on a car if your payment has to be less than $400. You can enter different amounts for the PV argument until you find the one that results in the PMT function being exactly $400.

You don't have to use the trial-and-error method to find the formula result you're after. You may prefer to use the Goal Seek feature in such situations to automatically set a certain variable to a certain amount in order to reach a certain goal.

In this exercise, you use Goal Seek to find the loan amount when the payment is a certain value.

Files needed: Lesson 6 Loans Practice.xlsx from the preceding exercise

1. **In** Lesson 6 Loans Practice.xlsx, **click the PMT worksheet tab and select cell B5.**

2. **Choose Data➪What-If Analysis➪Goal Seek.**

   The Goal Seek dialog box opens.

3. **In the Set Cell box, B5 is already entered, so leave that as-is; in the To Value box, type –400, making sure you type a – sign at the beginning to make it negative.**

   Here's an exception: If you used the ABS function to change the value in B5 to a positive number earlier, do not make the number negative here. That's why Figure 6-6 shows 400 as a positive number.

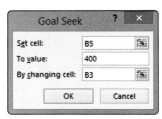

Figure 6-6

4. **In the By Changing Cell box, type** B3, **as shown in Figure 6-6.**

5. **Click OK and the value in cell B3 changes to $21,196, as shown in Figure 6-7. Click OK to accept the new values.**

6. **Save the workbook and close it.**

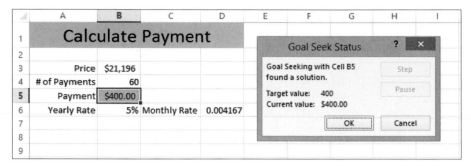

Figure 6-7

Leave Excel open for the next exercise.

Loading an add-in

Excel has some tools that are rather specialized, and rather than bog down the application by making them standard for everyone, Microsoft issued them as *add-ins* for Excel: You can load them only if you need them. An add-in is an optional feature that can be enabled or disabled in the application.

In this exercise, you load the Analysis ToolPak and the Solver add-ins, which you need for upcoming exercises.

Files needed: None

1. **Choose File⇨Options and in the Excel Options dialog box, click Add-Ins.**

   A list of active and inactive add-ins appears. (See Figure 6-8.)

2. **In the Manage drop-down list toward the bottom of the window, choose Excel Add-Ins (if it's not already selected) and then click the Go button.**

   The Add-Ins dialog box opens.

3. **Select the Analysis ToolPak check box.**

   You don't need to select the Analysis ToolPak – VBA check box.

4. **Select the Solver add-in if it's not already selected.**

   You use Solver later in this lesson. See Figure 6-9.

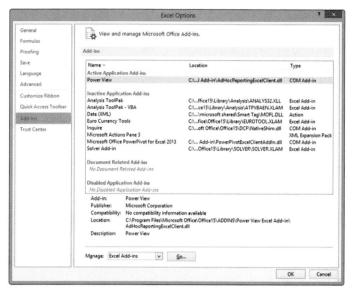

Figure 6-8

Figure 6-9

5. Click OK and then click the Data tab on the Ribbon.

Notice that a new Analysis group appears, with Data Analysis and Solver buttons in it. (See Figure 6-10.) You use this button in later exercises to select data analysis features.

Add-ins

Figure 6-10

Leave Excel open for the next exercise.

Calculating a moving average

When you look at all the data in an Excel worksheet, you may find some values in a data series that are not congruent with the surrounding ones. For example, you may see a particularly good or bad month for sales in an organization that usually has fairly consistent sales revenue. Excel helps you get a clearer picture of the data with its Moving Average feature in the Analysis ToolPak.

LINGO

A **moving average** is a sequence of averages computed from parts of a data series. A moving average smoothes out fluctuations in data to show a pattern or trend more clearly.

Calculating a moving average manually

You could calculate moving averages on your own, but it would be time-consuming. For example, suppose you wanted a moving average of the following numbers: 3, 5, 4, 7, 10, with an interval of 3. To calculate the moving average manually:

1. **Take the average of the first number (in this case, 3) with the two numbers that come before it. No two numbers come before the 3 in the sequence, so this produces nothing.**

2. **Take the average of the second number (in this case, 5) with the two numbers that come before it. Again, no two numbers come before the 5 in the sequence, so this produces nothing.**

3. **Take the average of the third number (in this case, 4) with the two numbers that come before it (in this case, 3 and 5):** $(3+5+4) \div 3 = 4$, **so the first number in the moving average is 4.**

4. **Take the average of the fourth number (in this case, 7) with the two numbers that come before it (in this case, 5 and 4):** $(5+4+7) \div 3 = 5^{1}/_{3}$, **so the second number in the moving average is 5.33.**

5. **Take the average of the fifth number (in this case, 10) with the two that come before it (in this case, 4 and 7):** $(4+7+10) \div 3 = 7$, **so the third number in the moving average is 7.**

Based on those calculations, the moving averages for this data are 4, 5.33, and 7. Overall the trend of this data is an increase of approximately 1.5 per movement, because there is about 1.5 difference between the three averages.

Calculating a moving average in Excel

I had you calculate a moving average manually in the preceding exercise to give you an appreciation of how much easier moving averages are to calculate with Excel.

In this exercise, you use the Moving Average feature of the Analysis ToolPak to calculate a moving average.

Files needed: Lesson 6 Analysis.xlsx

1. **Open** Lesson 6 Analysis.xlsx, **save it as** Lesson 6 Analysis Practice. xlsx, **and display the Revenue sheet if it's not already displayed.**

2. **Choose Data⇨Data Analysis. In the Data Analysis dialog box that appears, select Moving Average, as shown in Figure 6-11, and then click OK.**

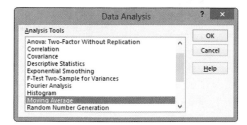

Figure 6-11

3. **In the Moving Average dialog box that appears, type** C1:C13 **in the Input Range box.**

   Alternatively, you can select the range C1:C13 behind the dialog box.

TIP

Excel fills in the dollar signs around the cell addresses automatically, creating absolute references.

4. **Select the Labels in First Row check box and then type** 3 **in the Interval box.**

5. **In the Output Range box, type** D2:D13 **(or select that range on the worksheet behind the dialog box) and then select the Chart Output check box.**

The completed dialog box resembles Figure 6-12.

Figure 6-12

The higher the interval, the more numbers adjacent to each value in the data series will be considered in the averaging, and the smoother the results will be. However, the higher the interval, the fewer usable values there will be in the results; Excel throws out a number of results at the beginning of the data series, equal to the interval you chose minus 1. So, for example, if you use an interval of 3, the first two rows will not have a moving average calculated for them.

6. **Click OK.**

The moving average values are filled into the range D4:D13 (cells D2 and D3 show the #N/A error message), and a chart is created on the worksheet (see Figure 6-13).

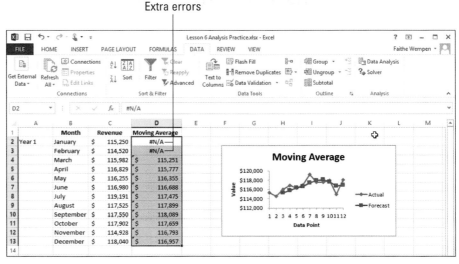

Figure 6-13

7. **Drag the border of the chart frame to expand it so you can see the chart more clearly.**

The blue line (Actual) is plotted from the Revenue column. The red line (Forecast) is plotted from the Moving Average column. (See Figure 6-14.) The Forecast line is much smoother because the moving average minimizes the variations.

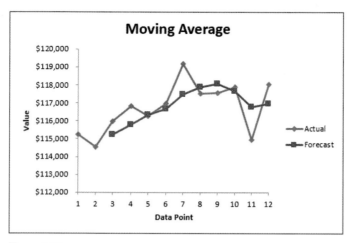

Figure 6-14

8. **Click cell D4 and notice the** =AVERAGE(C2:C4) **formula in the formula bar. Click cell D5 and notice the** =AVERAGE(C3:C5) **formula in the formula bar.**

This is congruent with the manual moving averaging you did earlier.

9. **Save the workbook.**

Leave the workbook open for the next exercise.

Using Solver to analyze complex problems

Using Solver to analyze complex problems works something like Goal Seek (as you see in the "Using Goal Seek to find a value" section). With Goal Seek, you find a certain value in one cell based on changing one other cell. Excel's Solver tool is somewhat like Goal Seek except that it solves problems that have multiple variables and constraints.

LINGO

A **constraint** is a rule that limits the range of values a cell may contain. For example, in a grade book worksheet, a constraint might be that scores on a test must not be negative numbers.

Suppose you run a factory that has a certain number of employees, and can produce different products, each of which has different manufacturing parts and labor costs and can be sold for a different price. Which products should you make, and how many, in order to produce the most profit? Solver can provide an answer to complex questions like this.

In this exercise, you use Solver to determine the optimal number of two products to produce.

Files needed: Lesson 6 Analysis Practice.xlsx from the preceding exercise

1. **Click the Production tab, and take a moment to familiarize yourself with the scenario outlined there, as shown in Figure 6-15:**

   - Each product takes both materials and labor to produce.

   - Each product has a fixed cost to produce that is based on the materials plus labor cost.

   - There is a limited number of man-hours per day because there are only 15 employees (see cell B3).

   - The profit for each product (cells F14 and F15) is the sales price minus all the manufacturing costs.

   - You need to determine which combination of product production will generate the maximum value in the Total Profit cell (F17).

	A	B	C	D	E	F
1	**Basic Assumptions**					
2	Labor Cost Per Hour	$25.00				
3	Employees	15				
4	Workday	8 hours				
5	Man-Hours/Day	120				
6						
7	**Per Unit Costs and Profits**					
8		Materials	Labor Hours	Labor Cost	Total Cost	Sales Price
9	Product A	$3.50	1.75	$43.75	$47.25	$55.12
10	Product B	$2.00	1.35	$33.75	$35.75	$44.80
11						
12	**Production Recommendation**					
13	Production	Units	Man/Hours	Cost to Make	Sales Revenue	Profit
14	Product A		0	$0.00	$0.00	$0.00
15	Product B		0	$0.00	$0.00	$0.00
16						
17		Total Man/Hours	0		Total Profit:	$0.00
18						

Figure 6-15

2. **In cell B14, type** 75 **as an experiment.**

   The worksheet shows how much profit would be made if you made 75 units of product A and none of product B.

3. **Notice, in cell C17, that Man/Hours is over the 120 limit specified in cell B5, so making 75 units of product A won't work.**

4. **Type** 68 **in cell B14.**

   Now Man/Hours is 119, which is within the limit.

5. **Type** 38 **in each of the cells B14 and B15.**

   Cell F17 now shows what the profit would be if you made equal numbers of each product, and kept the Man/Hours less than 120.

   As you can see, with so many factors involved, this is a very thorny problem to figure out on your own. Solver will make it much easier.

6. **Choose Data⇨Solver to open the Solver Parameters dialog box.**

7. **In the Set Objective box, type** F17 **and make sure the Max option button is selected in the To area.**

   Cell F17 contains the total profit, and you want to maximize it.

8. **In the By Changing Variable Cells box, type** B14:B15.

   These are the two cells that you want to find the correct values for — the number of units to produce of each product. The dialog box looks like Figure 6-16.

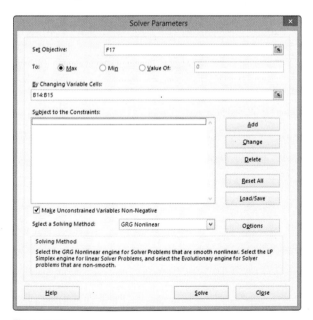

Figure 6-16

9. **Click the Add button to add a constraint, and in the Add Constraint dialog box that opens, type** C17 **in the Cell Reference box. The drop-down list is already set to Less Than Or Equal To (<=), so leave it as is.**

10. **In the Constraint box, type** B5 **(see Figure 6-17) and then click OK to add the constraint to the Subject to the Constraints list.**

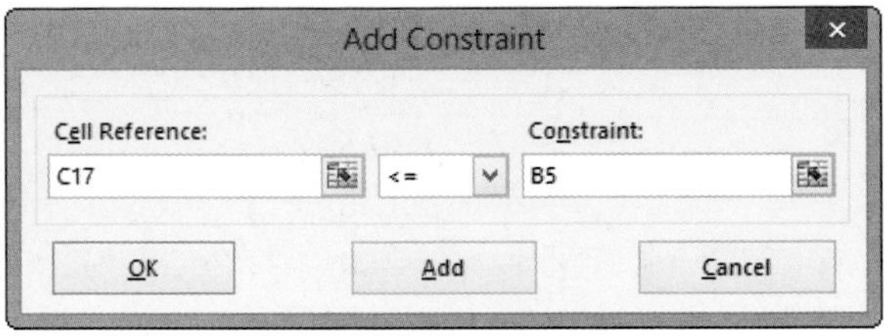

11. **Click the Solve button in the Solve Parameters dialog box.**

Figure 6-17

The values in cells B14 and B15 change, and the Solver Results dialog box opens. (See Figure 6-18.) Solver has determined that the maximum profit will be obtained by making 88 units of Product B and none of Product A.

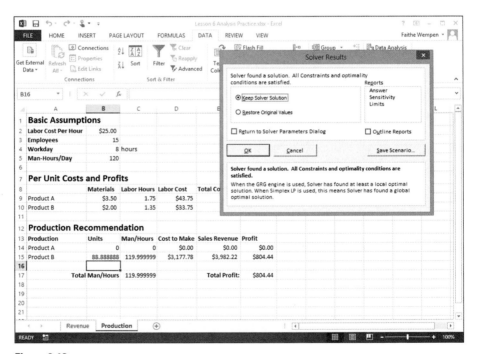

Figure 6-18

12. **In the Solver Results dialog box, click OK to keep the Solver solution.**

With the current data, it made more sense to not make any of Product A. But what if you needed to produce at least half as many of product A as you do Product B? Modify Solver to accommodate that additional constraint.

13. **Choose Data⇨Solver to open the Solver Parameters dialog box and then click the Add button to open the Add Constraint dialog box.**

14. **In the Cell Reference box, type** B14 **and choose >= from the drop-down list.**

15. **In the Constraint box, type** =B15/2 **and then click OK.**

   The new constraint is added, as shown in Figure 6-19.

Figure 6-19

16. **Click the Solve button in the Solver Parameters dialog box.**

   The Solver Results dialog box appears, and the values in cells B14 and B15 change to reflect the new constraints. (See Figure 6-20.)

17. **In the Solver Results dialog box, click the Save Scenario button to open the Save Scenario dialog box.**

   You learn more about scenarios in the next exercise.

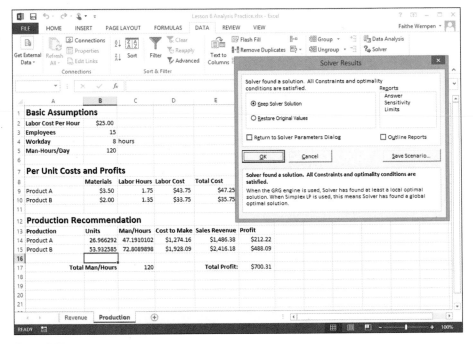

Figure 6-20

18. **Type 2X Product B in the Scenario Name field, as shown in Figure 6-21, and then click OK.**

19. **Click OK again to dismiss the Solver Results dialog box. Then save the workbook.**

Leave the workbook open for the next exercise.

Figure 6-21

Creating Scenarios

As you see in the earlier exercises, what-if analysis can be very useful. You can try different possibilities to see which one gives you the results you want. After you try a certain combination of values, you may want to revisit that combination at a later time. Using scenarios in Excel makes it possible to easily do so.

LINGO

A **scenario** is a stored set of values for particular cells. At the end of the preceding exercise, for example, you saved the Solver results as a scenario. You can recall this scenario at any time from the Scenario Manager. You can also create new scenarios and store them for later use.

Recalling a stored scenario

If you already have a scenario stored, you can easily recall it with the Scenario Manager.

In this exercise, you open a stored scenario.

Files needed: Lesson 6 Analysis Practice.xlsx from the preceding exercise

1. **On the Production tab, in cell B14, type** 0, **replacing the value there. In cell B15, type** 88, **replacing the value there.**

2. **Choose Data⇨What-If Analysis⇨Scenario Manager.**

   The 2X Product B scenario is there from the preceding exercise. (See Figure 6-22.)

Figure 6-22

3. **Click the 2X Product B scenario if it is not already selected and then click the Show button.**

   The stored scenario is loaded into the appropriate cells on the worksheet.

4. **Click the Close button in the upper-right of the Scenario Manager.**

5. **Save the workbook.**

Leave the workbook open for the next exercise.

Creating a scenario

When you were using Solver, you saw one way of creating a scenario — to save the Solver results as one. You can also manually create new scenarios.

In this exercise, you create a new scenario that looks at what would happen if the labor cost per hour changed.

Files needed: Lesson 6 Analysis Practice.xlsx from the preceding exercise

1. **Choose Data⇨What-If Analysis⇨Scenario Manager to open the Scenario Manager dialog box.**

2. **Click the Add button, and the Add Scenario dialog box opens.**

3. **In the Scenario Name box, replace the current name (if any) with** Labor Cost Decrease; **in the Changing Cells box, replace the current entry with** B2 **as shown in Figure 6-23.**

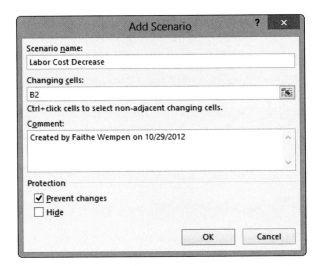

Figure 6-23

4. **Click OK, and in the Scenario Values dialog box that opens, change 25 (the current value in B2) to 20, as shown in Figure 6-24. Then click OK again.**

   The Scenario Manager dialog box reappears.

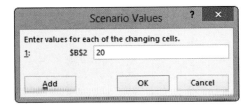

Figure 6-24

5. **Click the Show button.**

   The value in cell B2 changes to 20, and the cells that depend on that value also change.

6. **Click the Close button to close the Scenario Manager dialog box.**

For more practice, re-run Solver to update the quantities in cells B14 and B15 to reflect the new labor cost. The quantities will stay the same.

7. **Save the workbook.**

Leave the workbook open for the next exercise.

Working with Named Ranges

Naming a range can be helpful because you can refer to the range by a friendly name, rather than by the cell addresses, when constructing formulas and functions. That way you don't have to remember the exact cell addresses; you can construct formulas based on meaning.

For example, instead of remembering that the number of employees is stored in cell B3, you could name cell B3 *Employees.* Then in a formula that uses B3's value, such as `=B3*2`, you could use the name instead, such as `=Employees*2`.

Naming a range

Here are the three ways to name a range, each with pros and cons:

- ✔ **If the default names are okay to use, you can choose Formulas⇨Create from Selection.** With this method, Excel chooses the name for you, based on text labels it finds in an adjacent cell (above or to the left of the current cells). This method is very fast and easy, and works well when you have to create a lot of names at once and when the cells are well labeled with adjacent text.

- ✔ **You can select the range and then type a name in the Name box** (the area immediately above the column A heading, to the left of the Formula bar). With this fast and easy method, you get to choose the name. However, you have to do each range separately; you can't do a big batch at a time like you can by choosing Formulas⇨Create from Selection.

✔ **If you want to more precisely control the options for the name, choose Formulas⇨Define Name.** This method opens a dialog box from which you can specify the name, the scope, and any comments you might want to include.

In this exercise, you name several ranges using three methods.

Files needed: Lesson 6 Analysis Practice.xlsx from the preceding exercise

1. **On the Production tab, select the range A3:B4 and then choose Formulas⇨Create from Selection to open the Create Names from Selection dialog box.**

2. **Select the Left Column check box (see Figure 6-25) if it is not already selected and then click OK.**

   Cells C3 and C4 are assigned names based on the text in cells B3 and B4.

Figure 6-25

3. **Choose Formulas⇨Name Manager.**

   In the Name Manager dialog box that opens, the names appear on the list that you just created. See Figure 6-26.

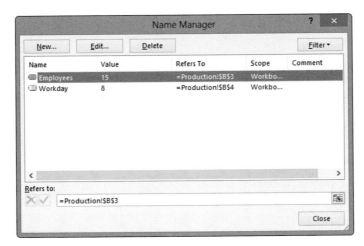

Figure 6-26

4. **Click Close to close the Name Manager dialog box.**

5. **Click cell F9; in the Name box above column A, type** SalesPriceA **(as shown in Figure 6-27) and press Enter.**

6. **Click cell F10; in the Name box, type** SalesPriceB **and press Enter.**

Name box

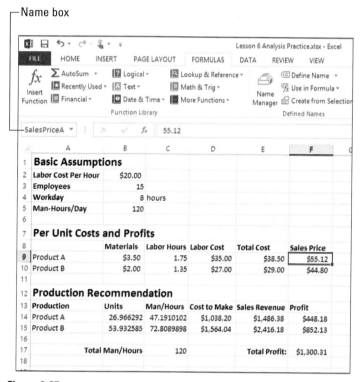

Figure 6-27

7. Click cell F17 and choose Formulas⇨Define Name.

The New Name dialog box opens. The `Total_Profit` name is suggested for you. That name works well enough, so don't change it.

8. Choose Production from the Scope drop-down list, as shown in Figure 6-28.

This name applies only to this worksheet.

9. Click OK to create the name and then choose Formulas⇨Name Manager.

The Name Manager dialog box reopens.

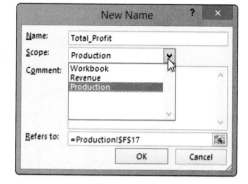

Figure 6-28

10. **Examine the list of all the named ranges you have created, and then click Close to close the dialog box.**

TIP

All the ranges you created in this exercise consist of a single cell, but ranges can consist of any number of cells. When a range contains multiple cells and you use the name in a formula, Excel treats it as if you had specified the range with the starting and ending cell addresses, such as A3:B6.

11. **Save the workbook.**

Leave the workbook open for the next exercise.

Using a named range in a formula

The main reason for naming a range is to refer to it in a formula. You can substitute the range name for the cell addresses in any situation where using a range would be appropriate.

WARNING!

Range names that refer to multiple cells may produce an error in a formula where a multi-celled range would not be an appropriate argument. For example, if the Sales range referred to B4:B8, the formula `=Sales` would result in an error because there's no math operation specified. (The formula `=B4:B8` would produce the same error.) However, `=SUM(Sales)` would work just fine, as would `=SUM(B4:B8)`.

In this exercise, you use range names in formulas.

Files needed: Lesson 6 Analysis Practice.xlsx from the preceding exercise

1. **Click cell B5 to select it and then replace its formula with the following:**

   `=Employees*Workday`

2. **Select cell E14, click in the Formula bar, and edit the formula as follows:**

   `=B14*SalesPriceA`

3. **Select cell E15, click in the Formula bar, and edit the formula as follows:**

   `=B15*SalesPriceB`

4. **Save the workbook and close it.**

5. **Exit Excel.**

Summing Up

Here are the key points you learned about in this lesson:

- The functions PV, FV, PMT, RATE, and NPER are all for calculating different parts of a loan's terms. PV is present value; FV is future value. PMT is payment amount. RATE is interest rate. NPER is number of periods.

- The Goal Seek feature helps you adjust the value in one cell by solving for a particular value in another dependent cell. To access Goal Seek, choose Data⇨What-If Analysis⇨Goal Seek.

- Some features in Excel are add-ins. To load an add-in, choose File⇨Add-Ins, and in the Manage box, select Excel Add-Ins, and click Go.

- One of the Data Analysis add-in features is Moving Average, which calculates a sequence of averages to smooth out fluctuations in data.

- Another add-in is Solver, which is like Goal Seek except it solves problems that have multiple variables and constraints.

- A scenario is a stored set of values for particular cells. You can save and load scenarios to try and re-try different possibilities. Access them from Data⇨What-If Analysis⇨Scenario Manager.

- You can name ranges and then use the names in formulas and functions instead of the cell references. One way to name a range is to select it and then type a name in the Name box (to the left of the Formula bar).

Try-it-yourself lab

1. **Start Excel, and create a worksheet that uses the RATE function to calculate the interest rate on a loan given a present value of $150,000, a term of 360 payments, and a payment of $1,000. Make the present value negative in the worksheet so the rate comes out positive.**

In the cell where you place the RATE function, you may need to increase the number of decimal places shown in order to see the rate correctly. Choose Home⇨Increase Decimal. You may also want to format the rates as percentages; choose Home⇨Percentage.

2. **(Optional) Look up the PPMT function in the Excel Help system, and then use it to create an amortization table for the loan. If you don't know what an amortization table is, research it online.**

Figure 6-29 shows an example of the completed project.

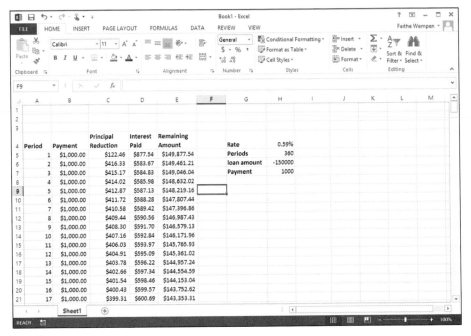

Figure 6-29

Excel has an interest calculation function, IPMT, but you don't have to use it to calculate the interest. You can just subtract the principal amount from the payment.

As you are entering the arguments for the PPMT function, make sure you use absolute references for any of the cells that shouldn't change when that function is copied. That way you can easily fill in the rest of the amortization table by copying.

Know this tech talk

add-in: An optional feature that can be enabled or disabled in an application.

constraint: A rule that limits the range of values a cell may contain.

FV: A function that calculates the future value of a loan or savings account.

Goal Seek: A feature that forces a certain cell to be a certain value by changing the values in dependent cells.

moving average: A sequence of averages computed from parts of a data series.

NPER: A function that calculates the number of periods in a loan.

PMT: A function that calculates the payment to be made per period for a loan.

PV: A function that calculates the present value or principal amount for a loan or savings account.

RATE: A function that calculates the interest rate to be charged per period, or the percentage of amortization or depreciation per period.

scenario: A stored set of values for particular cells in a worksheet.

Solver: An Excel add-in that solves for a certain value by manipulating one or more variables or constraints.

Working with Math, Statistical, and Text Functions

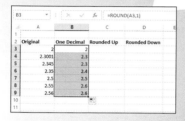

✔ You can exponentiate a number by any multiple with the POWER function.

✔ You can quickly determine a number's square root with the SQRT function.

✔ The ROUND functions enable you to round numbers to a certain number of decimal places.

✔ You can calculate sine, cosine, and tangent with Excel's trigonometry functions SIN, COS, and TAN.

✔ The AVERAGE and MEDIAN functions help you find the average and midpoint values in data series.

✔ The MAX and MIN functions report the highest and lowest values in a series of numbers.

✔ The COUNT function counts the number of values in a specified range.

✔ You can change the case of text with the UPPER, LOWER, and PROPER functions.

✔ The TRIM function removes extra spaces in text strings, and the CLEAN function removes non-printing characters from text strings.

✔ You can combine the contents of two or more cells with the CONCATENATE function.

Excel offers hundreds of functions in various categories. In this lesson, I show you a sampling of the functions in three of those categories: math, statistics, and text. You learn how to do exponentiation and square roots by using functions; how to compute sines, cosines, and tangents; and how to format and manipulate text by using functions.

Using Math Functions

Excel uses basic math operators in formulas, and you're probably already familiar with these:

- ✔ **Addition:** +
- ✔ **Subtraction:** –
- ✔ **Multiplication:** *
- ✔ **Division:** /
- ✔ **Exponentiation:** ^

If you want to go beyond these basic calculations, you must rely on functions. In the next several exercises, you explore Excel's math functions and try a few examples.

Use the POWER and SQRT functions

The POWER function takes the number to the nth power, where n is a number you specify. For example, if cell A1 contains 7, and you enter =POWER(A1,2) in some other cell, the result is 49, which is 7 to the 2nd power (7×7). The function =POWER(A1,3) would result in 343, which is $7 \times 7 \times 7$.

LINGO

Exponentiation is another name for power. You can do exponentiation with the ^ math operator in Excel instead of using the POWER function if you prefer. For example, instead of =POWER(A1,2), you could use =A1^2.

Square root is the opposite of exponentiation; it's the number that, when multiplied by itself, equals the original value. For example, 4 is the square root of 16 because $4 \times 4 = 16$.

The SQRT function finds the square root of a number. For example, if cell A1 contains 49, the function =SQRT(A1) would produce a result of 7.

In this exercise, you practice using the POWER and SQRT functions.

Files needed: Lesson 7 Functions.xlsx

1. **Open** Lesson 7 Functions.xlsx, **save it as** Lesson 7 Functions Practice.xlsx, **and click the Power worksheet tab to display that sheet.**

2. **In cell A3, type** =SQRT(B3) **and then press Enter. Click cell A3 again and drag the fill handle down to cell A12 to copy the function, as shown in Figure 7-1.**

| A3 | ▼ | ⋮ | ✕ | ✓ | f_x | =SQRT(B3) |

◢	A	B	C	D	E
1					
2	**Square Root**	**Original**	**2nd Power**	**3rd Power**	
3	1	1			
4	1.414213562	2			
5	1.732050808	3			
6	2	4			
7	2.236067977	5			
8	2.449489743	6			
9	2.645751311	7			
10	2.828427125	8			
11	3	9			
12	3.16227766	10			
13					
14					

Figure 7-1

3. **In cell C3, type** =POWER(B3,2) **and then press Enter. Click cell C3 again and drag the fill handle down to cell C12 to copy the function, as shown in Figure 7-2.**

4. **In cell D3, type** =POWER(B3,3) **and then press Enter. Click cell D3 again and drag the fill handle down to cell D12 to copy the function, as shown in Figure 7-3.**

5. **Save the workbook.**

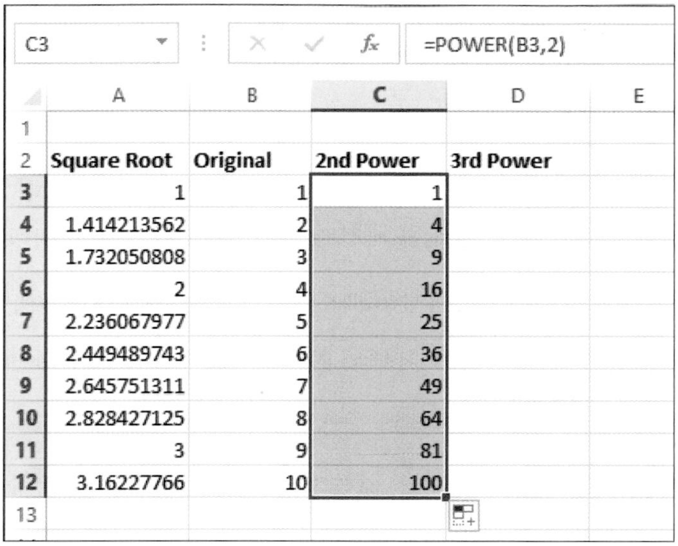

C3		:	×	✓	*fx*	=POWER(B3,2)	

▲	A	B	C	D	E
1					
2	Square Root	Original	2nd Power	3rd Power	
3	1	1	1		
4	1.414213562	2	4		
5	1.732050808	3	9		
6	2	4	16		
7	2.236067977	5	25		
8	2.449489743	6	36		
9	2.645751311	7	49		
10	2.828427125	8	64		
11	3	9	81		
12	3.16227766	10	100		
13					

Figure 7-2

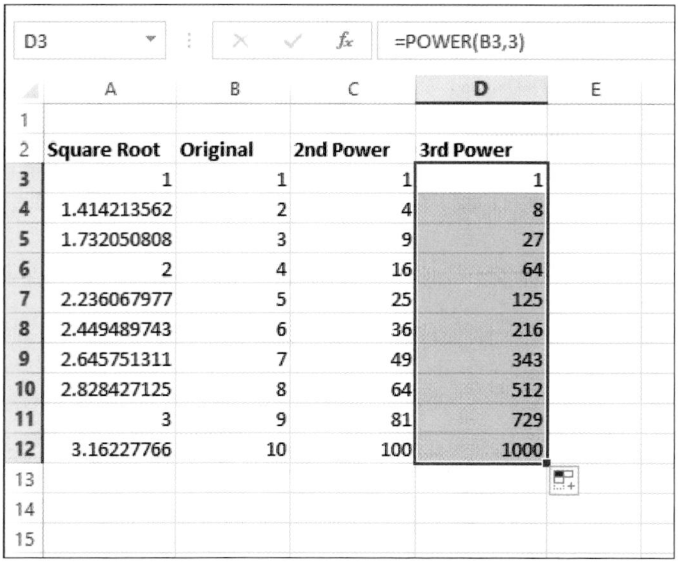

D3		:	×	✓	*fx*	=POWER(B3,3)	

▲	A	B	C	D	E
1					
2	Square Root	Original	2nd Power	3rd Power	
3	1	1	1	1	
4	1.414213562	2	4	8	
5	1.732050808	3	9	27	
6	2	4	16	64	
7	2.236067977	5	25	125	
8	2.449489743	6	36	216	
9	2.645751311	7	49	343	
10	2.828427125	8	64	512	
11	3	9	81	729	
12	3.16227766	10	100	1000	
13					
14					
15					

Figure 7-3

Leave the workbook open for the next exercise.

Use the ROUND functions

The ROUND function rounds a number either up or down, depending on the number, to a specified number of decimal points. For example, if cell A1 contains 3.244, the function =ROUND(A1,2) rounds this number to two decimal places, resulting in 3.24. The final 4 is rounded down to 0 because the value of that digit (4) is less than 5. If the value of the digit removed is greater than or equal to 5, the number is rounded up. If the number does not have as many decimal places as the function specifies, the ROUND function makes no change to the number.

If you want to round a number down, regardless of whether the digit being rounded is greater than or less than 5, use the ROUNDDOWN function. Conversely, to round up no matter what the number is, use ROUNDUP.

LINGO

To **round** a number is to limit a number to a certain number of decimal places, increasing the last visible decimal place digit by one if the first decimal place removed was greater than or equal to 5. For example, when rounding 1.252 to 2 decimal places, the result would be 1.25 because the removed number (2) is less than 5. However, rounding 1.256 to 2 decimal places would result in 1.26 because the removed number (6) is greater than 5.

In this exercise, you practice using rounding functions.

Files needed: Lesson 7 Functions Practice.xlsx from the preceding exercise

1. **Click the Rounding worksheet tab to switch to that sheet.**

2. **In cell B3, type** =ROUND(A3,1) **and then press Enter. Click cell B3 again and drag the fill handle down to cell B9 to copy the function, as shown in Figure 7-4.**

B3	▼	:	×	✓	f_x	=ROUND(A3,1)	
◢	A		B		C	D	E
1							
2	Original		One Decimal		Rounded Up	Rounded Down	
3	2		2				
4	2.3001		2.3				
5	2.345		2.3				
6	2.35		2.4				
7	2.5		2.5				
8	2.55		2.6				
9	2.56		2.6				
10							
11							

Figure 7-4

3. **In cell C3, type** =ROUNDUP(A3,1) **and then press Enter. Click cell C3 again and drag the fill handle down to cell C9 to copy the function, as shown in Figure 7-5.**

C3	▼	⋮	×	✓	fx	=ROUNDUP(A3,1)	

	A	B	C	D	E
1					
2	Original	One Decimal	Rounded Up	Rounded Down	
3	2	2	2		
4	2.3001	2.3	2.4		
5	2.345	2.3	2.4		
6	2.35	2.4	2.4		
7	2.5	2.5	2.5		
8	2.55	2.6	2.6		
9	2.56	2.6	2.6		
10					
11					
12					

Figure 7-5

4. **In cell D3, type** =ROUNDDOWN(A3,1) **and then press Enter. Click cell D3 again and drag the fill handle down to cell D9 to copy the function, as shown in Figure 7-6.**

D3	▼	⋮	×	✓	fx	=ROUNDDOWN(A3,1)	

	A	B	C	D	E
1					
2	Original	One Decimal	Rounded Up	Rounded Down	
3	2	2	2	2	
4	2.3001	2.3	2.4	2.3	
5	2.345	2.3	2.4	2.3	
6	2.35	2.4	2.4	2.3	
7	2.5	2.5	2.5	2.5	
8	2.55	2.6	2.6	2.5	
9	2.56	2.6	2.6	2.5	
10					
11					
12					

Figure 7-6

5. **Save the workbook.**

Leave the workbook open for the next exercise.

Use trigonometry functions

Sine, cosine, and tangent are three essential calculations used in trigonom-etry. Excel has a function for each of them: SIN, COS, and TAN. You can use them to create a reference table for solving trigonometry problems, or for solving individual trig problems.

In this exercise, you practice using trigonometry functions.

Files needed: Lesson 7 Functions Practice.xlsx from the preceding exercise

1. **Click the Trig worksheet tab to switch to that sheet.**

2. **In cell B3, type** =SIN(A3) **and then press Enter. In cell C3, type** =COS(A3) **and then press Enter. In cell D3, type** =TAN(A3) **and then press Enter, as shown in Figure 7-7.**

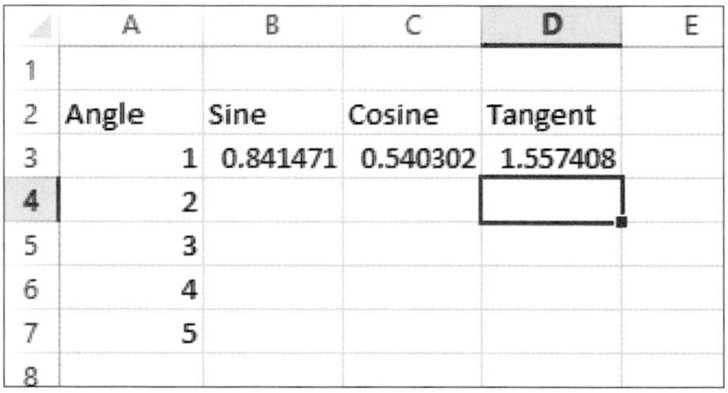

	A	B	C	D	E
1					
2	Angle	Sine	Cosine	Tangent	
3	1	0.841471	0.540302	1.557408	
4	2				
5	3				
6	4				
7	5				
8					

Figure 7-7

3. **Select the range B3:D3 and drag the fill handle down to cell D23, copy-ing the functions.** See Figure 7-8.

4. **Save the workbook.**

Leave the workbook open for the next exercise.

	A	B	C	D	E
2	Angle	Sine	Cosine	Tangent	
3	1	0.841471	0.540302	1.557408	
4	2	0.909297	-0.41615	-2.18504	
5	3	0.14112	-0.98999	-0.14255	
6	4	-0.7568	-0.65364	1.157821	
7	5	-0.95892	0.283662	-3.38052	
8	6	-0.27942	0.96017	-0.29101	
9	7	0.656987	0.753902	0.871448	
10	8	0.989358	-0.1455	-6.79971	
11	9	0.412118	-0.91113	-0.45232	
12	10	-0.54402	-0.83907	0.648361	
13	11	-0.99999	0.004426	-225.951	
14	12	-0.53657	0.843854	-0.63586	
15	13	0.420167	0.907447	0.463021	
16	14	0.990607	0.136737	7.244607	
17	15	0.650288	-0.75969	-0.85599	
18	16	-0.2879	-0.95766	0.300632	
19	17	-0.9614	-0.27516	3.493916	
20	18	-0.75099	0.660317	-1.13731	
21	19	0.149877	0.988705	0.151589	
22	20	0.912945	0.408082	2.237161	
23	21	0.836656	-0.54773	-1.5275	
24					

Figure 7-8

TIP

Many other math functions are available. To find a complete list of Excel's math-based functions, choose Formulas➪Math & Trig. Then click the formula you're interested in using to open a dialog box where you can enter its arguments.

Using Statistical Functions

Statistical functions help you interpret a data set, providing useful information about the data that might not be obvious at a glance. When many people hear *statistics,* they automatically think about advanced statistical analysis like standard deviation and variance (and Excel offers many functions to do those calculations). But statistics is a much larger tent than that and also includes more basic calculations such as averages, medians, and counts as well. You find out how to set up these basic calculations in Excel in the following sections.

Use the AVERAGE and MEDIAN functions

The AVERAGE and MEDIAN functions are two ways of looking at data that consists of a common score or response. Neither is better than the other; they are simply two different ways of analyzing data.

In this exercise, you practice using the AVERAGE and MEDIAN functions.

Files needed: Lesson 7 Functions Practice.xlsx from the preceding exercise

1. **Click the Stats worksheet tab to switch to that sheet.**

2. **In cell B2, type** =AVERAGE(**and drag across the range B10:B35. Then press Enter.**

   Excel adds the closing parenthesis for you automatically. The average for Test 1 appears in cell B2.

3. **Click cell B2 to see the formula in the Formula bar, as shown in Figure 7-9.**

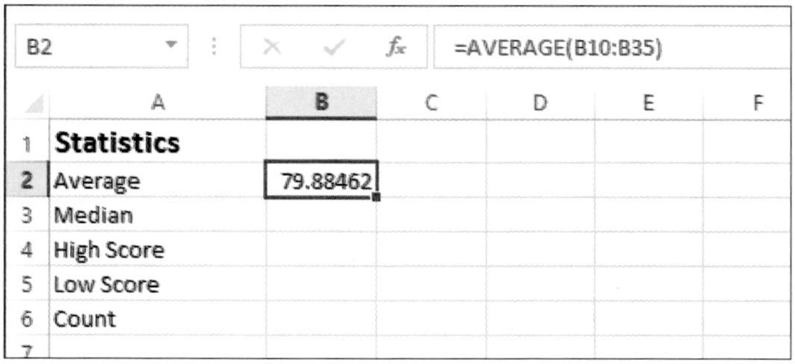

B2	▾	⋮	✕	✓	*fx*	=AVERAGE(B10:B35)		
	A		**B**	C	D	E	F	
1	**Statistics**							
2	Average		79.88462					
3	Median							
4	High Score							
5	Low Score							
6	Count							
7								

Figure 7-9

4. **In cell B3, type** =MEDIAN(B10:B35) **and press Enter.**

   You could drag across the range again as you did in Step 2, but typing is sometimes easier.

5. **Click cell B3 to see the formula in the Formula bar, as shown in Figure 7-10.**

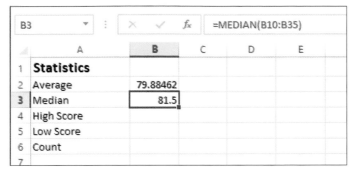

Figure 7-10

6. Save the workbook.

Leave the workbook open for the next exercise.

Use the MAX, MIN, and COUNT functions

The MIN, MAX, and COUNT functions provide a specific piece of information about a data set.

In this exercise, you practice using the COUNT, MIN, and MAX functions.

Files needed: Lesson 7 Functions Practice.xlsx from the preceding exercise

1. **On the Stats tab, in cell B4, type** =MAX(B10:B35) **and then press Enter.**

   The largest value from the range appears in cell B4.

2. **Click cell B4 again to see the completed function in the Formula bar, as shown in Figure 7-11.**

3. **In cell B5, type** =MIN(B10:B35) **and then press Enter.**

   The smallest value from the range appears in cell B5.

LINGO

MIN determines the lowest (minimum) value in the set, and **MAX** determines the highest (maximum). **COUNT** counts the number of cells in a range that contains numeric values.

EXTRA INFO

There are other counting functions, and each one puts a slightly different spin on things. For example, COUNTA counts the number of non-blank cells in the range, regardless of whether they contain text or numbers, and COUNTBLANK counts the number of blank cells. COUNTIF counts the number of cells that meet a condition you specify, and DCOUNT counts the cells containing numbers that also match conditions you specify.

4. **In cell B6, type** =COUNT(B10:B35) **and then press Enter.**

5. **Click cell B6 again to see the completed function in the formula bar, as shown in Figure 7-12.**

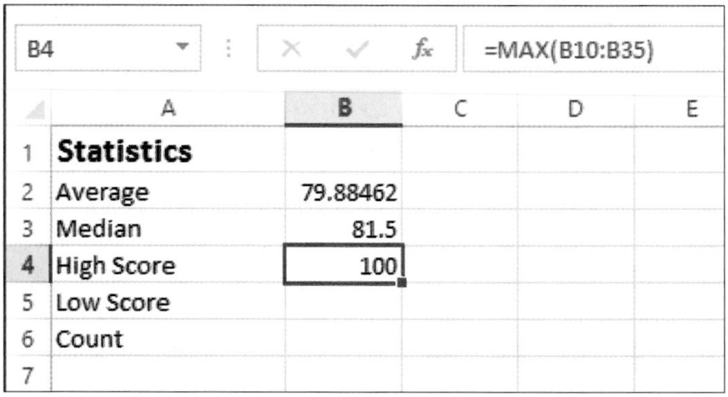

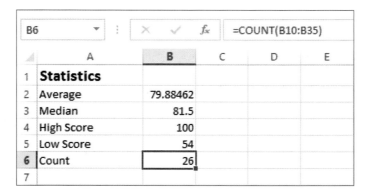

B4		:	×	✓	fx	=MAX(B10:B35)	

	A	B	C	D	E
1	**Statistics**				
2	Average	79.88462			
3	Median	81.5			
4	High Score	100			
5	Low Score				
6	Count				
7					

Figure 7-11

B6		:	×	✓	fx	=COUNT(B10:B35)	

	A	B	C	D	E
1	**Statistics**				
2	Average	79.88462			
3	Median	81.5			
4	High Score	100			
5	Low Score	54			
6	Count	26			
7					

Figure 7-12

PRACTICE

For more practice, repeat these steps for the data in column C, placing the functions in cells C2:C6.

6. **Save the workbook.**

Leave the workbook open for the next exercise.

Many other statistical functions are available in Excel, including several that are specific to calculating probability, such as standard deviation and variance. For example, for standard deviation, Excel 2013 breaks variants into separate functions: STDEV.S (based on a sample) and STDEV.P (based on an entire population). For compatibility with Excel 2007 and earlier, Excel 2013 also supports a simpler and more generic version: STDEV, which calculates standard deviation based on a sample and ignores logical values and text. An STDEVA version is the same except it includes logical values and text.

Formatting Data with Text Functions

Functions usually work with numbers, but some functions are designed specifically for use with text. For example, if you have a list of data in which the capitalization is not consistent, you could use the UPPER function to make all the text uppercase.

Text functions can be used to

- ✔ **Standardize capitalization.** Use the UPPER, LOWER, and PROPER functions to correct data entry errors or apply capitalization conventions.

- ✔ **Clean up text.** Use CLEAN and TRIM to remove extra spaces or unwanted characters that may end up in your worksheet when you bring text into Excel from other sources.

- ✔ **Evaluate a text string.** The LEFT, MID, or RIGHT function can report on the characters at certain positions in a cell; LEN can report the length of the text string overall, and the T function tells whether a cell's content is a text string at all.

- ✔ **Merge cell contents.** With the CONCATENATE function, you can join the content of two or more cells into a single cell.

Replacing cell content by using a text function is typically a multi-step process. When you modify a cell's content with a text function, you have to place the new entry in a separate cell from the original. Then, if you want the new entry to appear in the original location, you have to copy the function to the Clipboard and then use Paste Special to paste its value back to the original location. Finally, you can delete the function that you used to make the change. Some of the upcoming exercises demonstrate this process.

Standardize capitalization

Often, when different people enter data into a worksheet, they have different ideas about the correct capitalization, or they simply get sloppy about entering data consistently. You can clean up data by standardizing the capitalization using a text function. The UPPER function converts all text to uppercase, LOWER converts all text to lowercase, and PROPER capitalizes only the first letter in each word, as if each word were a proper noun.

In this exercise, you practice using the PROPER and LOWER functions to standardize text capitalization.

Files needed: Lesson 7 Functions Practice.xlsx from the preceding exercise

1. **Click the Text worksheet tab to display that worksheet.**

2. **In cell G3, type** =PROPER(A3) **and then press Enter.**

   The name *Amy* appears in G3. Amy doesn't change in cell A3 because it was already capitalized correctly. (See Figure 7-13.)

	A	B	C	D	E	F	G	H
1								
2	First	Last	Status	Address	Access Code			
3	Amy	adams	active	124 Ravinia Road Box 25A	F34872A		Amy	
4	Brent	Brown	inactive	1616 West Washington	F95777B			
5	charlie	cutler	ACTIVE	411 South Main Street	F05827A			
6	dawn	damery	Active	3536 West 14th Street	F85721A			
7	ETHAN	ELLIS	Active	4857 Kayla Road #2	L58347B			
8	FAITH	FARRIS	inactive	788 Macon Lane	L05827B			

Figure 7-13

3. **Select cell G3 and drag the fill handle to cell H3, copying the function.**

   Notice that because the reference to cell A3 was relative, H3 now contains =PROPER(B3).

4. **Select the range G3:H3 and drag the fill handle down to cell H26, copying the function to all the intervening cells.**

   All the names appear in consistently capitalized form in columns G and H. See Figure 7-14.

5. **Press Ctrl+C to copy the selected cells to the Clipboard and then click cell A3.**

6. **From the Home tab, click the down arrow on the Paste button, as shown in Figure 7-15, and choose the first icon in the Paste Values section.**

   This pastes the results of the functions, rather than the functions themselves.

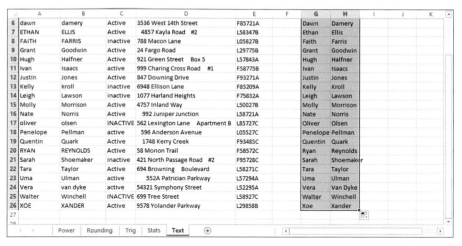

Figure 7-14

Click here.

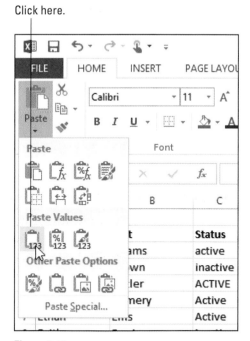

Figure 7-15

7. **Select G3:H26 again, and then press the Delete key to clear the contents.**

8. **In the now-empty cell G3, type** =LOWER(C3) **and then press Enter.**

Cell G3 displays the word *active* — the same as what's in cell C3 — because C3 already contained a lowercase entry.

9. **Select cell G3 and drag the selection handle down to cell G26, copying the function.**

All the statuses from column C appear in column G in consistently lower-cased format. (See Figure 7-16.)

	A	B	C	D	E	F	G	H	I	J	K
5	Charlie	Cutler	ACTIVE	411 South Main Street	F05827A		active				
6	Dawn	Damery	Active	3536 West 14th Street	F85721A		active				
7	Ethan	Ellis	Active	4857 Kayla Road #2	L58347B		active				
8	Faith	Farris	inactive	788 Macon Lane	L05827B		inactive				
9	Grant	Goodwin	Active	24 Fargo Road	L29775B		active				
10	Hugh	Halfner	Active	921 Green Street Box 5	L57843A		active				
11	Ivan	Isaacs	active	999 Charing Cross Road #1	F58775B		active				
12	Justin	Jones	Active	847 Downing Drive	F93271A		active				
13	Kelly	Kroll	inactive	6948 Ellison Lane	F85209A		inactive				
14	Leigh	Lawson	inactive	1077 Harland Heights	F75832A		inactive				
15	Molly	Morrison	Active	4757 Inland Way	L50027B		active				
16	Nate	Norris	Active	992 Juniper Junction	L58721A		active				
17	Oliver	Olsen	INACTIVE	562 Lexington Lane Apartment B	L85727C		inactive				
18	Penelope	Pellman	active	596 Anderson Avenue	L05527C		active				
19	Quentin	Quark	Active	1748 Kerry Creek	F93485C		active				
20	Ryan	Reynolds	Active	58 Monon Trail	F58572C		active				
21	Sarah	Shoemaker	inactive	421 North Passage Road #2	F95728C		inactive				
22	Tara	Taylor	Active	694 Browning Boulevard	L58271C		active				
23	Uma	Ulman	active	552A Patrician Parkway	L57294A		active				
24	Vera	Van Dyke	active	54321 Symphony Street	L52295A		active				
25	Walter	Winchell	INACTIVE	699 Tree Street	L58927C		inactive				
26	Xoe	Xander	Active	9578 Yolander Parkway	L29858B		active				

Power | Rounding | Trig | Stats | **Text** | +

Figure 7-16

10. **Press Ctrl+C to copy the selection to the Clipboard and then click cell C3.**

11. **From the Home tab, click the down arrow on the Paste button and choose the first icon in the Paste Values section, pasting the values.**

12. **Select the range G3:G26 and then press the Delete key to remove the functions from column G.**

TIP

You might be thinking, "Why not use Ctrl+X for Cut instead of copying in Step 10?" Then you wouldn't have to delete the range in Step 12. That won't work, though, because Paste Values is not available as an option in Step 11 if you choose Cut in Step 10.

13. **Save the workbook.**

Leave the workbook open for the next exercise.

Clean up text

Sometimes, when you bring in text to Excel from other sources, you end up with extra characters. These could be multiple extra spaces, or they could be non-printing "junk" characters such as tabs, page-break characters, paragraph breaks, line breaks, and non-ASCII characters. Non-printing characters sometimes occur when you import data from obscure data formats, for example, or when Excel misidentifies the data type when importing data.

Excel gives you two functions for cleaning up text. The TRIM function removes extra spaces anywhere that they occur in the entry, replacing them with a single space. The CLEAN function removes any non-printing characters from the entry.

If there are multiple spaces in a row in a cell, the TRIM function removes all except one of them in each spot. One exception, though: If blank spaces are at the beginning of the cell's content, it removes them all. That's actually very handy because then you don't have to worry about some entries having a blank space at the beginning that you would have to manually remove.

In this exercise, you clean up some text entries using the TRIM function.

Files needed: Lesson 7 Functions Practice.xlsx from the preceding exercise

1. On the Text worksheet, in cell G3, type =TRIM(D3) **and then press Enter.**

The same text in cell D3 appears in cell G3, except without the extra spaces.

2. Click cell G3 and check the formula in the Formula bar.

See Figure 7-17.

G3				*fx*	=TRIM(D3)								
	A	B	C	D		E	F	G	H	I	J	K	
1													
2	First	Last	Status	Address		Access Code							
3	Amy	Adams	active	124 Ravinia Road Box 25A		F34872A		124 Ravinia Road Box 25A					
4	Brent	Brown	inactive	1616 West Washington		F95777B							
5	Charlie	Cutler	active	411 South Main Street		F05827A							
6	Dawn	Damery	active	3536 West 14th Street		F85721A							
7	Ethan	Ellis	active	4857 Kayla Road #2		L58347B							
8	Faith	Farris	inactive	788 Macon Lane		L05827B							
9	Grant	Goodwin	active	24 Fargo Road		L29775B							

Figure 7-17

3. **Drag the fill handle from cell G3 down to cell G26.**

   All the addresses are cleaned up, with extra spaces removed.

4. **With the range G3:G26 selected, press Ctrl+C to copy to the Clipboard and then click cell D3.**

5. **From the Home tab, click the down arrow on the Paste button and choose the first icon in the Paste Values section.**

   The cleaned-up addresses are pasted into column D. See Figure 7-18.

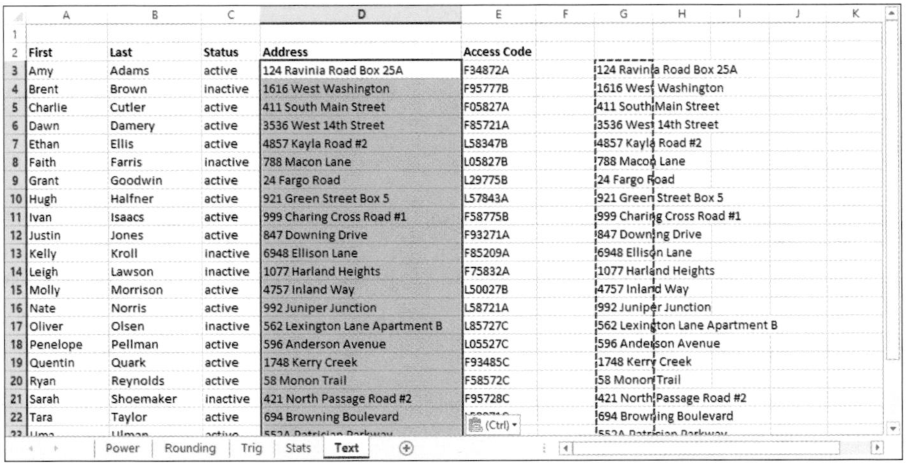

	A	B	C	D	E	F	G	H	I	J	K
1											
2	First	Last	Status	Address	Access Code						
3	Amy	Adams	active	124 Ravinia Road Box 25A	F34872A		124 Ravinia Road Box 25A				
4	Brent	Brown	inactive	1616 West Washington	F95777B		1616 West Washington				
5	Charlie	Cutler	active	411 South Main Street	F05827A		411 South Main Street				
6	Dawn	Damery	active	3536 West 14th Street	F85721A		3536 West 14th Street				
7	Ethan	Ellis	active	4857 Kayla Road #2	L58347B		4857 Kayla Road #2				
8	Faith	Farris	inactive	788 Macon Lane	L05827B		788 Macon Lane				
9	Grant	Goodwin	active	24 Fargo Road	L29775B		24 Fargo Road				
10	Hugh	Halfner	active	921 Green Street Box 5	L57843A		921 Green Street Box 5				
11	Ivan	Isaacs	active	999 Charing Cross Road #1	F58775B		999 Charing Cross Road #1				
12	Justin	Jones	active	847 Downing Drive	F93271A		847 Downing Drive				
13	Kelly	Kroll	inactive	6948 Ellison Lane	F85209A		6948 Ellison Lane				
14	Leigh	Lawson	inactive	1077 Harland Heights	F75832A		1077 Harland Heights				
15	Molly	Morrison	active	4757 Inland Way	L50027B		4757 Inland Way				
16	Nate	Norris	active	992 Juniper Junction	L58721A		992 Juniper Junction				
17	Oliver	Olsen	inactive	562 Lexington Lane Apartment B	L85727C		562 Lexington Lane Apartment B				
18	Penelope	Pellman	active	596 Anderson Avenue	L05527C		596 Anderson Avenue				
19	Quentin	Quark	active	1748 Kerry Creek	F93485C		1748 Kerry Creek				
20	Ryan	Reynolds	active	58 Monon Trail	F58572C		58 Monon Trail				
21	Sarah	Shoemaker	inactive	421 North Passage Road #2	F95728C		421 North Passage Road #2				
22	Tara	Taylor	active	694 Browning Boulevard			694 Browning Boulevard				
23	Uma	Ulman	active	552A Patrician Parkway			552A Patrician Parkway				

Power | Rounding | Trig | Stats | **Text** | ⊕

Figure 7-18

6. **Select the range G3:G26 and then press the Delete key to clear those cells.**

7. **Save the workbook.**

Leave the workbook open for the next exercise.

Extract characters

The LEFT, RIGHT, and MID functions extract a character from a specific point in the text string. LEFT extracts from the beginning, RIGHT from the end, and MID from the midpoint. You can specify the number of characters to include. These functions are handy when you need to distill text entries down to just a few characters at the beginning or end of the string, or to truncate text strings that are longer than a certain number of characters.

In this exercise, you extract the suffix character (A, B, or C) from a list of access codes.

Files needed: Lesson 7 Functions Practice.xlsx from the preceding exercise

1. **On the Text worksheet, in cell F2, type** Code Type.

2. **In cell F3, type** =RIGHT(E3,1) **and then press Enter.**

REMEMBER

The RIGHT function has two arguments. The first one specifies the cell containing the text to be evaluated, and the second one specifies the number of characters to extract. The LEFT and MID functions take the same arguments.

3. **Click cell F3 again and notice its function in the Formula bar, as shown in Figure 7-19.**

F3	▼	:	×	✓	*fx*	=RIGHT(E3,1)		

	A	B	C	D	E	F	G
1							
2	**First**	**Last**	**Status**	**Address**	**Access Code**	**Code Type**	
3	Amy	Adams	active	124 Ravinia Road Box 25A	F34872A	A	
4	Brent	Brown	inactive	1616 West Washington	F95777B		
5	Charlie	Cutler	active	411 South Main Street	F05827A		
6	Dawn	Damery	active	3536 West 14th Street	F85721A		
7	Ethan	Ellis	active	4857 Kayla Road #2	L58347B		
8	Faith	Farris	inactive	788 Macon Lane	L05827B		

Figure 7-19

4. **Drag the fill handle down to F26 to complete the column, as shown in Figure 7-20.**

	A	B	C	D	E	F	G	H	I	J	K
5	Charlie	Cutler	active	411 South Main Street	F05827A	A					
6	Dawn	Damery	active	3536 West 14th Street	F85721A	A					
7	Ethan	Ellis	active	4857 Kayla Road #2	L58347B	B					
8	Faith	Farris	inactive	788 Macon Lane	L05827B	B					
9	Grant	Goodwin	active	24 Fargo Road	L29775B	B					
10	Hugh	Halfner	active	921 Green Street Box 5	L57843A	A					
11	Ivan	Isaacs	active	999 Charing Cross Road #1	F58775B	B					
12	Justin	Jones	active	847 Downing Drive	F93271A	A					
13	Kelly	Kroll	inactive	6948 Ellison Lane	F85209A	A					
14	Leigh	Lawson	inactive	1077 Harland Heights	F75832A	A					
15	Molly	Morrison	active	4757 Inland Way	L50027B	B					
16	Nate	Norris	active	992 Juniper Junction	L58721A	A					
17	Oliver	Olsen	inactive	562 Lexington Lane Apartment B	L85727C	C					
18	Penelope	Pellman	active	596 Anderson Avenue	L05527C	C				⊕	
19	Quentin	Quark	active	1748 Kerry Creek	F93485C	C					
20	Ryan	Reynolds	active	58 Monon Trail	F58572C	C					
21	Sarah	Shoemaker	inactive	421 North Passage Road #2	F95728C	C					
22	Tara	Taylor	active	694 Browning Boulevard	L58271C	C					
23	Uma	Ulman	active	552A Patrician Parkway	L57294A	A					
24	Vera	Van Dyke	active	54321 Symphony Street	L52295A	A					
25	Walter	Winchell	inactive	699 Tree Street	L58927C	C					
26	Xoe	Xander	active	9578 Yolander Parkway	L29858B	B					

| Power | Rounding | Trig | Stats | **Text** | ⊕ |

Figure 7-20

5. **Save the workbook.**

Leave the workbook open for the next exercise.

Concatenate text

In some worksheets, you may find that you have split data into multiple columns that would make more sense in a single column. For example, perhaps you entered first and last names in separate cells, but now you prefer to have them both in a single cell. To fix such problems, you can use the CONCATENATE function.

When concatenating values from cells, you specify the cells as you normally would — by their addresses (such as cell A1). In between the cell contents, you probably want to insert some literal text, such as a blank space. You enclose any literal text in quotation marks within the function's arguments; so if you wanted to include a space, you'd enclose a single space in quotation marks like this: " ".

In this exercise, you concatenate first and last names into a single column.

Files needed: Lesson 7 Functions Practice.xlsx from the preceding exercise

1. **On the Text worksheet, in cell G3, type the following:**

   =CONCATENATE(

2. **Type A3, type a comma, type a quotation mark, press the spacebar, type another quotation mark, and then type a comma.**

   The actual text that you type looks like this:

   ," ",

3. **Click cell B3 and then press Enter.**

   Excel inserts the closing parenthesis automatically for you.

4. **Click cell G3 and look at the** =CONCATENATE(A3," ",B3) **function in the Formula bar, as shown in Figure 7-21.**

5. **Drag the fill handle down to G26, copying the function.**

   All the names appear in column G.

6. **Press Ctrl+C to copy the selection to the Clipboard and then click cell A3.**

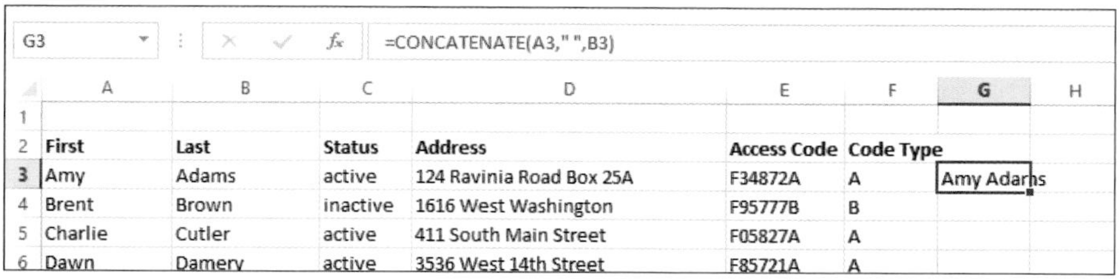

	A	B	C	D	E	F	G	H
G3				fx	=CONCATENATE(A3," ",B3)			
1								
2	First	Last	Status	Address	Access Code	Code Type		
3	Amy	Adams	active	124 Ravinia Road Box 25A	F34872A	A	Amy Adams	
4	Brent	Brown	inactive	1616 West Washington	F95777B	B		
5	Charlie	Cutler	active	411 South Main Street	F05827A	A		
6	Dawn	Damery	active	3536 West 14th Street	F85721A	A		

Figure 7-21

7. **From the Home tab, click the down arrow on the Paste button and choose the first icon in the Paste Values section, as shown in Figure 7-22.**

   The names are pasted into column A.

8. **Select the range G3:G26 and then press the Delete key to clear those cells.**

9. **Click the column heading for column B to select that column and then choose Home⇨Delete to remove it.**

10. **Double-click between column headings A and B to auto-resize column A to fit the widest entry.**

11. **Click cell A2 and type** Name, **replacing the earlier entry in that cell.**

    Figure 7-23 shows the completed worksheet.

12. **Save the worksheet and close it. Exit Excel.**

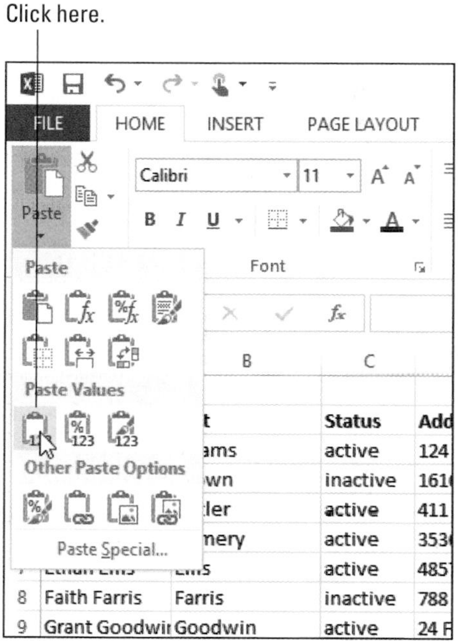

Click here.

Figure 7-22

	A	B	C	D	E	F	G	H	I	J	K
1											
2	Name	Status	Address	Access Code	Code Type						
3	Amy Adams	active	124 Ravinia Road Box 25A	F34872A	A						
4	Brent Brown	inactive	1616 West Washington	F95777B	B						
5	Charlie Cutler	active	411 South Main Street	F05827A	A						
6	Dawn Damery	active	3536 West 14th Street	F85721A	A						
7	Ethan Ellis	active	4857 Kayla Road #2	L58347B	B						
8	Faith Farris	inactive	788 Macon Lane	L05827B	B						
9	Grant Goodwin	active	24 Fargo Road	L29775B	B						
10	Hugh Halfner	active	921 Green Street Box 5	L57843A	A						
11	Ivan Isaacs	active	999 Charing Cross Road #1	F58775B	B						
12	Justin Jones	active	847 Downing Drive	F93271A	A						
13	Kelly Kroll	inactive	6948 Ellison Lane	F85209A	A						
14	Leigh Lawson	inactive	1077 Harland Heights	F75832A	A						
15	Molly Morrison	active	4757 Inland Way	L50027B	B						
16	Nate Norris	active	992 Juniper Junction	L58721A	A						
17	Oliver Olsen	inactive	562 Lexington Lane Apartment B	L85727C	C						
18	Penelope Pellman	active	596 Anderson Avenue	L05527C	C						
19	Quentin Quark	active	1748 Kerry Creek	F93485C	C						
20	Ryan Reynolds	active	58 Monon Trail	F58572C	C						
21	Sarah Shoemaker	inactive	421 North Passage Road #2	F95728C	C						
22	Tara Taylor	active	694 Browning Boulevard	L58271C	C						
23	Uma Ulman	active	552A Patrician Parkway	L57294A	A						
24	Vera Van Dyke	active	54321 Symphony Street	L52295A	A						

Power Rounding Trig Stats **Text**

Figure 7-23

Summing Up

Here are the key points you learned in this lesson:

✔ The POWER function multiplies a number (the first argument) by itself, the number of times specified in its second argument. For example, =POWER(A1,3) multiplies A1 × A1 × A1.

✔ The SQRT function finds the square root of the number specified in its argument; it takes only one argument.

✔ The ROUND function rounds a number (the first argument) to the number of decimal places specified in its second argument. For example, =ROUND(A1,3) rounds the number in A1 to 3 decimal places.

✔ The ROUNDUP and ROUNDDOWN functions round in a specific direction, but otherwise work like ROUND.

✔ The SIN, COS, and TAN functions perform the trigonometric functions of sine, cosine, and tangent, respectively.

✔ AVERAGE sums all the values and divides by the total number of values.

✔ MEDIAN finds the midpoint value when the list of values is arranged from smallest to largest, or largest to smallest.

✔ The MIN and MAX functions find the smallest and largest values in a data set, respectively.

✔ The COUNT function counts the number of numeric values in a range. COUNTA counts the number of non-blank cells, regardless of content type.

✔ The UPPER and LOWER functions convert text to uppercase or lowercase, respectively. The PROPER function capitalizes the first letter of each word.

✔ To remove extra spaces, use TRIM. To remove non-printing characters, use CLEAN.

✔ To extract a certain number of characters from one end of a text string, use the LEFT or RIGHT function. The MID function extracts a certain number of characters from the center.

✔ To combine the contents of multiple cells, use the CONCATENATE function and separate the pieces to be concatenated by commas, like this: =CONCATENATE(A1,A2). If you want a space between the values that make up the cell's contents, include a space in quotation marks as an argument, like this: =CONCATENATE(A1," ",A2).

Try-it-yourself lab

In this lab, you try some of the functions that were mentioned in this lesson but not included in exercises:

1. **Start Excel, open** Lesson 7 Cleanup.xlsx, **and save it as** Lesson 7 Cleanup Practice.xlsx.

   This file contains some non-printing junk characters that you can get rid of with the CLEAN function.

2. **In column B, use the** CLEAN **function to clean up the data from column A. Then using Copy and Paste Special, replace the data in column A with the new values from the function results from column B.**

3. **Delete the contents of column B.**

4. **In column B, use the** LEN **function to find the length of each of the text strings in column A.**

   Hint: They are all between 13 and 17 characters.

5. **In cell A8, use the** COUNTA **function to count the number of non-blank cells in the range A1:A7. Reduce the number of decimal places displayed to zero.**

6. **Save the workbook and close Excel.**

*I*s a picture really worth a thousand words? Just ask anyone who has been faced with a spreadsheet full of numbers to analyze. Creating charts that summarize data is a quick way to make sense of data — or to present data to someone else.

In this lesson, you learn how to create several types of charts, and how to add and remove chart elements such as legends, data labels, and data tables. You learn how to move and resize charts, how to place a chart on its own separate tab in a workbook, and how to apply a variety of formatting to a chart.

Creating a Basic Chart

Excel offers various chart types, each suited for a different type of data analysis: Pie charts show how parts contribute to a whole, line and column charts compare values over time, stock charts show daily pricing information, and so on. You don't have to know a lot about charts to start creating them, though, so I want to knock out a few simple charts right off the bat. You then spend the rest of the lesson manipulating them in various ways.

Create a pie chart

Pie charts are good for situations in which the relationship among the values being charted is the most significant thing. For example, suppose Kris sold 15 cars, Dave sold 7, and Tom sold 8. If the important thing is that Kris sold 50 percent of all the cars, a pie chart is ideal. Pie charts are limited in that they can handle only one data series. For example, you couldn't use a single pie chart to show Kris, Dave, and Tom's sales for several different periods; you'd have to do a separate pie chart for each period.

LINGO

A **pie chart** shows a circle divided into slices. The relative size of each slice represents a data point's contribution to the whole. Each pie chart shows one **data series** — that is, only one related set of numeric values.

In the following exercise, you create a basic pie chart.

Files needed: Lesson 8 Publishing.xlsx

1. **Start Excel, if needed, open** `Lesson 8 Publishing.xlsx`**, and save it as** Lesson 8 Publishing Plan.xlsx**.**

2. **Select cells A5:A10. Hold down the Ctrl key and select cells E5:E10.**

   The first selection is the labels for the chart; the second selection is the data. The labels and the data do not have to be contiguous.

3. **Choose Insert⇨Insert Pie or Doughnut Chart⇨3-D Pie.**

   3-D Pie is the only icon in the 3-D section of the menu, as shown in Figure 8-1.

   A floating pie chart appears on the worksheet.

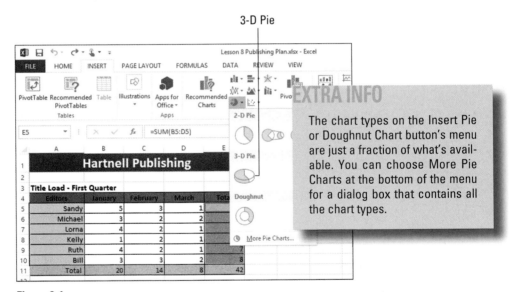

Figure 8-1

4. **Point at the chart's border (but not on a selection handle) and drag it to the right of the Title Load data, as shown inFigure 8-2.**

For more practice, select the new chart and press the Delete key to remove it. Then re-create the chart by choosing More Pie Charts in Step 3 and then choosing a different chart type. Repeat this operation a few times, each time picking a different chart type; then repeat Steps 3–4, exactly as written, to finalize the chart.

Leave the workbook open for the next exercise.

Drag the chart's border to move the chart.

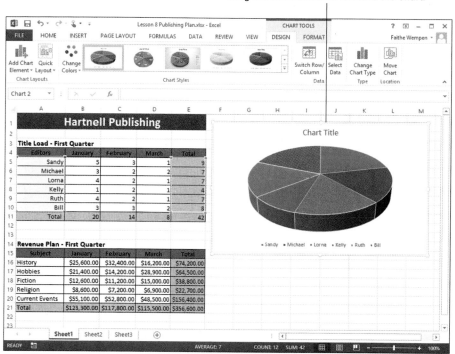

Figure 8-2

Create a column chart

A column chart is good for showing multiple data series on a two-axis grid, just as in geometry class. For example, in Figure 8-2, notice that each editor has different values for each month. Depending on how you plot the data, each month could be a data series or each editor could be a data series. (You can switch back and forth between plotting by rows or by columns after you create the chart. You learn to do that later in this lesson, in the section "Switch rows and columns.")

In the following exercise, you create a basic column chart.

Files needed: Lesson 8 Publishing Plan.xlsx from the preceding exercise

1. **In** `Lesson 8 Publishin Plan.xlsx,` **select the range A15:D20 and then choose Insert⇨Insert Column Chart⇨3-D Clustered Column.**

    3-D Clustered Column is the first chart in the 3-D Column section of the menu. A new column chart appears in the center of the worksheet.

2. Drag the chart by its border (but not by a selection handle) to place it below the pie chart. (See Figure 8-3.)

Position the column chart below the pie chart.

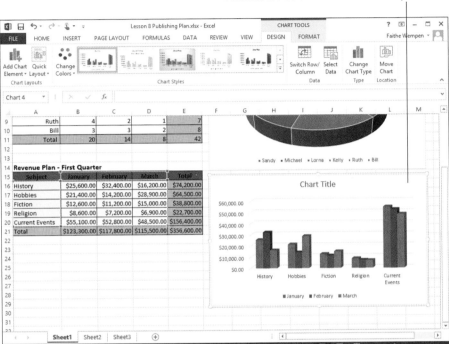

Figure 8-3

3. Save the workbook.

Leave the workbook open for the next exercise.

Changing a Chart

Now that you have a couple of charts under your belt, take a closer look at some chart types. Figure 8-4 shows four chart types created from the same data, so you can compare their look and presentation. In the next few sections, you learn about the elements of a chart, switch chart types, and make some changes to your charts.

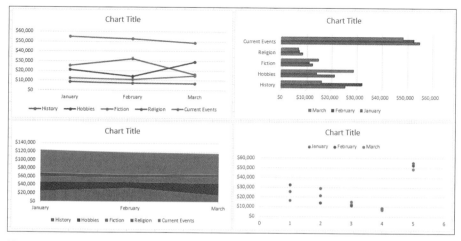

Figure 8-4

Understand the elements of a chart

Each chart has many elements — and you can customize each element separately. Learning the names for the elements of a chart helps you understand what's going on later in the lesson, in "Adding and Positioning Chart Elements," when I cover customization. Figure 8-5 points out some key elements of a chart, and Table 8-1 describes them.

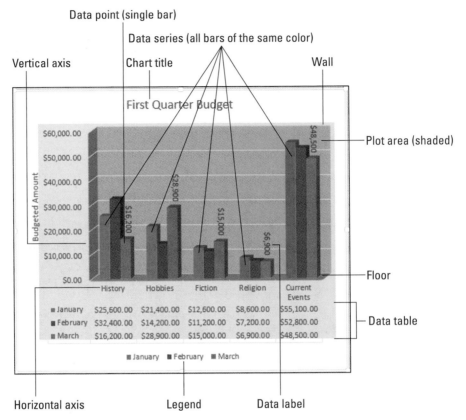

Figure 8-5

Table 8-1		The Elements of a Chart
Element	***What It Is***	***Usage***
Chart area	The entire contents of the chart frame	Everything in Figure 8-5 is considered part of the chart area.
Chart title	A title that identifies the chart	Use if it's not already obvious what the chart represents.
Data point	A single bar, line, column, pie slice, and so on	Each column is a data point in Figure 8-5.
Data series	All the bars (lines, columns, and so on) of a common color	All the blue columns are a data series in Figure 8-5.

Element	What It Is	Usage
Data table	An optional table that appears below the chart, showing the data that it comprises	Used mostly when a chart is on a separate tab from the data.
Floor	On a 3-D chart, the area that the 3-D bars rest on	A floor can give a 3-D chart an additional appearance of being three-dimensional.
Horizontal axis	The axis that runs side to side	In Figure 8-5, the horizontal axis shows the book types.
Legend	The key that tells what each data series represents	The legend can appear at the bottom (as in Figure 8-5) or in any other position around the plot area. When the data table duplicates the legend, as in Figure 8-5, the legend can be omitted.
Plot area	The area of the chart that contains the data, the axes, and the data table (if present)	In Figure 8-5, the plot area is shaded to distinguish it from the chart area.
Vertical axis	The axis that runs up and down	In Figure 8-5, vertical axis shows the numeric values and is the value axis.
Vertical axis title	A text label that explains what the vertical axis represents	In Figure 8-5, the vertical axis title is Budgeted Amount.
Wall	The area directly behind the data	In Figure 8-5, the wall is shaded light gray to distinguish it from the plot area.
Data labels	Numeric values on or adjacent to a data point	In Figure 8-5, the green series of bars has data labels.

Edit the chart data range

You can decide after initially creating a chart that you want a different data range to be plotted in it. For example, you might want to add or remove a data series or exclude certain data points.

In the following exercise, you change the data range on a chart.

Files needed: Lesson 8 Publishing Plan.xlsx from the preceding exercise

1. **In** Lesson 8 Publishing Plan.xlsx, **select the column chart.**

   The range B16:D20 is outlined with a blue border, as shown in Figure 8-6, and the range A16:A20 is outlined with a purple border, indicating it is being used for category axis labels. The range B15:D15 is outlined with a red border, indicating it is being used for series names.

14	Revenue Plan - First Quarter			
15	Subject	January	February	March	Total
16	History	$25,600.00	$32,400.00	$16,200.00	$74,200.00
17	Hobbies	$21,400.00	$14,200.00	$28,900.00	$64,500.00
18	Fiction	$12,600.00	$11,200.00	$15,000.00	$38,800.00
19	Religion	$8,600.00	$7,200.00	$6,900.00	$22,700.00
20	Current Events	$55,100.00	$52,800.00	$48,500.00	$156,400.00
21	Total	$123,300.00	$117,800.00	$115,500.00	$356,600.00
22					

Figure 8-6

2. **Drag the bottom-right corner selection handle of the blue-selected area (currently B16:D20) upward so the blue outline excludes the Current Events row (row 20).**

   The range is now B16:D19, and the chart changes immediately to show the new range. See Figure 8-7.

3. **Choose Chart Tools Design⇨Select Data.**

   The Select Data Source dialog box opens.

The Current Events bars are not displayed.

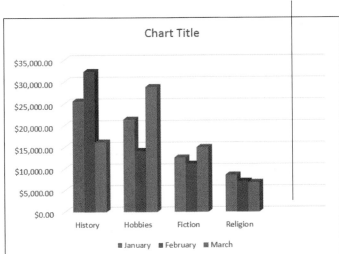

Figure 8-7

4. **Click the Collapse Dialog button to the right of the Chart Data Range box (see Figure 8-8).**

The dialog box collapses.

Collapse Dialog button

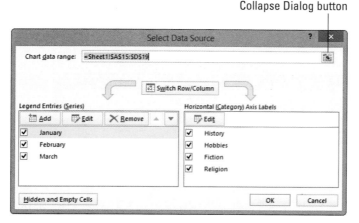

Figure 8-8

5. **Select the range A15:D20, and then press Enter to reopen the Select Data Source dialog box.**

Notice that column A and row 15 are included in this selection because they are used for the data labels. The chart data range as selected here includes not only the data but the labels too.

6. **Click OK to accept the new chart range.**

The Current Events data is shown again in the chart.

7. **Save the workbook.**

Leave the workbook open for the next exercise.

Change the chart type

Rather than completely re-creating a chart if you decide you didn't choose the right type initially, you can change the chart's type. In fact, it's so easy to change the chart type that you might want to experiment with several chart types before you make the final decision on which one to use.

In the following exercise, you change the chart type for two charts.

Files needed: Lesson 8 Publishing Plan.xlsx from the preceding exercise

1. **In** `Lesson 8 Publishing Plan.xlsx`**, select the pie chart and then choose Chart Tools Design⇨Change Chart Type.**

   The Change Chart Type dialog box opens.

2. **Click the first Pie icon at the top, as shown in Figure 8-9, and then click OK.**

   The pie chart changes to show the new type. The pie in your spreadsheet is now two-dimensional, as in Figure 8-10.

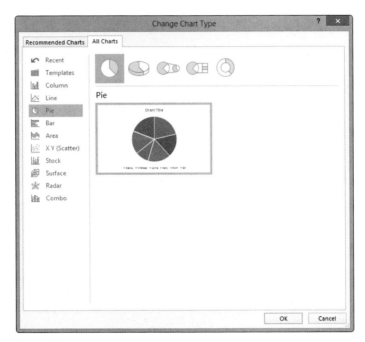

Figure 8-9

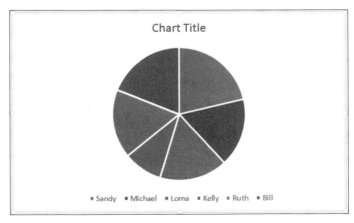

Figure 8-10

3. **Click the column chart on the worksheet, right-click the chart's border, and choose Change Chart Type.**

The Change Chart Type dialog box opens.

4. **In the list of categories at the left, click Area; then click 3-D Stacked Area icon at the top of the dialog box.**

Two samples appear: one plots the data by rows and the other plots the data by columns. See Figure 8-11.

Figure 8-11

5. **Click the sample on the left, and click OK.**

The chart changes to the new type, as shown in Figure 8-12.

Re-open the Change Chart Type dialog box and click the Recommended Charts tab. Then choose one of the recommended chart types and click OK. Press Ctrl+Z to undo the change.

6. **Save the workbook.**

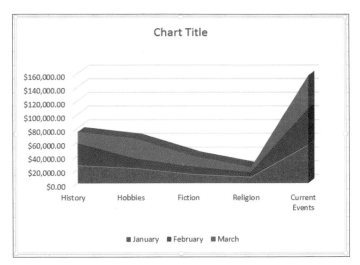

Figure 8-12

Leave the workbook open for the next exercise.

Switch rows and columns

Numbers don't lie, but presenting the numbers in different ways can make your audience think about the numbers differently. For example, in Figure 8-12, the area chart invites the audience to consider each book category separately, looking at the sum total of that category's performance over three months. If you wanted the audience to compare the different categories with one another for each month, you could switch the rows and columns so that the series become the categories rather than the months. That's what you do in the following exercise.

In the following exercise, you switch a chart's rows and columns.

Files needed: Lesson 8 Publishing Plan.xlsx from the preceding exercise

1. **In** `Lesson 8 Publishing Plan.xlsx`**, select the area chart and then choose Chart Tools Design⇨Switch Row/Column.**

   The chart changes to show the categories as the series. (See Figure 8-13.)

REMEMBER

Charts that consist of a single data series, such as pie charts, change to something unusable if you try to switch their rows/columns.

2. Click the pie chart and then choose Chart Tools Design⇨Switch Row/Column.

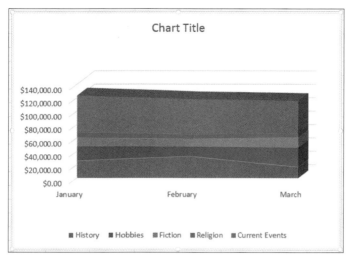

Figure 8-13

The chart changes to a single pie with only one big slice because this chart has only one category.

3. Choose Chart Tools Design⇨Switch Row/Column again to change the pie chart back to its original appearance.

4. Save the changes to the workbook.

Leave the workbook open for the next exercise.

Resize a chart

You can resize a chart by dragging a selection handle on the border of its frame in any direction. Selection handles are marked with small dots; the side selection handles are in the center of each side, and the corner selection handles are in each corner. You can also specify an exact size for a chart's frame by using the Height and Width text boxes on the Chart Tools Format tab.

In the following exercise, you resize charts.

Files needed: Lesson 8 Publishing Plan.xlsx from the preceding exercise

1. **In** `Lesson 8 Publishing Plan.xlsx`**, select the pie chart; then point the mouse pointer at the bottom-right corner of the chart's frame, so the mouse pointer becomes a double-headed arrow.**

2. **Drag inward so the bottom-right corner of the chart aligns with the bottom-right corner of cell K11, as shown in Figure 8-14.**

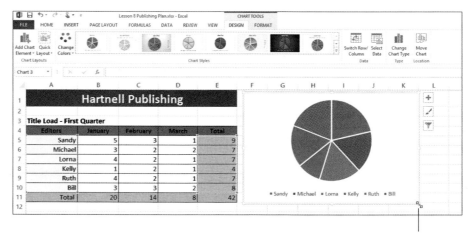

Mouse pointer

Figure 8-14

3. **Select the area chart and then on the Chart Tools Format tab, type** 2.5" **in the Shape Height box.**

4. **Type** 5.25" **in the Shape Width box.**

   The chart's frame adjusts to the specified dimensions. (See Figure 8-15.)

5. **Save the workbook.**

Shape Height

Shape Width

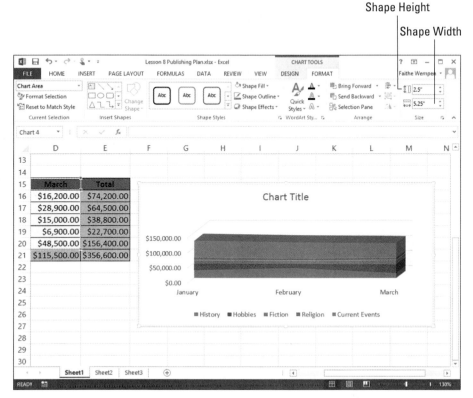

Figure 8-15

Leave the workbook open for the next exercise.

Move a chart to its own worksheet

On a crowded worksheet, you may not have much room for a chart, and as a result, the chart might need to be resized down to a size where it's not as easy to read as it might otherwise be. To solve this problem, you might want to move a chart to its own sheet.

TIP

When a chart is on its own sheet, a data table is sometimes useful to remind the reader what data the chart represents, such as the one you saw in Figure 8-5. See "Add a data table," later in this lesson, to learn how to add one.

In the following exercise, you move a chart to its own worksheet tab.

Files needed: Lesson 8 Publishing Plan.xlsx from the preceding exercise

1. **In** `Lesson 8 Publishing Plan.xlsx`**, right-click the frame of the area chart and choose Move Chart.**

   The Move Chart dialog box opens.

2. **Select the New Sheet option, and in the New Sheet text box, type** Revenue Plan Chart**, as shown in Figure 8-16.**

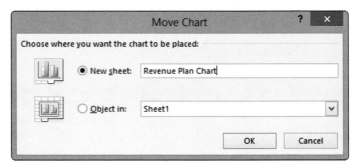

Figure 8-16

3. **Click OK.**

   The chart is placed on its own sheet in the workbook. See Figure 8-17.

   Notice that the chart still has a chart frame where the white of the chart-area background intersects the gray of the sheet background.

4. **Right-click the area chart's frame and choose Move Chart.**

   The Move Chart dialog box reopens.

5. **Select the Object In option, and choose Sheet2 from the Object In drop-down list. Click OK.**

   The chart moves to Sheet2 as a floating object.

6. **Move the chart on Sheet2 so its upper-left corner aligns with the upper-left corner of cell A1.**

   To move a chart, drag its border, but not a selection handle.

7. **Resize the chart on Sheet2 so that the chart covers cells A1:M22.**

   As Figure 8-18 shows, to resize a chart, drag one of the selection handles on its border.

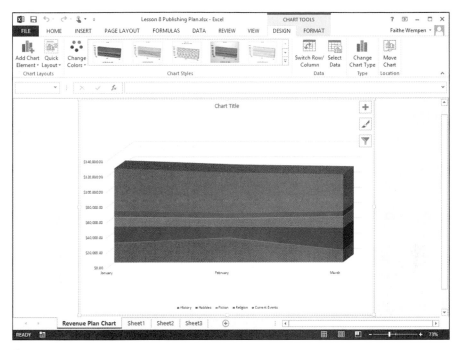

Figure 8-17

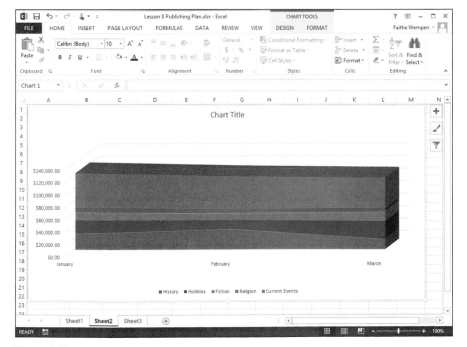

Figure 8-18

8. **Save the workbook.**

Leave the workbook open for the next exercise.

Adding and Positioning Chart Elements

As I hint earlier in the lesson, when reviewing the elements of a chart (refer to Figure 8-5), each element is individually customizable. You can turn elements on and off, change their positions, and so on. In the next exercises, you add and position a legend, data table, and data labels.

Add a legend

By default, a legend is positioned to the right of the chart, but you can place it anywhere. When a legend is placed at the top or bottom of a chart, it's laid out horizontally; when placed at the side of a chart, it's laid out vertically.

In the following exercise, you remove and then re-add a legend on a chart, and position it below the chart.

Files needed: Lesson 8 Publishing Plan.xlsx from the preceding exercise

> **LINGO**
>
> The **legend** is the key that tells what each color (or pattern, or shade of gray) represents on a chart. Legends are useful for pie charts, for example, and for most multi-series charts, such as the bar and column charts you have worked with throughout this lesson. A legend is not particularly useful on a chart that contains only one series, such as a bar chart that consists of a single set of bars, all the same color.

1. **In** Lesson 8 Publishing Plan.xlsx, **on Sheet2, click the chart's legend to select it.**

   Selection handles appear around the legend. See Figure 8-19.

2. **Press the Delete key to remove the legend.**

   The chart expands vertically to fill in the space.

3. **Choose Chart Tools Design⇨Add Chart Element⇨Legend⇨Right.**

   As shown in Figure 8-20, the legend appears to the right of the chart.

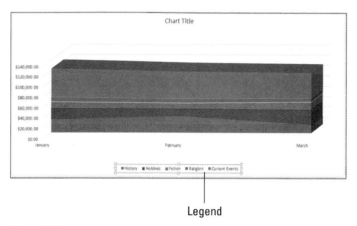

Legend

Figure 8-19

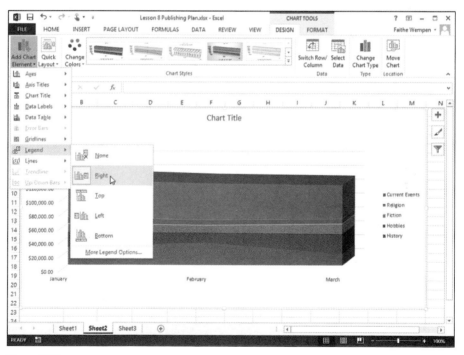

Figure 8-20

For more practice, try each of the other legend positions on the menu.

4. Select the legend and drag it up, so its top edge aligns with the top-most gridline of the chart's plot area, as shown in Figure 8-21.

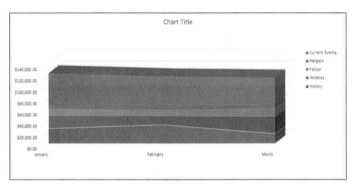

Figure 8-21

5. Save the workbook.

Leave the workbook open for the next exercise.

Add a data table

In the following exercise, you add a data table with a legend key to a chart.

Files needed: Lesson 8 Publishing Plan.xlsx from the preceding exercise

1. In Lesson 8 Publishing Plan.xlsx, **on Sheet2, click the legend and press the Delete key.**

You don't need the legend because the data table you create provides colored squares for each series that duplicate the functionality of a legend.

2. Choose Chart Tools Design⇨Add Chart Element⇨Data Table⇨With Legend Keys.

The data table appears below the chart, as shown in Figure 8-22.

3. Turn off the data table again. To do so, choose Chart Tools Design⇨ Add Chart Element⇨Data Table⇨None.

LINGO

A **data table** repeats the data on which the chart is based. A data table is helpful when the cells containing the data and the chart are not simultaneously visible onscreen.

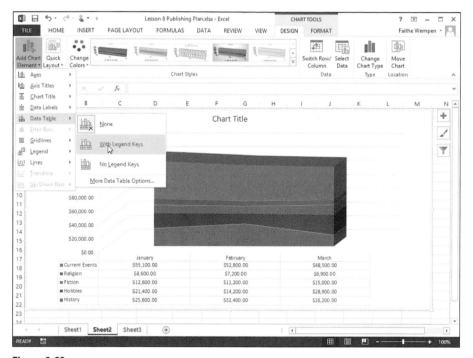

Figure 8-22

4. **Turn the legend back on again. To do so, choose Chart Tools Design⇨ Add Chart Element⇨Legend⇨Right.**

5. **Save the workbook.**

Leave the workbook open for the next exercise.

Add data labels

Data labels are used whenever the exact value of a data point is significant. You can add data labels for the entire chart, a single series, or a single data point. On a pie chart, you can either show the exact value of each slice or the percentage of the whole that it represents. Depending on what you want to show with the chart, one or the other may be more valuable.

In the following exercise, you add data labels to a chart.

Files needed: Lesson 8 Publishing Plan.xlsx from the preceding exercise

1. **In** `Lesson 8 Publishing Plan.xlsx`, **on Sheet2, change the chart type to Clustered Bar as follows:**

    a. Select the chart, and then choose Chart Tools Design⇨Change Chart Type.

    b. In the Change Chart Type dialog box, click Bar. Clustered Bar is the default subtype selected. See Figure 8-23.

    c. Click OK.

Figure 8-23

2. **Click one of the light blue bars on the chart (one of the Current Events cones).**

    All the light blue bars become selected.

3. **Choose Chart Tools Design⇨Add Chart Element⇨Data Labels⇨Center.**

    The data labels appear in the middle of the bars, for only the selected series. See Figure 8-24.

Data label

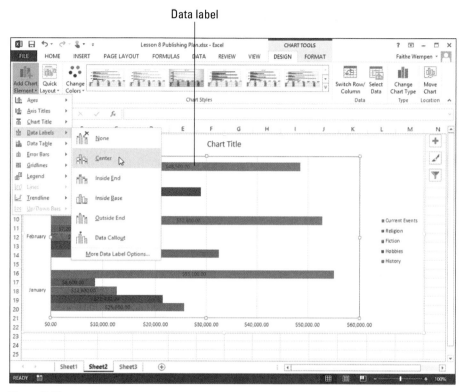

Figure 8-24

TIP

If you want to use data labels, a bar chart is a good choice for the chart type because the bars run horizontally. Column charts don't display data labels as easily; you have to do some manual formatting to get them to fit on the column bars.

4. **Click the Sheet1 tab and select the pie chart. Drag the bottom-right corner of the chart frame down to cell M19 to enlarge the chart so it's easier to work with.**

Now you'll add data labels to the pie chart, but this time you'll use a different method.

5. **Click the Chart Elements button to the right of the pie chart, select the Data Labels check box, and then click the right-pointing arrow next to Data Labels to display the submenu.**

6. **Click Center.**

Data labels appear in the centers of each slice, as shown in Figure 8-25.

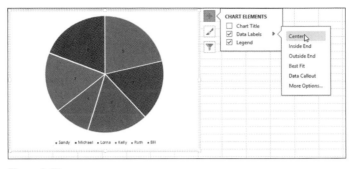

Figure 8-25

Next you will modify what the data labels show on the pie chart.

7. **Click the Chart Elements button again, point to Data Labels, click the right-pointing arrow, and click More Options.**

   The Format Data Labels task pane opens.

8. **Select the Percentage check box, deselect the Value check box, and select the Category Name check box.** Each slice shows the person's name and the percentage, as shown in Figure 8-26.

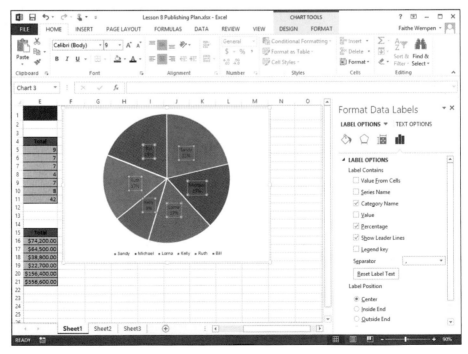

Figure 8-26

9. **Close the task pane.**

   You no longer need the legend on this chart because the data labels serve the same purpose.

10. **Click the Chart Elements button again, and clear the Legend check box, as shown in Figure 8-27.**

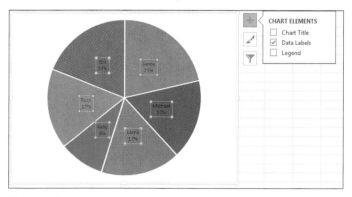

Figure 8-27

This is an alternate way of turning off the legend; you can also select the legend and press the Delete key, as you did in an earlier exercise.

11. **Save the workbook.**

Leave the workbook open for the next exercise.

Formatting a Chart

Chart formatting can make a big difference in a chart's attractiveness and readability. Depending on the look you're after, you may prefer to make blanket formatting changes to the entire chart by applying a chart style, or to select and make changes to individual elements. For each individual part of the chart, you can change its fill color, its outline, and its text (including font, size, color, attributes, alignment, and so on).

Apply chart styles

In the following exercise, you change the style of two charts.

Files needed: Lesson 8 Publishing Plan.xlsx from the preceding exercise

> **LINGO**
>
> **Chart styles** are collections of formatting presets that you can apply to the entire chart at once. Each chart style can be applied in a variety of color combinations, all based on the theme colors for the workbook.

1. **In** Lesson 8 Publishing Plan.xlsx, **on Sheet1, click the pie chart's frame to select the chart and then choose Chart Tools Design⇨More in the Chart Styles group.**

   The More button is the down-pointing arrow that opens the Chart Styles gallery, as shown in Figure 8-28.

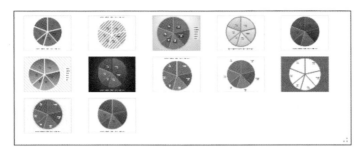

Figure 8-28

2. **Click Style 7 (the black-background sample in the second row).**

   The style changes to the colors and shape style represented by that sample.

For more practice, try several of the other chart styles.

3. **Click the Sheet2 tab and then click the chart to select it.**

4. **Choose Chart Tools Design⇨More in the Chart Styles group to open the palette of styles.**

   Notice that the styles are different because this is a different chart type.

5. **Click Style 12 (the last style in the bottom row).**

   The chart changes to use that style. (See Figure 8-29.)

6. **Save the workbook.**

Style 12

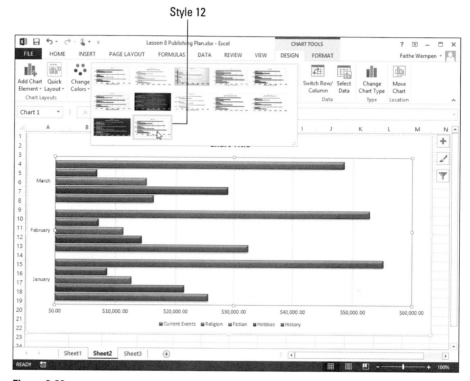

Figure 8-29

Leave the workbook open for the next exercise.

Format text on a chart

When you resize a chart, some of the text in it resizes also. If you want certain text to be larger or smaller in relation to the chart size, though, you can manually change its font size. You can also change the font's color, typeface, and attributes.

TIP
When formatting a chart, you'll likely want to increase the legend's text size because by default, Excel's legends are a bit small.

In the following exercise, you resize the text on a chart.

Files needed: Lesson 8 Publishing Plan.xlsx from the preceding exercise

1. **In** `Lesson 8 Publishing Plan.xlsx`, **on Sheet1, click the pie chart's frame to select the chart and then click the data label on one of the pie slices.**

   The labels on all the pie slices are selected.

2. **Choose Home⇨Increase Font Size until the font size is 12 point. Choose Home⇨Bold to make the text bold.**

3. **Click the text on the largest slice (Sandy 21%).**

4. **On the Home tab, click the down arrow to the right of the Font Color button, opening its color palette; then, click the Yellow square in the Standard colors section.**

   The selected data label (and only that one) becomes yellow. Figure 8-30 shows the completed formatting.

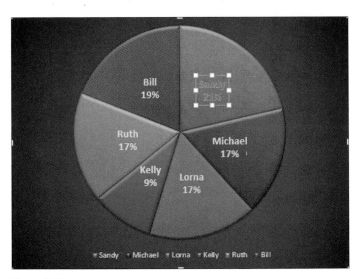

Figure 8-30

5. **Click the Sheet2 tab, select the chart, and choose Chart Tools Design⇨Add Chart Element⇨Legend⇨Right to move the legend.**

6. **Click the legend to select it, and on the Home tab, open the Font Size drop-down list and choose 12.**

7. **Click one of the month names on the left.**

   All three month names are selected in a single frame.

8. **Choose Home⇨Increase Font Size until the font size for the month names is 12 point.**

9. **Choose Home⇨Orientation⇨Angle Counterclockwise.**

   The month names rotate by 45 degrees, as shown in Figure 8-31.

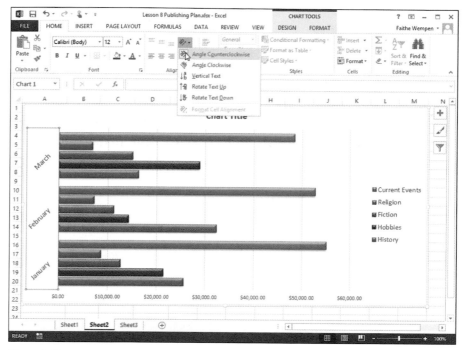

Figure 8-31

10. **Save the workbook.**

Leave the workbook open for the next exercise.

Change the color of a chart element

Each element of a chart can be recolored individually. This includes the data points and series, the chart's walls, its plot area, the entire chart area, the legend, and all the text used for every purpose.

It's common to change the colors of one or more of the data series in a bar chart, or to change one or more pie slice colors in a pie chart.

Usually, when you change the color of a data bar (or other data-related object), you want to change the color for the entire series, not just for one individual data point. If you have a legend that shows what each color means and then you change the color of the whole series, the legend updates automatically. However, if you change the color of only one data point, the legend still shows the color for the other bars in the series, and that one data point does not match up with anything in the legend.

In the following exercise, you change the colors of some elements in a chart.

Files needed: Lesson 8 Publishing Plan.xlsx from the preceding exercise

1. **In** `Lesson 8 Publishing Plan.xlsx`, **on Sheet2, click the chart's legend to select it.**

   On the Chart Tools Format tab, in the Current Selection group, the Chart Elements box shows *Legend.* The Chart Elements box provides the name of the selected element.

2. **Choose Series "History" from the Chart Elements drop-down list on the Chart Tools Format tab.**

   The bars that represent History are selected. See Figure 8-32.

3. **Choose Chart Tools Format⇨Shape Fill⇨Orange, Accent 6.**

   (You can point to a fill color to see a ScreenTip that tells its name.) All the bars in the selected series change to that color, as does the legend key for that series.

4. **Click the legend to select it.**

   Note that Legend appears again in the Chart Elements drop-down list.

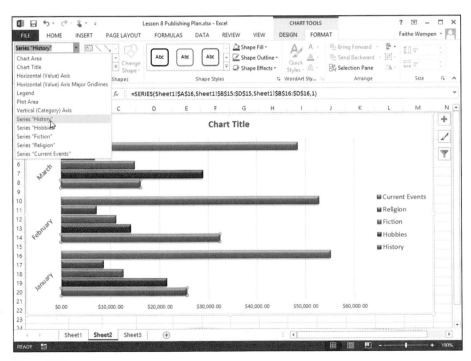

Figure 8-32

5. **Choose Chart Tools Format⇨More in the Shape Styles group, opening a palette.**

6. **Click Moderate Effect, Red, Accent 2.**

   (It's the red sample in the next-to-last row.) The legend formats to that shape style, which includes a red gradient background. See Figure 8-33.

7. **With the legend still selected, choose Chart Tools Format⇨Shape Outline⇨Red Accent 2, Darker 50%.**

   (You can point to a fill color to see a ScreenTip that tells its name.)

8. **Choose Plot Area from the Chart Elements drop-down list.**

9. **Choose Chart Tools Format⇨Format Selection.**

   The Format Plot Area task pane opens.

10. **Click the Fill heading to expand its options, click Gradient Fill, and from the Preset Gradients drop-down list, choose Bottom Spotlight - Accent 3 (the next-to-last green preset).**

    The chart's plot area changes to the gradient fill. See Figure 8-34.

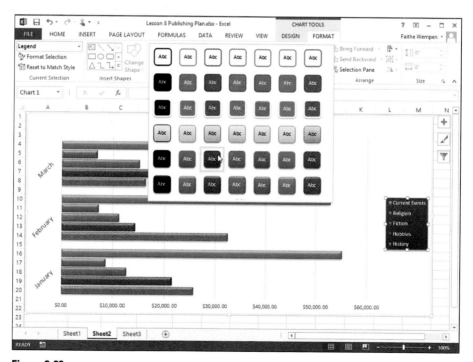

Figure 8-33

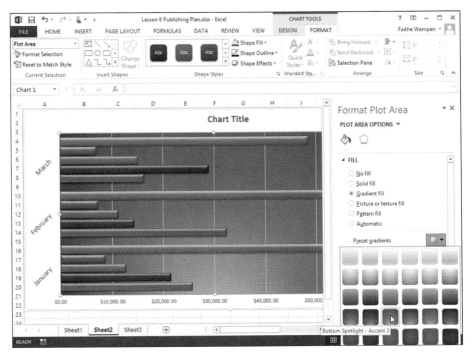

Figure 8-34

11. **Click Close to close the dialog box.**

12. **Save the workbook and close it. Exit Excel.**

 Summing Up

Here are the key points you learned in this lesson:

- ✔ To insert a chart, select the data, click the appropriate chart type on the Insert tab, and then select a subtype from the menu that appears.

- ✔ To change a chart's data range, choose Chart Tools Design⇨Select Data.

- ✔ To change the chart type, choose Chart Tools Design⇨Change Chart Type.

- ✔ To switch rows and columns, choose Chart Tools Design⇨Switch Row/Column.

- ✔ To resize a chart, drag a selection handle on its frame. To move a chart, drag the frame anywhere except on a selection handle.

- ✔ To move a chart to its own tab, right-click its frame and choose Move Chart.

✔ To add, remove, or modify a legend, choose Chart Tools Design⇨Add Chart Element⇨Legend.

✔ To add or remove a data table, choose Chart Tools Design⇨Add Chart Element⇨Data Table.

✔ To add or remove data labels, select the data series or points to affect and then choose Chart Tools Design⇨Add Chart Element⇨Data Labels.

✔ To apply a style to a chart, on the Chart Tools Design tab, click a style in the Chart Styles group. Open the full gallery with the More button, if needed.

✔ To format text on a chart, use the commands in the Font group on the Home tab.

✔ To modify an element of a chart, select it and then choose Chart Tools Format⇨Format Selection.

Try-it-yourself lab

1. **Start Excel, open the file** Lesson 8 Try It Publishing.xlsx, **and save it as** Lesson 8 Charts.xlsx.

2. **Create a column chart using the Clustered Column type that shows each week's sales for Mondays only. Do not include a legend. Place the new chart on its own separate sheet, and name that sheet Monday Sales.**

3. **Change the chart style to Chart Style 16.**

4. **Create a column chart that uses the 3-D Stacked Column type and includes all the data on Sheet1. Each column should represent a different week. Place the new chart on its own separate sheet and name the sheet Overall.**

5. **Add a data table to the Overall chart that includes a legend key and then remove the separate legend.**

6. **Format each chart to make them as attractive as possible. This may include increasing font sizes and changing colors or chart styles.**

7. **Save the workbook and close Excel.**

Know this tech talk

area chart: Like a line chart, except the space below the line is filled in as an area.

bar chart: A column chart that runs horizontally rather than vertically.

chart style: A collection of formatting presets you can apply to an entire chart at once.

column chart: A chart that uses vertical bars to represent data points on a two-dimensional or three-dimensional grid.

data labels: Labels that show the individual values on each data point.

data series: A related set of numeric values in a chart.

data table: A table under a chart that repeats the data on which the chart is based.

legend: The color key that tells what each color, pattern, or shade represents on a chart.

line chart: Like a column chart, except dots represent the data points, and the dots are connected by a line.

pie chart: A circle that's divided into wedges that represent parts of the whole.

scatter chart: Like a line chart, but there's no line; data points are represented by dots.

value axis: The axis that contains the numeric values.

Lesson 9

Working with PivotTables and PivotCharts

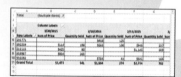

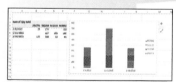

- PivotTables allow you to analyze and summarize data without disturbing the original data set.

- Sorting data in a PivotTable makes it easier to look up data in chronological order.

- Filtering a PivotTable limits its scope to certain values you specify.

- Using summary functions in a PivotTable allows you to average data, count records, or perform other calculations.

- A PivotChart presents PivotTable information in a graphical way.

_P_ivotTables are summary grids that display information in different ways from the default way it is presented on the worksheet. They enable you to glean meaningful information from a data set by summarizing, sorting, and filtering the data, without disturbing the original data set. In this lesson, you learn how to create PivotTables and PivotCharts, format them, and use the summarizing, sorting, and filtering options to manipulate the data to extract useful facts from it.

Creating a PivotTable

You create PivotTables within the workbook that contains the data you want to analyze. The PivotTable typically is placed on its own worksheet. After creating the PivotTable, you can drag fields onto it.

Create a PivotTable from worksheet data

To create a PivotTable, start with a worksheet that already contains data in row-and-column format. A table like the ones you created in Lesson 5 would be appropriate, for example. Typically the field names should appear at the top, across a single row, with the records beneath those headings. After making sure the data is ready, you can insert a PivotTable to summarize it.

In this exercise, you create a PivotTable.

Files needed: Lesson 9 Data.xlsx

1. **Open** `Lesson 9 Data.xlsx` **and save it as** Lesson 9 Data Pivot.xlsx.

2. **On Sheet1, select the range A1:E29 and then choose Insert⇨PivotTable.**

   The Create PivotTable dialog box opens. (See Figure 9-1.)

PivotTable button

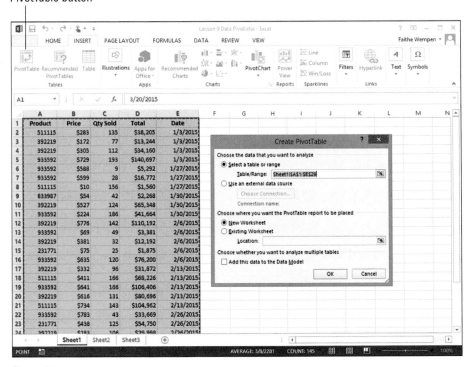

Figure 9-1

3. **Click OK to accept the default settings.**

   The default settings use the selected range and place the PivotTable on a new worksheet. A new sheet appears. A PivotTable empty placeholder appears at the left, and on the right is a PivotTable Fields task pane. (See Figure 9-2.)

4. **In the PivotTable Fields task pane, drag the Product field from the top section of the pane to the Rows area at the bottom.**

   The product codes appear in the PivotTable, in a single column on the left. In Figure 9-3, notice that each product appears only once in this summary; in the original data, each product appeared multiple times.

Empty PivotTable

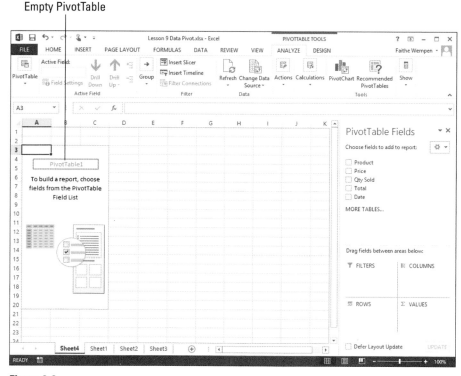

Figure 9-2

Drag the Product field...

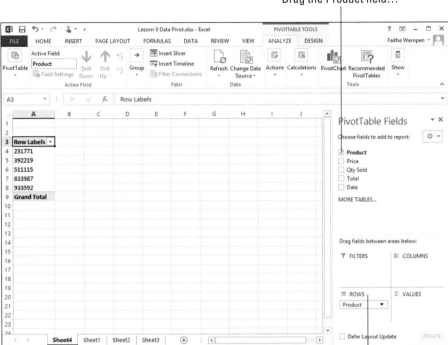

...to the Rows area.

Figure 9-3

5. **Drag the Date field to the Columns area at the bottom.**

The dates appear across the top of the PivotTable, in a single row (see Figure 9-4).

Drag the Date field...

Figure 9-4

...to the Columns area.

6. **Drag the Total field to the Values area at the bottom.**

The totals appear at the intersection of the row and column labels on the PivotTable (see Figure 9-5).

Drag the Total field...

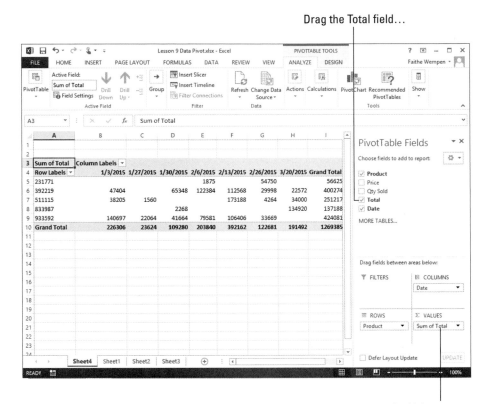

...to the Values area.

Figure 9-5

7. **In the Values area at the bottom of the task pane, click Sum of Total and choose Remove Field (see Figure 9-6).**

   The field is removed from the PivotTable.

8. **In the upper part of the task pane, click the Price and Qty Sold check boxes.**

   These fields are added to the Values area at the bottom of the task pane, just as if you had dragged them there, and to the PivotTable. This is an alternate method for specifying fields for the Values part of the report. See Figure 9-7.

Figure 9-6

Mark the Price and Qty Sold check boxes.

```
Choose fields to add to report:          ☼ ▾

  ☑ Product
  ☑ Price
  ☑ Qty Sold
  ☐ Total
  ☑ Date
  MORE TABLES...




  Drag fields between areas below:

  ▼ FILTERS          ▥ COLUMNS
                     ┌──────────────┐
                     │ Date       ▾ │
                     ├──────────────┤
                     │ Σ Values   ▾ │
                     └──────────────┘

  ☰ ROWS             Σ VALUES
  ┌──────────────┐   ┌──────────────┐
  │ Product    ▾ │   │ Sum of Price ▾ │
  └──────────────┘   ├──────────────┤
                     │ Sum of Qty S... ▾ │
                     └──────────────┘

  ▨ Defer Layout Update          UPDATE
```

Figure 9-7

Notice in Figure 9-7 that an additional item has been added in the Column area of the task pane: Values. This allows sub-headings based on the Values fields under the main column headings for Date.

9. Save the workbook.

Leave the workbook open for the next exercise.

Format PivotTables

When you create a PivotTable from existing data, the PivotTable might not pick up the formatting correctly from the original data. For example, currency values may not be formatted as Currency anymore, and font sizes and colors may be lost. You can easily reapply any formatting you like.

In this exercise, you format a PivotTable.

Files needed: Lesson 9 Data Pivot.xlsx from the preceding exercise

1. **Rename the worksheet tab** PivotTable **by double-clicking the worksheet tab for the PivotTable's sheet, typing** PivotTable, **and pressing Enter.**

2. **In the Values section of the task pane, click Sum of Price, as shown in Figure 9-8, and choose Value Field Settings.**

   The Value Field Settings dialog box opens. See Figure 9-9.

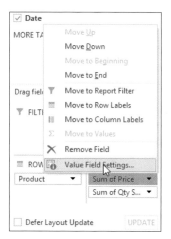

Figure 9-8

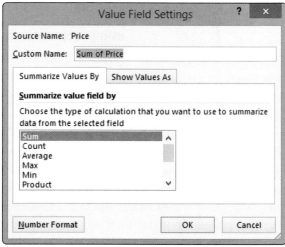

Figure 9-9

3. **Click the Number Format button.**

   The Format Cells dialog box opens. This is a custom version of the dialog box, with only the Number tab.

4. **Select Currency in the Category list. In the Decimal Places box, click the down-increment arrow twice to decrease the number of decimal places to 0, as shown in Figure 9-10, and then click OK.**

5. **Click OK again to close the Value Field Settings dialog box.**

   The numbers in the Sum of Price columns appear as currency.

6. **Choose PivotTable Tools Analyze⇨Show⇨Field Headers to toggle off the field headers, as shown in Figure 9-11.**

Depending on the width of the Excel window, Show may be a group instead of a button, and you may not have to click Show in order to access Field Headers.

Set Decimal Places to 0.

Figure 9-10

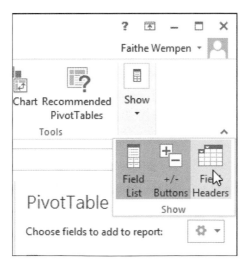

Figure 9-11

7. **Click cell C4 and type** Quantity Sold, **replacing the previous entry.**

   All the cells containing this same heading also change (cells E4, G4, I4, and so on).

8. **Select row 4 by clicking its row header and then choose Home⇔Center, as shown in Figure 9-12, to horizontally center all the headings in that row.**

Center button

Figure 9-12

9. **Select row 3 by clicking its row header and then choose Home⇔Increase Font Size twice to increase the font size in that row to 14 pt.**

10. **Select the range A5:Q9 and then choose Home⇔Borders⇔All Borders, as shown in Figure 9-13.**

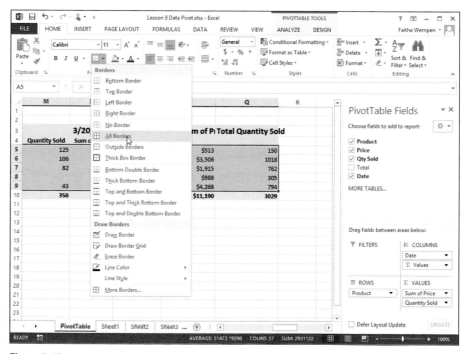

Figure 9-13

11. **If hashmarks (#####) appear in D4 and J4, double-click the divider between the D and E column headings, and between the J and K column headings, to widen columns D and J as needed so that the dates display correctly.**

12. **Click away from the PivotTable to deselect it.**

    Notice that the PivotTable Tools tabs no longer appear on the Ribbon and the task pane closes.

13. **Save the workbook.**

Leave the workbook open for the next exercise.

Sorting and Filtering PivotTable Data

Like tables, PivotTables can be sorted and filtered to make the meaning of the data more apparent. In the following exercises, you learn how to sort and filter a PivotTable.

Sort a PivotTable

You can sort by any field, in either ascending or descending order.

In this exercise, you sort a PivotTable.

Files needed: Lesson 9 Data Pivot.xlsx from the preceding exercise

> ### LINGO
> An **ascending** sort sorts from oldest to newest, or from A to Z. In an ascending sort, symbols and numbers (0 to 9) come before letters. A **descending** sort sorts from newest to oldest, or from Z to A. In a descending sort, numbers (9 to 0) and symbols come after letters.

1. **Click inside the PivotTable to re-select it and then choose PivotTable Tools Analyze⇨ Show⇨Field Headers to turn on the display of field headers.**

    (You turned them off in the preceding exercise.)

2. **Click the down arrow on the Column Labels field header and choose Sort Newest to Oldest, as shown in Figure 9-14.**

    The dates are reordered in the PivotTable.

Column Labels field header

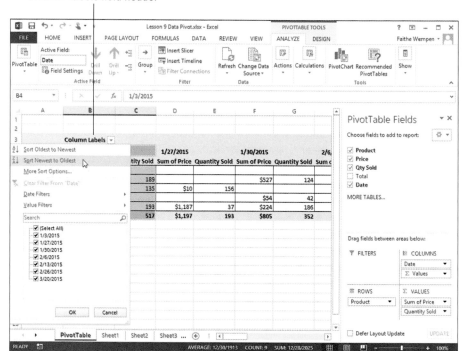

Figure 9-14

3. **Click the down arrow on the Row Labels field header and choose Sort Smallest to Largest, as shown in Figure 9-15.**

   The product numbers are sorted in ascending order.

4. **Save the workbook.**

Leave the workbook open for the next exercise.

Row Labels field header

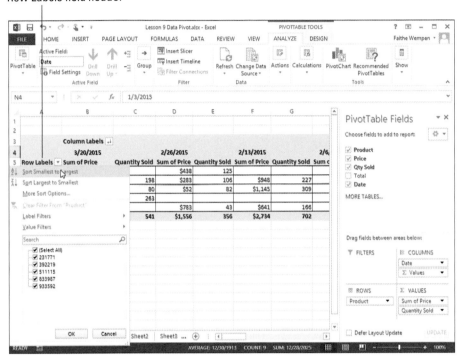

Figure 9-15

Filter a PivotTable

One way to filter a PivotTable is to apply a report filter. You can apply a report filter by adding a field to the Report Filter section of the PivotTable Fields task pane and then specifying the values (or range of values) to include. You must use this method if you want to filter by a field that's not part of the PivotTable. For example, you might want to filter by a specific date, but not include the Date field in the PivotTable grid itself.

In this exercise, you filter a PivotTable.

Files needed: Lesson 9 Data Pivot.xlsx from the preceding exercise

1. **In the PivotTable Fields task pane, drag the Total field to the Filters section.**

   A filter appears in row 1. (See Figure 9-16.)

TIP

   Dragging a field to the Filters section is useful for filtering by a field that doesn't appear already in the PivotTable.

2. **Click the down arrow to the right of (All) in cell B1 and select the Select Multiple Items check box.**

   Each of the values now appears with a check box next to it.

3. **Deselect the check boxes for all values less than $5,000, as shown in Figure 9-17, and click OK to apply the filter.**

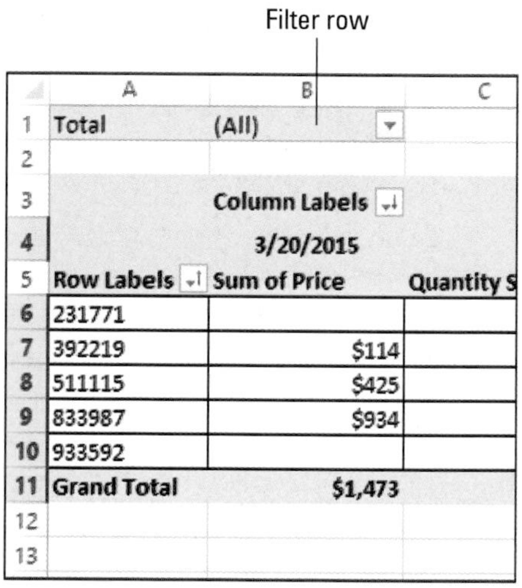

Filter row

	A	B	C
1	Total	(All)	▼
2			
3		Column Labels ↓	
4		3/20/2015	
5	Row Labels ↓	Sum of Price	Quantity S
6	231771		
7	392219	$114	
8	511115	$425	
9	833987	$934	
10	933592		
11	Grand Total	$1,473	
12			
13			

Figure 9-16

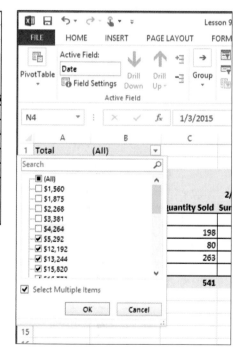

Figure 9-17

The data is filtered to show only totals more than $5,000, and the filter in cell B1 appears as (Multiple Items). A funnel (filter) symbol appears next to Total in the task pane. (See Figure 9-18.)

Funnel indicates filtering.

	A	B	C	D	E	F	G	
1	Total	(Multiple Items) ⊤						
2								
3		Column Labels ↓						
4		3/20/2015		2/26/2015		2/13/2015		2/
5	Row Labels ↓	Sum of Price	Quantity Sold	Sum of Price	Quantity Sold	Sum of Price	Quantity Sold	Sum
6	231771			$438	125			
7	392219	$114	198	$283	106	$948	227	
8	511115	$425	80			$1,145	309	
9	833987	$934	263					
10	933592			$783	43	$641	166	
11	Grand Total	$1,473	541	$1,504	274	$2,734	702	
12								
13								

Figure 9-18

4. **Save the workbook.**

Leave the workbook open for the next exercise.

Filter individual column and row fields

Another way to filter a PivotTable is to select specific values for individual fields by using the Column Labels or Row Labels menus. Each filter you apply for different fields combines with other filters already in place so that only records that match all the criteria you specify appear.

In this exercise, you filter individual fields on a PivotTable.

Files needed: Lesson 9 Data Pivot.xlsx from the preceding exercise

1. **Click the down arrow on the Column Labels field header, point to Date Filters, and choose After, as shown in Figure 9-19.**

2. **In the Date Filter (Date) dialog box that appears, type** 1/31/2015, **as shown in Figure 9-20, and click OK.**

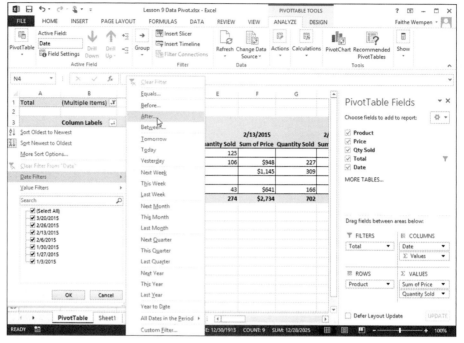

Figure 9-19

Figure 9-20

3. **Scroll the worksheet to the right to confirm that no dates appear that are earlier than 1/31/2015. Then scroll back so column A is visible again.**

4. **Save the workbook.**

Leave the workbook open for the next exercise.

Modifying a PivotTable

PivotTables are famous for their flexibility. No matter how you want to analyze your data, a PivotTable can probably accommodate your wishes. In this section, you learn how to change the summary functions that the PivotTable uses and how to set PivotTable options.

Change the summary functions

When you include numeric values in a PivotTable, Excel automatically assigns a summary function of SUM to the field. You may have noticed in the file you've been working with, for example, that the Price field was assigned Sum of Price, and the Quantity field was assigned Sum of Quantity. (You changed the latter's heading to different text, but the data still sums the quantities.)

Sometimes, though, sum is not a meaningful statistic for a particular field. For example, when summarizing orders, Sum of Price is not helpful. A more useful statistic might be the average price. You can choose any of these math operations for the summary: SUM, AVERAGE, MAX, MIN, PRODUCT, COUNT (numbers), STDEV (standard deviation), or VAR (variance).

In this exercise, you change a field's summary function.

Files needed: Lesson 9 Data Pivot.xlsx from the preceding exercise

1. **In the PivotTable Fields task pane, in the Values section, click Sum of Price, as shown in Figure 9-21, and choose Value Field Settings.**

   The Value Field Settings dialog box opens.

2. **On the Summarize Values By tab, click Average, and in the Custom Name box, delete the word *of* so that the name reads Average Price, as shown in Figure 9-22.**

3. **Click OK to apply the change.**

4. **Save the workbook.**

Leave the workbook open for the next exercise.

Figure 9-21

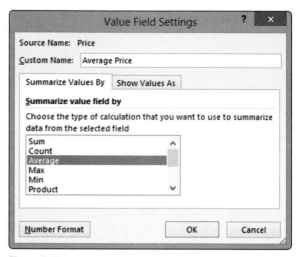

Figure 9-22

Change PivotTable options

You can set many options for a PivotTable — so many that covering them all would consume a whole lesson! On the PivotTable Tools Options tab, the commands enable you to take actions, such as moving the PivotTable, displaying or hiding the field list and field headers, and more. In the PivotTable Options dialog box, you can control dozens of other settings.

In this exercise, you set PivotTable options.

Files needed: Lesson 9 Data Pivot.xlsx from the preceding exercise

1. **Choose PivotTable Tools Analyze ⇨Show⇨Field List to deselect it, as shown in Figure 9-23.**

   The PivotTable Fields task pane closes.

2. **Choose PivotTable Tools Analyze⇨Show⇨Field Headers button to deselect it.**

   The field headers disappear from the PivotTable.

3. **Choose PivotTable Tools Analyze⇨Actions⇨Move PivotTable.**

   The Move PivotTable dialog box opens.

4. **Behind the dialog box, click the Sheet1 worksheet tab and then click cell G2.**

   In the Location text box in the Move PivotTable dialog box, a new location is filled in: Sheet1!$G$2. (See Figure 9-24.)

5. **Click OK.**

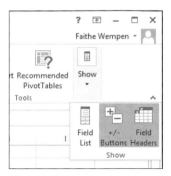

Figure 9-23

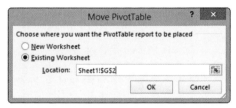

Figure 9-24

The PivotTable moves to Sheet1. Notice that some of the columns aren't wide enough, and some entries are truncated, as shown in Figure 9-25.

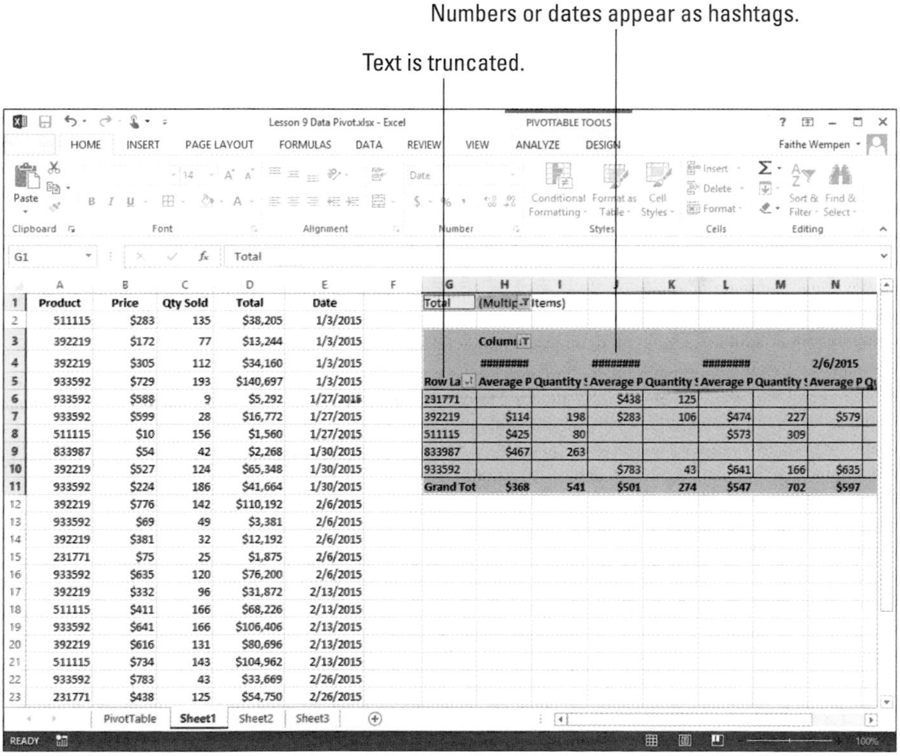

Numbers or dates appear as hashtags.

Text is truncated.

	A	B	C	D	E	F	G	H	I	J	K	L	M	N
1	Product	Price	Qty Sold	Total	Date		Total	(Multip Items)						
2	511115	$283	135	$38,205	1/3/2015									
3	392219	$172	77	$13,244	1/3/2015			Columr T						
4	392219	$305	112	$34,160	1/3/2015			########		########		########		2/6/2015
5	933592	$729	193	$140,697	1/3/2015		Row La	Average P	Quantity S	Average P	Quantity S	Average P	Quantity S	Average P Q
6	933592	$588	9	$5,292	1/27/2015		231771			$438	125			
7	933592	$599	28	$16,772	1/27/2015		392219	$114	198	$283	106	$474	227	$579
8	511115	$10	156	$1,560	1/27/2015		511115	$425	80			$573	309	
9	833987	$54	42	$2,268	1/30/2015		833987	$467	263					
10	392219	$527	124	$65,348	1/30/2015		933592			$783	43	$641	166	$635
11	933592	$224	186	$41,664	1/30/2015		Grand Tot	$368	541	$501	274	$547	702	$597
12	392219	$776	142	$110,192	2/6/2015									
13	933592	$69	49	$3,381	2/6/2015									
14	392219	$381	32	$12,192	2/6/2015									
15	231771	$75	25	$1,875	2/6/2015									
16	933592	$635	120	$76,200	2/6/2015									
17	392219	$332	96	$31,872	2/13/2015									
18	511115	$411	166	$68,226	2/13/2015									
19	933592	$641	166	$106,406	2/13/2015									
20	392219	$616	131	$80,696	2/13/2015									
21	511115	$734	143	$104,962	2/13/2015									
22	933592	$783	43	$33,669	2/26/2015									
23	231771	$438	125	$54,750	2/26/2015									

Figure 9-25

6. **Click the PivotTable to select it, and then widen the columns in the PivotTable so that no text is truncated.**

One way to do this is to double-click the divider between the column headings to auto-size each column. You can also select all the columns that need to be wider and then choose Home⇨Format⇨AutoFit Column Width.

7. **Click PivotTable Tools Analyze⇨PivotTable⇨Options to open the PivotTable Options dialog box.**

8. **In the PivotTable Name box at the top, type** Sales Information, **replacing the default entry, as shown in Figure 9-26.**

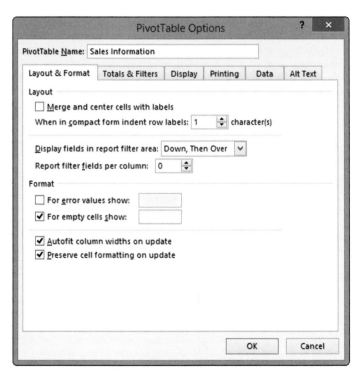

Figure 9-26

9. **Click the Totals & Filters tab, deselect both check boxes in the Grand Totals section, and click OK.**

The Grand Total row and column are hidden.

10. **Save the workbook.**

Leave the workbook open for the next exercise.

Creating a PivotChart

PivotCharts enable you to easily experiment with charting different data. Although you could do this with regular charts, PivotCharts are more flexible than regular charts. With PivotCharts, you can more easily select different data and filter the data included in the chart.

Define a PivotChart

Creating a PivotChart is very much like creating a PivotTable. The main difference is that instead of clicking the PivotTable button on the Insert tab, you open the PivotTable button's drop-down list and choose PivotChart.

In the following steps, you create a PivotChart.

Files needed: Lesson 9 Data Pivot.xlsx from the preceding exercise

LINGO

A **PivotChart** is like a PivotTable except it appears in graphical chart format rather than as a report. Actually each PivotChart also has an associated PivotTable, where the data used to make the chart is stored. You could think of a PivotChart as an optional extension of a PivotTable.

1. **On the Sheet1 tab, select the range A1:E29.**

2. **On the Insert tab, click the down arrow on the PivotChart button and choose PivotChart, as shown in Figure 9-27.**

    The Create PivotChart dialog box opens. See Figure 9-28.

PivotChart button

Figure 9-27

3. **Click OK to accept the default settings in the dialog box.**

    A new worksheet is created, and on it, an empty PivotTable and PivotChart. (See Figure 9-29.)

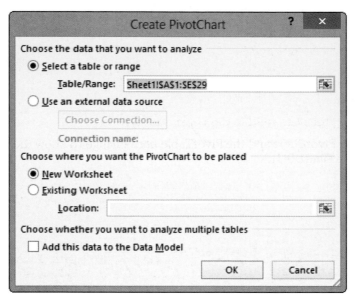

Figure 9-28

Empty PivotChart

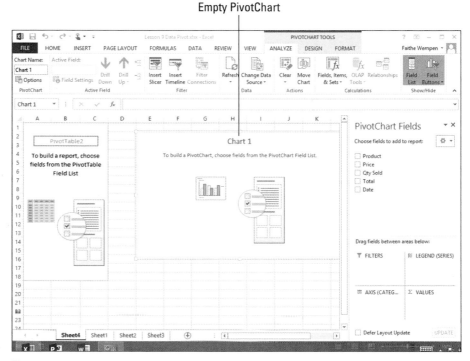

Figure 9-29

4. **In the PivotChart Fields task pane, drag the Product field to the Axis area at the bottom.**

5. **Drag the Qty Sold field to the Values area at the bottom.**

   The chart shows the quantities sold by product, and a PivotTable appears to the left of the chart showing the data being used for the chart. (See Figure 9-30.)

6. **Drag the Date field to the Legend area.**

   The PivotChart and the PivotTable both change to show the new data. (See Figure 9-31.)

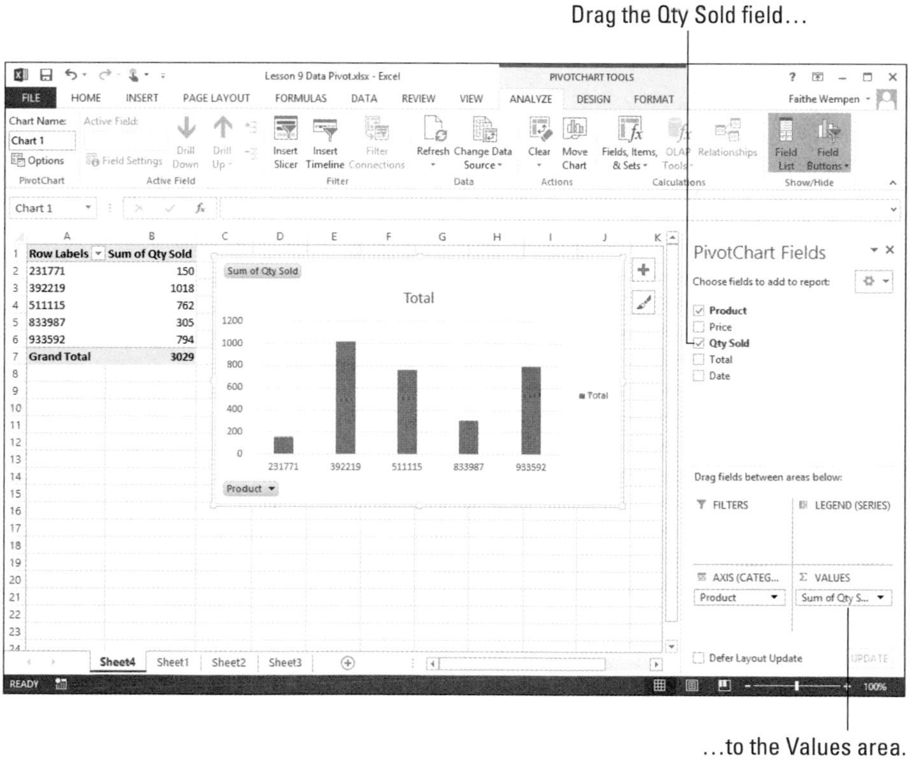

Drag the Qty Sold field...

...to the Values area.

Figure 9-30

Drag the Date field...

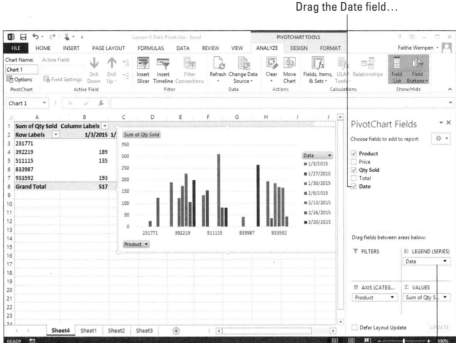

...to the Legend area.

Figure 9-31

7. **In the Legend area, click Date and choose Remove Field.**

   The PivotTable and PivotChart go back to the way they were in Figure 9-30.

8. **Save the workbook.**

Leave the workbook open for the next exercise.

Filter a PivotChart

Just like with a PivotTable, you can filter a PivotChart to show only certain values. For example, you can filter a chart to show only certain dates, or only certain products.

In the following steps, you filter a PivotChart.

Files needed: Lesson 9 Data Pivot.xlsx from the preceding exercise

1. **In the PivotChart Fields task pane, drag the Date field to the Filters area.**

   A Date button with drop-down list arrow appears in the chart. (See Figure 9-32.)

2. **Click the Date button on the chart, and the menu shown in Figure 9-33 appears.**

3. **Click 1/3/2015 and then click OK.**

   The chart changes to show only the products sold for that date. (See Figure 9-34.)

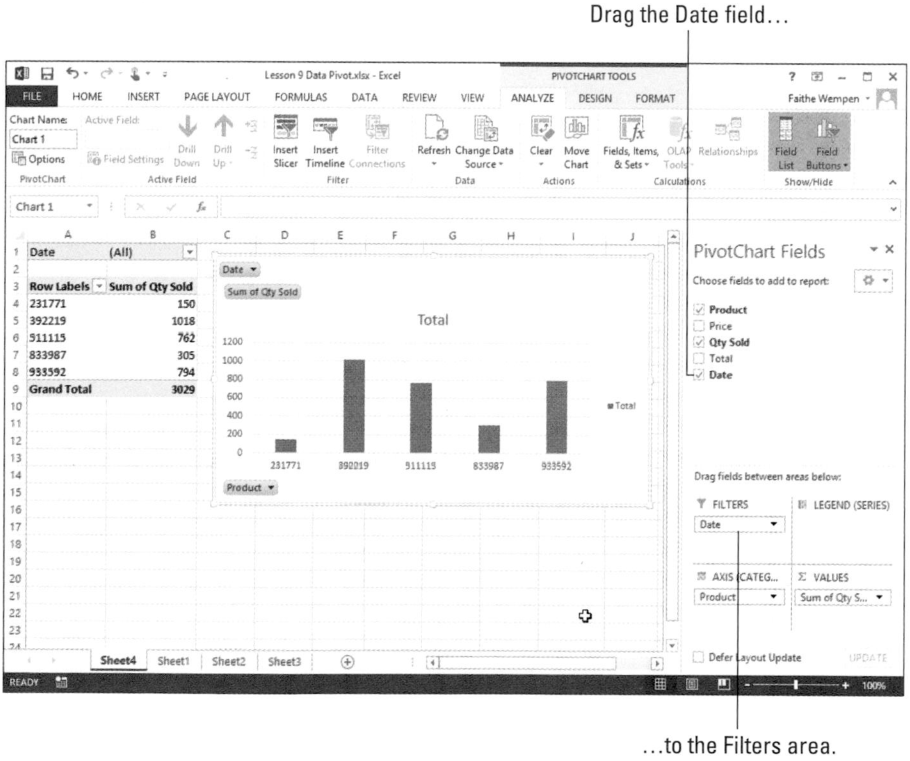

Drag the Date field...

...to the Filters area.

Figure 9-32

Select 1/3/2015   Click the Date button.

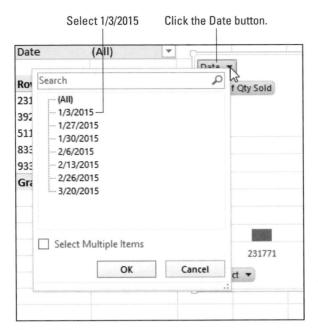

Figure 9-33

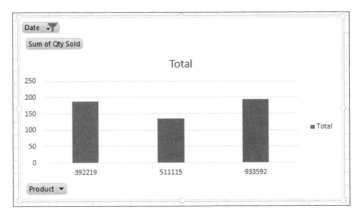

Figure 9-34

4. **Click the Date button on the chart again and select the Select Multiple Items check box so that individual check boxes appear for each date.**

5. **Select the 1/27/2015 and 1/30/2015 check boxes so that all the dates in January are selected, as shown in Figure 9-35, and then click OK.**

The chart changes to show the products for the chosen dates.

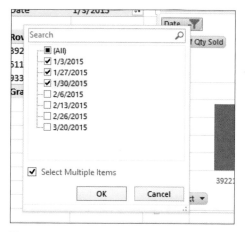

Figure 9-35

6. **In the Filters area of the task pane, click Date and choose Remove Field.**

The filter is removed from the chart.

7. **Save the workbook.**

Leave the workbook open for the next exercise.

Format a PivotChart

Formatting a PivotChart is much like formatting any other chart (see Lesson 8), except you use Ribbon tabs related to PivotCharts. The commands are mostly the same.

Here are the three PivotChart Tools tabs you have to work with:

- ✔ **PivotChart Tools Analyze:** From this tab, you can modify the chart's data in various ways, including changing the data source. This tab also provides controls for displaying and hiding the field buttons and field list.

- ✔ **PivotChart Tools Design:** You can change the chart type, layout, and style from this tab. You can modify the individual elements of the chart, including the legend, title, and so on from the Add Chart Element button's menu on this tab.

- ✔ **PivotChart Tools Format:** Use this tab to modify the attributes of individual chart items. For example, change the font for a title or color a bar on the chart differently from the others.

In the following steps, you format a PivotChart.

Files needed: Lesson 9 Data Pivot.xlsx from the preceding exercise

1. **With the PivotChart selected, choose PivotChart Tools Analyze⇨Field List to turn off the PivotChart Fields task pane.**

2. **Choose PivotChart Tools Analyze⇨Field Buttons to turn off the field buttons.**

   The PivotChart looks very much like a regular chart. See Figure 9-36.

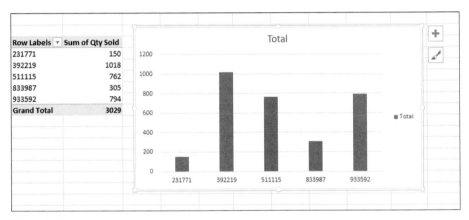

Figure 9-36

3. **Choose PivotChart Tools Design⇨Change Chart Type.**

   The Change Chart Type dialog box opens.

4. **In the list at the left, click Pie; then click the 3-D Pie icon, as shown in Figure 9-37; and click OK.**

5. **Choose PivotChart Tools Design⇨Add Chart Element⇨Chart Title⇨ None, as shown in Figure 9-38.**

   The chart's title is removed.

6. **Choose PivotChart Tools Design⇨Add Chart Element⇨Data Labels⇨Outside End, as shown in Figure 9-39.**

   The data labels are added to the chart.

3-D Pie icon

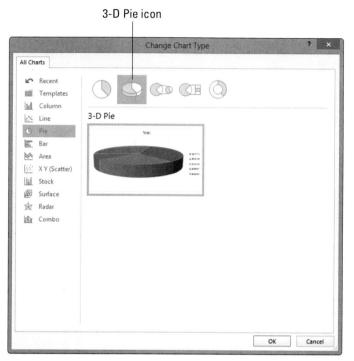

Figure 9-37

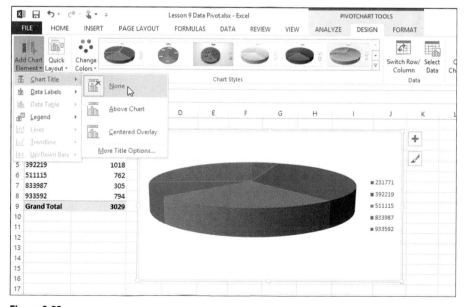

Figure 9-38

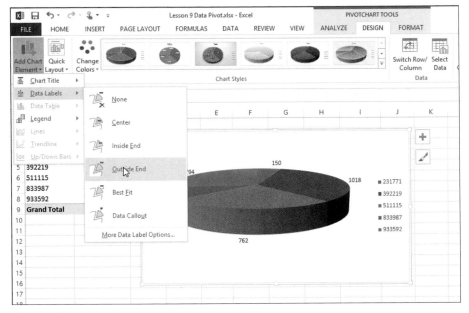

Figure 9-39

7. **Right-click the chart's frame and choose Format Chart Area, opening the Format Chart Area task pane.**

8. **Click the Effects icon.**

9. **Click the 3-D Rotation heading to expand those options.**

10. **Click the Perspective up-arrow button until the setting is 0.1°, as shown in Figure 9-40.**

    This decreases the tilt on the pie so it's easier to read.

11. **Close the task pane, and then click the red pie slice on the chart twice to select only that slice.**

Size and Properties

Click heading to expand section.

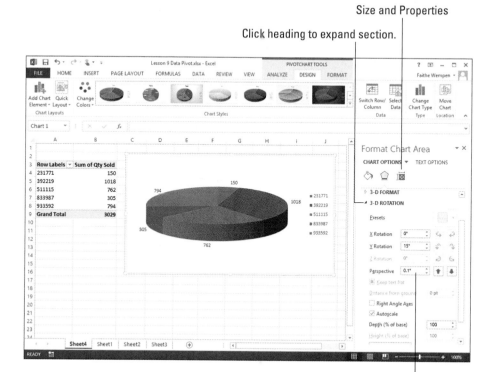

Set Perspective to 0.1.

Figure 9-40

12. **Choose PivotChart Tools Format⇨Shape Fill and then click the Orange, Accent 6 theme color.**

    The color you want is the orange square in the top line of the Theme Colors section.

    The red slice changes to orange. (See Figure 9-41.)

13. **Save the workbook and close it.**

14. **Exit Excel.**

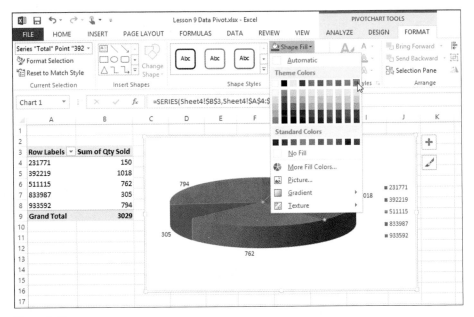

Figure 9-41

Summing Up

Here are the key points you learned about in this lesson:

- PivotTables are summary grids that display information in different ways, to help users understand their meaning.

- When analyzing data in a PivotTable, a field is a type of data that is consistent for each record. For example, for a list of products, Product Number would be a field because each product has one.

- To create a PivotTable, select the data and choose Insert⇨PivotTable. Then use the PivotTable Fields task pane to add fields to the PivotTable.

- To sort a PivotTable, open the menu for the field on the PivotTable and choose one of the Sort commands.

- To filter a PivotTable, drag a field to the Filters section of the task pane. Alternatively, you can open the menu for the field on the PivotTable and select a filter.

- To change which summary function is used for a value, click a field in the Values area of the task pane, choose Value Field Settings, and in the dialog box that appears, choose a different function.

✔ A PivotChart is like a PivotTable except it's a chart instead of a report. To create one, select the data and on the Insert tab, choose PivotChart⇨PivotChart.

✔ You can filter a PivotChart by dragging a field to the Filters area of the task pane.

✔ To format a PivotChart, use the commands on the PivotChart Tools tabs: Analyze, Design, and Format.

Try-it-yourself lab

In this lab, you try some of the functions that I mention in this lesson but didn't include in the exercises:

1. **Reopen the original** `Lesson 9 Data.xlsx` **file for this lesson and save it as** Lesson 9 Try It Pivot.xlsx.

2. **Using the range A1:E29, create a new PivotTable and PivotChart that looks like Figure 9-42.**

   This chart is a Stacked Column chart that shows the quantities sold of each product on each date in February. The Grand Totals for both rows and columns have been turned off, and the field headers (on the PivotTable) and field buttons (on the PivotChart) have been hidden. (*Hint:* To do that, right-click the cell containing Grand Total and choose Remove Grand Total.)

3. **Save and close the workbook.**

4. **Exit Excel.**

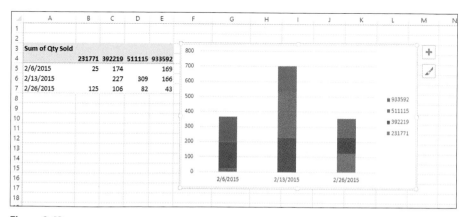

Figure 9-42

Know this tech talk

field: A type of data in a data range that stores data records, such as ID, Product Name, or Price.

PivotChart: A chart layout associated with a PivotTable, in which you can easily customize and modify the fields being plotted.

PivotTable: A customizable table view that displays and analyzes information from a range in a worksheet.

report: A completed PivotTable or PivotChart.

Correcting and Validating Data

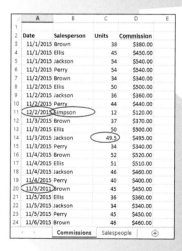

✔ Formula error checking helps find and fix common errors in formulas and functions.

✔ Showing formulas in their cells makes it easy to browse the formulas in an entire worksheet at once.

✔ Evaluating a formula provides a step-by-step picture of how a formula arrives at its result.

✔ Tracing precedents and dependents helps you determine how a formula arrives at its result.

✔ Data validation helps minimize data-entry errors by limiting what data a cell accepts.

espite your best efforts, your worksheets may contain errors. And they may not be your fault! Other users might introduce errors into your work, for example, if you allow them editing privileges. Excel has lots of features to help you fix errors; in this lesson, you learn how to fix them and create validation rules that prevent some data-entry mistakes.

Finding and Fixing Errors in Formulas

In a large or complicated workbook with multiple dependent formulas and functions, the location of errors that prevent the workbook from delivering accurate results isn't always obvious. Excel offers a variety of error-correction tools, which you learn about in the following sections.

Use formula error checking

Excel has an Error Check utility that analyzes an entire worksheet and reports the errors it finds, one by one, for you to deal with. These are some of the errors that Error Check may find:

- ✔ **Circular references:** A cell's formula refers to that cell, which places it into an endless loop. For example, if you place =C3 in cell C3, you get a circular reference.

- ✔ #NAME **errors:** This error occurs when the formula references a named range or cell address that's invalid. For example, if you have a named ELX range, but you accidentally type ELY in a formula, this error would occur.

- ✔ #VALUE **errors:** This error occurs when the formula can't calculate a valid result. You might get this error if one of the cells you're trying to perform a math operation upon contains text, for example.

- ✔ **Inconsistent formulas:** In a table or a range that contains a series of similar formulas in adjacent cells, if one of the cells in that range contains a formula that's unlike the others, Excel may flag it for closer inspection. This isn't necessarily an error; it's just a warning.

In this exercise, you correct errors in a worksheet.

Files needed: Lesson 10 Errors.xlsx

1. **Open** Lesson 10 Errors.xlsx. **Click OK to close the circular reference warning. Save the workbook as** Lesson 10 Errors Fixed.xlsx.

2. **On the Formulas tab, click the down arrow on the Error Checking button and point to Circular References.**

   A list of the circular reference errors appears. (See Figure 10-1.) In this example, you see that cell C1 contains a circular reference to $C$1. (Remember that dollar signs indicate an absolute reference.)

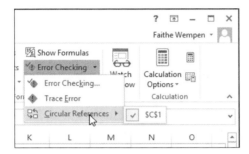

Figure 10-1

3. **Click $C$1 on the list of circular references.**

   The cell cursor moves to cell C1. In the Formula bar, cell C1 contains =COM and so does the Name box. This cell has been named COM, so the formula =COM is equivalent to =C1. That's why the result shows $0. (See Figure 10-2.)

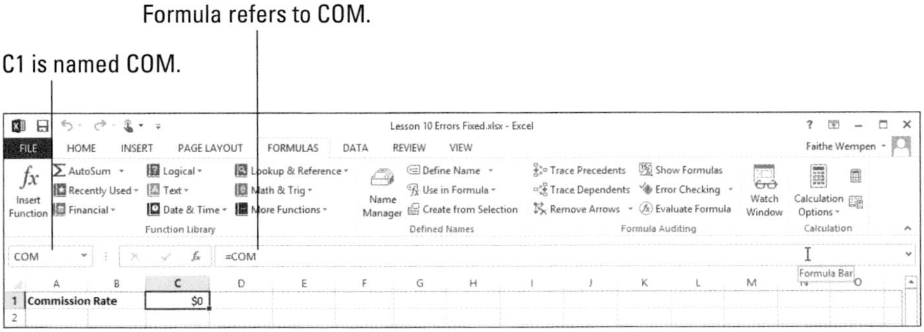

C1 is named COM.

Formula refers to COM.

Figure 10-2

4. **In C1, type** 15, **replacing the current entry, and the circular reference error is corrected.**

5. **Choose Formulas⇨Error Checking.**

The Error Checking dialog box opens. See Figure 10-3. The first error it finds is an inconsistent formula in cell G5. You'd expect the formula to be =F5-E5, but there's a typo in it, so it reads =F4-E5 instead.

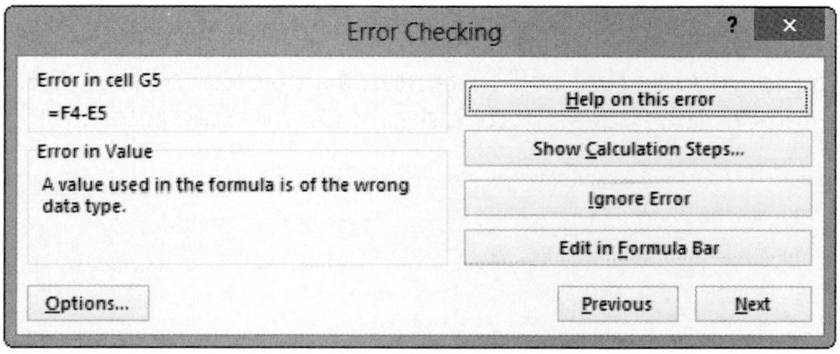

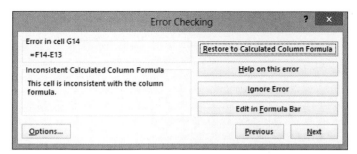

Figure 10-3

6. **Click the Edit in Formula Bar button, and then in the Formula bar change F4 to F5 and press Enter.**

The error is corrected.

7. **In the Error Checking dialog box, click Resume.**

The next error is an inconsistent formula in G14. This formula should be =F14-E14, but there is a typo in it, so it reads =F14-E13. (See Figure 10-4.)

Error Checking	? ✕
Error in cell G14	Restore to Calculated Column Formula
=F14-E13	
Inconsistent Calculated Column Formula	Help on this error
This cell is inconsistent with the column formula.	Ignore Error
	Edit in Formula Bar
Options...	Previous Next

Figure 10-4

8. **Click the Restore to Calculated Column Formula button.**

The error is corrected.

The next error appears in cell E30. In this cell, cell C3 (named COM) has been referred to incorrectly as COMM. (See Figure 10-5.)

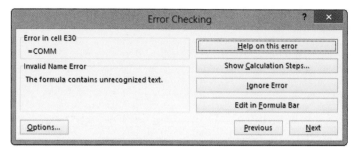

Figure 10-5

9. **Click the Edit in Formula Bar button so that the insertion point moves to the Formula bar and then press the Backspace key to remove the extra letter M from the end of the cell name.**

10. **In the Error Checking dialog box, click the Resume button.**

A dialog box appears that error checking is complete.

11. **Click OK.**

12. **Save the workbook.**

Leave the workbook open for the next exercise.

Show formulas

By default, Excel shows a formula's result in the cell itself and the formula behind that result in the Formula bar when the cell is selected. When you search for an error, it may be tedious to click each cell individually to see its formula. You may find it easier to temporarily show all the formulas at once in their cells.

In this exercise, you display and hide formulas in cells.

Files needed: Lesson 10 Errors Fixed.xlsx from the preceding exercise

1. **Choose Formulas⇨Show Formulas.**

The formulas appear in the cells. (See Figure 10-6.) Notice that the columns widen as needed to show the formulas.

Ctrl+` (the accent mark key above the Tab key) also toggles between showing and hiding formulas.

Show Formulas

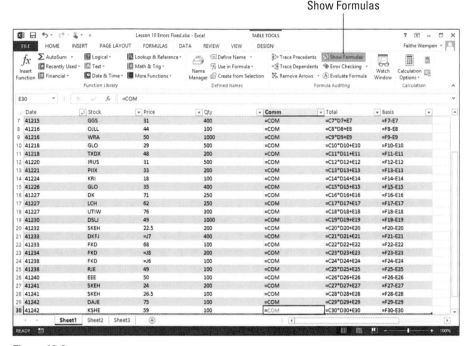

Figure 10-6

2. Choose Formulas⇨Show Formulas again to return to normal viewing.

Leave the workbook open for the next exercise.

Evaluate individual formulas

When you troubleshoot a complicated formula that refers to several cells, you may find it helpful to walk through the formula's execution one step at a time, as if you were solving a math problem by hand. The Evaluate Formula feature does just that — it walks you through a formula, showing the interim results at each step.

In this exercise, you evaluate a formula.

Files needed: Lesson 10 Errors Fixed.xlsx from the preceding exercise

1. **Click cell F5, examine its formula in the Formula bar, and then choose Formulas⇨Evaluate Formula to open the Evaluate Formula dialog box.**

   The first cell reference in the formula (C5) is underlined. See Figure 10-7.

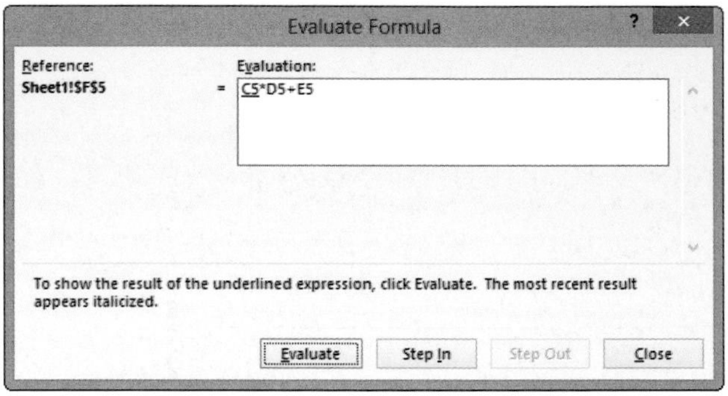

Figure 10-7

2. Click the Evaluate button.

In place of C5 in the formula, the result of C5 appears, and D5 becomes underlined. See Figure 10-8.

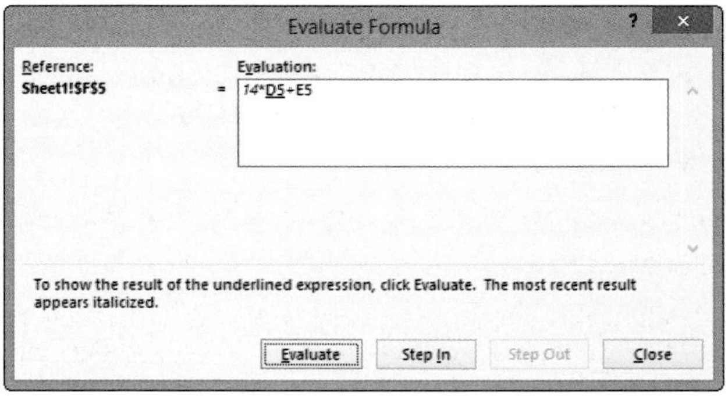

Figure 10-8

3. Click the Step In button.

A box appears below the formula, showing that D5 contains a *constant* (that is, a number, rather than another formula). (See Figure 10-9.)

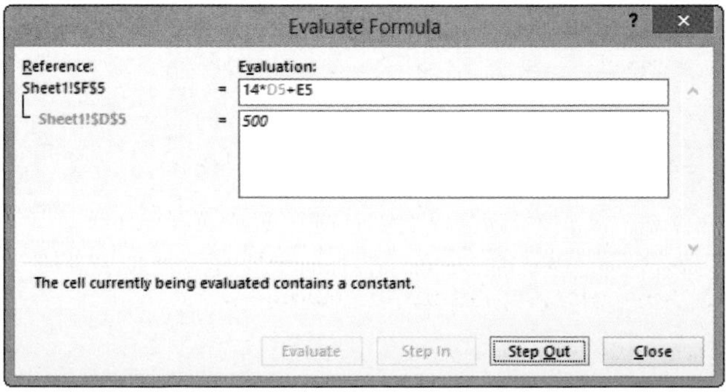

Figure 10-9

4. Click the Step Out button.

The values for both C5 and D5 appear in the formula in the dialog box. (See Figure 10-10.)

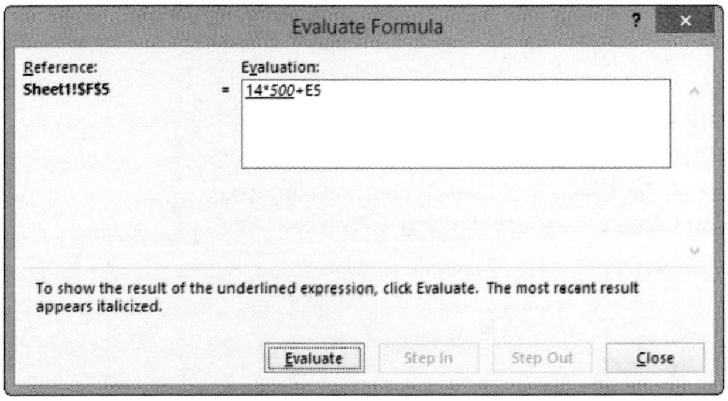

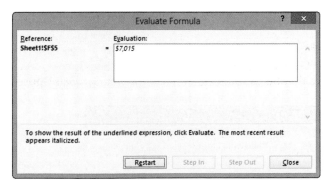

Figure 10-10

5. Click the Evaluate button.

The first math operation in the formula is performed (14 x 500), and the result is shown in the dialog box (7000+E5).

6. Click the Evaluate button.

The value of E5 is substituted for the cell reference: 7000+15.

7. Click the Evaluate button.

The next math operation is performed (7000+15), and the result appears in the dialog box. (See Figure 10-11.) You've just seen, step by step, how Excel arrived at the value.

Figure 10-11

8. Click the Close button to close the dialog box.

9. Save the workbook.

Leave the workbook open for the next exercise.

Trace precedents and dependents

Some formulas in complex worksheets can be difficult to troubleshoot when you don't get the expected results because they may refer to cells that in turn, refer to other cells. To facilitate the process of troubleshooting in such situations, Excel enables you to trace the precedents and dependents of a formula.

In this exercise, you trace the precedents and dependents of a formula.

Files needed: Lesson 10 Errors Fixed.xlsx from the preceding exercise

1. **Click cell F5, which contains the formula** =C5*D5+E5, **and then choose Formulas⇨Trace Precedents.**

   A blue arrow appears pointing from cell C5 to cell F5, with a blue dot in cells C5, D5, and E5 to indicate that each of those cells is included.

2. **Choose Formulas⇨Trace Precedents again, and another arrow is added to show the next level of precedents: from cell C1 to cell E5.**

   This happens because the formula in E5 refers to C1. See Figure 10-12.

> **LINGO**
>
> A **precedent** is a cell that contributes to a formula's calculation — in other words, a backward reference. For example, in the formula =A1+A2, cells A1 and A2 are precedents of that formula. If cell A1, in turn, contains the formula =C1+C2, cells C1 and C2 are precedents of A1. A **dependent** is a cell that depends upon a certain cell's content to report its own result — in other words, a forward reference. For example, if cell G9 contains =F9+10, cell G9 depends on F9.

F5		:	×	✓	fx	=C5*D5+E5		
	A	B	C	D	E	F	G	H
1	Commission Rate		$15					
2								
3								
4	Date	Stock	Price	Qty	Comm	Total	Basis	
5	11/1/2012	TRU	14	500	$15	$7,015	$7,000	
6	11/2/2012	DFS	57	300	$15	$17,115	$17,100	
7	11/2/2012	GGS	31	400	$15	$12,415	$12,400	
8	11/3/2012	OJLL	44	100	$15	$4,415	$4,400	

Figure 10-12

3. **Choose Formulas⇨Remove Arrows to make the arrows disappear and then choose Formulas⇨Trace Dependents.**

   Two arrows appear: from cell F5 to cell G5, and from F5 to cell F32. This happens because F5 is referenced in formulas in those two cells.

4. **Choose Formulas⇨Trace Dependents again.**

Nothing happens, and an error sound plays (if you have sound support enabled on your·PC), indicating that there are no further dependents.

5. Choose Formulas⇨Remove Arrows.

The arrows are cleared.

6. Save and close the workbook.

Leave Excel open for the next exercise.

Validating Data

When you use Excel to store database data, it can be a challenge to maintain consistency in the data formatting and content, especially if multiple people help with the data entry. For example, some people might enter a state's full name (such as *Indiana*) but others might enter the abbreviation (such as *IN*). You might also end up with duplicate data records, which can be difficult to find just by browsing through the data. In the following sections, you learn several ways to make your data more consistent.

Create data validation rules

In this exercise, you create data validation rules.

Files needed: Lesson 10 Validation.xlsx

1. Open Lesson 10 Validation.xlsx, **save it as** Lesson 10 Validation Checked.xlsx, **and on the Commissions tab, select the range A3:A50.**

LINGO

Validation rules can help ensure consistency by limiting what can be entered into certain cells. You can restrict a cell to a certain type of data, such as dates, numbers, or text, and you can specify a certain number of characters (or text length) for an entry.

In Step 1 (and also Step 7), you select extra rows at the bottom so that if you enter new records later, the rules also apply to them. You could select all the way down to row 100, or even further, if you had a lot more records to enter. You could even apply the validation rule to the entire column.

2. Choose Data⇨Data Validation.

The Data Validation dialog box opens.

3. From the Allow drop-down list, choose Date.

4. In the Start Date text box, type 11/1/2015; **in the End Date text box, type** 12/1/2015 **(see Figure 10-13).**

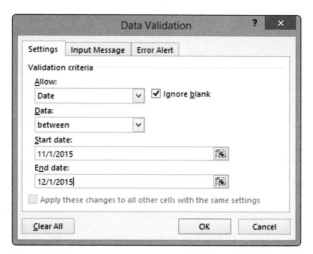

Figure 10-13

5. **Click OK; in cell A22, type** 1/2/2003 **and press Enter.**

   An error appears because the rule is violated. (See Figure 10-14.)

6. **Click the Cancel button.**

7. **Select the range C3:C50 and then choose Data⇨Data Validation to open the Data Validation dialog box.**

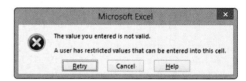

Figure 10-14

8. **From the Allow drop-down list, choose Whole Number; from the Data drop-down list, choose Greater Than or Equal To.**

9. **In the Minimum box, type** 0.

   You can see the filled-out dialog box in Figure 10-15.

10. **Click the Error Alert tab and type** Entry Error **in the Title text box.**

11. **In the Error Message box, type** Units must be in whole numbers.

    You can see the filled out Error Alert tab in Figure 10-16.

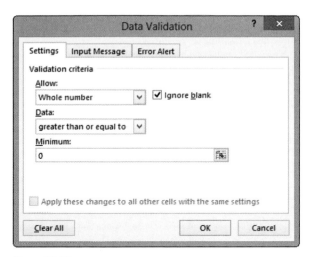

Figure 10-15

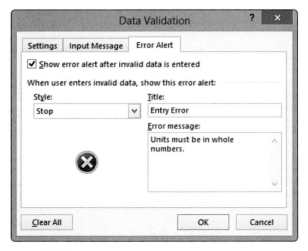

Figure 10-16

12. **Click OK; in cell C45, type** 12.5 **and press Enter.**

    The custom Entry Error dialog box opens, as shown in Figure 10-17. (You created this dialog box in Steps 10–12.)

13. **Click the Cancel button.**

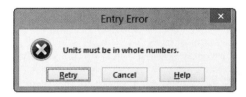

Figure 10-17

For more practice, create a validation rule for the names in column B using the List type of rule, and specify the list on the Salespeople tab as the range from which to draw the valid names. To do this, start a new data validation rule for B3:B50 on the Commissions tab and set the Allow value to List. Set the Source to the salespeople's names on the Salespeople tab (A1:A4 on that tab).

14. **Save the workbook.**

Leave the workbook open for the next exercise.

Circle invalid data

You can create data validation rules either before or after you enter data. If you create the validation rules on cells that already contain data, the existing data in them may violate the rules. You can check for violations via the Circle Invalid Data feature.

In this exercise, you circle invalid data.

Files needed: Lesson 10 Validation Checked.xlsx from the preceding exercise

1. **On the Data tab, click the down arrow on the Data Validation button, as shown in Figure 10-18, and then choose Circle Invalid Data.**

   Excel circles data that violates the data validation rules. (See Figure 10-19.)

Figure 10-18

2. **Change the value in cell A11 to 11/2/2015; change the value in cell A20 to 11/5/2015; change the value in cell C14 to 49.**

   The circles disappear on these cells.

   Note: If you did the optional Practice step in the previous exercise to place a validation rule on the entries in column B, cell B11's value shows as an error. You can choose to correct it by changing to some other salesperson name or leave it with the error.

	A	B	C	D	E
1					
2	Date	Salesperson	Units	Commission	
3	11/1/2015	Brown	38	$380.00	
4	11/1/2015	Ellis	45	$450.00	
5	11/1/2015	Jackson	54	$540.00	
6	11/1/2015	Perry	54	$540.00	
7	11/2/2015	Brown	34	$340.00	
8	11/2/2015	Ellis	50	$500.00	
9	11/2/2015	Jackson	36	$360.00	
10	11/2/2015	Perry	44	$440.00	
11	12/2/2015	Simpson	12	$120.00	
12	11/3/2015	Brown	37	$370.00	
13	11/3/2015	Ellis	50	$500.00	
14	11/3/2015	Jackson	49.5	$495.00	
15	11/3/2015	Perry	34	$340.00	
16	11/4/2015	Brown	52	$520.00	
17	11/4/2015	Ellis	51	$510.00	
18	11/4/2015	Jackson	46	$460.00	
19	11/4/2015	Perry	40	$400.00	
20	11/5/2011	Brown	45	$450.00	
21	11/5/2015	Ellis	36	$360.00	
22	11/5/2015	Jackson	34	$340.00	
23	11/5/2015	Perry	45	$450.00	
24	11/6/2015	Brown	46	$460.00	

| Commissions | Salespeople | ⊕ |

Figure 10-19

3. **Save the workbook.**

Leave the workbook open for the next exercise.

Copy validation rules

You can copy validation rules from one cell to another using Copy and Paste Special. This method is handy when you need to extend the range that contains the data in a list, for example, or if you created the validation rules in the wrong range to begin with.

In this exercise, you copy validation rules.

Files needed: Lesson 10 Validation Checked.xlsx from the preceding exercise

1. **Select cell A3 and then press Ctrl+C to copy it.**

2. **Select the range A51:A60.**

   (Column A already has the validation rules in place for rows up through 50 from a previous exercise.)

3. **On the Home tab, click the down arrow on the Paste button, as shown in Figure 10-20, and choose Paste Special.**

   The Paste Special dialog box opens.

4. **Select the Validation option, as shown in Figure 10-21, and then click OK.**

   The validation rule is pasted to the destination cells you selected in Step 2.

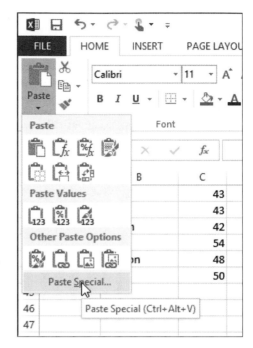

Figure 10-20

Figure 10-21

5. **Select cell A51, type** 12/01/2012, **and press Enter.**

An error box appears, which proves that the rule was copied success-
fully. Any date that is not in the range specified will generate this error
box. The valid date range is 1/1/2015 to 2/1/2015, because of the validation rule you created earlier in this lesson.

6. **Click the Cancel button.**

7. **Save the workbook.**

Leave the workbook open for the next exercise.

Remove duplicate data

In a long list of worksheet data, you might find that the existence of duplicate
data isn't obvious. For example, if each salesperson on each date should
have only one sales record and you have dozens of records, you might not
be able to tell at a glance which records duplicate both the Salesperson and
Date fields.

Excel's Find Duplicates feature makes it easy to identify records (rows) that
have identical values in the fields (columns) that you specify.

In this exercise, you find and remove duplicate data.

Files needed: Lesson 10 Validation Checked.xlsx from the preceding exercise

1. **Select cell A3 and choose Data⇨Remove Duplicates.**

The Remove Duplicates dialog box opens, as shown in Figure 10-22.

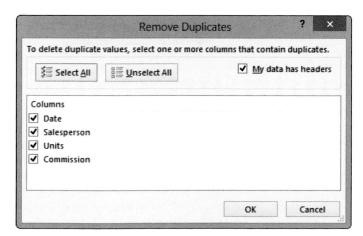

Figure 10-22

2. Deselect the Units and Commission check boxes. Then click OK.

TIP

You're looking for records that have the same Salesperson and Date; they might or might not have the same Units or Commission.

A message box appears saying that a duplicate was found and removed. (See Figure 10-23.)

3. Click OK to close the message box.

4. Save the workbook and close it.

5. Close Excel.

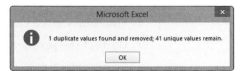

Microsoft Excel

ⓘ 1 duplicate values found and removed; 41 unique values remain.

OK

Figure 10-23

Summing Up

Here are the key points you learned in this lesson:

✔ On the Formulas tab are several tools for finding and fixing errors.

✔ Choosing Formulas⇨Error Checking finds many different types of formula errors.

✔ To show formulas in cells, choose Formulas⇨Show Formulas or press Ctrl+`.

✔ To evaluate a formula, choose Formulas⇨Evaluate Formula.

✔ To trace a formula's precedents or dependents, choose Formulas⇨Trace Precedents or Formulas⇨Trace Dependents, respectively.

✔ A data validation rule restricts what can be entered into a cell. Choose Data⇨Data Validation to set up rules.

✔ Choose Data⇨Data Validation⇨Circle Invalid Data to find cells that violate data validation rules.

✔ To copy a validation rule, use Paste Special and select the Validation option.

✔ Choose Data⇨Remove Duplicates to clean out duplicate entries from a data list.

Try-it-yourself lab

In this lab, you make corrections to a worksheet that has several problems in its formulas.

1. **Open** `Lesson 10 Try It Errors.xlsx` **file and save it as** Lesson 10 Try It Fixed.xlsx.

2. **Find and fix the circular reference.**

3. **Correct the problem with the function name in column E.**

4. **Correct the problem with the calculation of Roommates 2 and 3's share of the expenses.**

5. **Correct the problem with the formula in cell B12 not containing the right range.**

6. **Save the workbook and close it.**

7. **Exit Excel.**

Know this tech talk

circular reference: An error in which a cell's formula refers to its own cell address.

dependent: A cell that depends on a certain cell's content to report its own result.

#NAME **error:** An error that occurs when a formula references an invalid named range or cell address.

precedent: A cell that contributes to a formula's calculation.

validation rule: A rule that limits what can be entered into a certain cell.

#VALUE **error:** An error that occurs when a formula can't calculate a valid result.

Protecting and Sharing Data

✔ Protect a worksheet to prevent changes from being made to it.

✔ Unlocking cells makes them editable when the rest of the worksheet is protected.

✔ Encrypting a workbook password-protects it to secure sensitive information.

✔ Mark a workbook as final to discourage further editing of an approved draft.

✔ Tracking changes made to a workbook enables you to manage changes from multiple users.

I n Lesson 10, you saw that Excel offers features to guard against your own mistakes, but it also includes features that minimize other people's ability to mess up your worksheets. Suppose you want to share a workbook with others and track the changes made to it; in this lesson, you see how Excel helps you do so. You also learn how to encrypt a workbook with a password, and how to mark it as the final draft.

Protecting Ranges

Excel offers a variety of tools and commands for protecting your work from being altered, either accidentally or on purpose. Furthermore, you don't have to protect the entire workbook, or even the entire sheet, just to get protection on certain cells. You can protect a little or a lot.

Locking and unlocking cells

By default, every cell on a worksheet is set to be locked. You don't notice this because the worksheet itself is unprotected, so the locking of the individual cells doesn't take effect. Only when the worksheet is protected does a cell's Locked status become important.

Because of this, locking cells actually works backward from the way you might think. On a given worksheet, you unlock the cells that you still want to be able to change when the worksheet is protected. Then you protect the worksheet, and the protection doesn't apply to the cells you unlocked.

In this exercise, you unlock some cells.

Files needed: Lesson 11 Loans Unlock.xlsx

1. **Open** `Lesson 11 Loans Unlock.xlsx` **and save it as** Lesson 11 Loans Protection.xlsx**.**

2. **Click the Payments tab and select the range B3:B4; then right-click the selection and choose Format Cells to open the Format Cells dialog box.**

3. **Click the Protection tab, deselect the Locked check box (see Figure 11-1), and then click OK.**

Clear the locked check box.

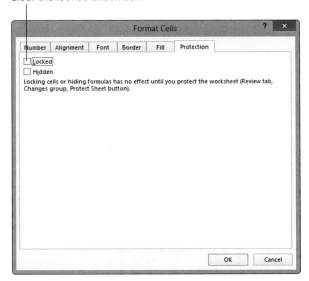

Figure 11-1

Locking is an on/off toggle. To relock a cell, select the Locked check box.

4. **Click the Amount tab and select the range B4:B5; then right-click the range and choose Format Cells.**

5. **In the Format Cells dialog box, click the Protection tab, deselect the Locked check box, and click OK.**

6. **Save the workbook.**

Leave the workbook open for the next exercise.

Protecting a worksheet

When you protect a worksheet, you make it uneditable, except for any cells that have been unlocked (as described in the preceding exercise). Protection is not an all-or-nothing thing. You can choose specific editing actions to allow or disallow on a protected worksheet. For example, you might choose to allow data to be edited, but no rows or columns to be added or removed.

You can also specify a protection password for the sheet. That way, anyone who knows the password can unprotect it. If you decline to use a password, anyone may unprotect the sheet.

TIP

As you plan protection for a worksheet, think about why you want to protect it. Are you more concerned about avoiding accidental changes? If so, no password is necessary. Are you worried about unauthorized users making intentional changes that would ruin the sheet? Use a password.

In this exercise, you protect a worksheet.

Files needed: Lesson 11 Loans Protection.xlsx from the preceding exercise

1. **Click the Payments worksheet tab and choose Review⇨Protect Sheet.**

   The Protect Sheet dialog box opens.

2. **In the Password to Unprotect Sheet text box, type** Unprotect.

3. **Select the Format Cells, Format Columns, and Format Rows check boxes (see Figure 11-2) and then click OK.**

   The Confirm Password dialog box opens.

4. **Type** Unprotect **and click OK.**

5. **Click cell B5 and try to type something. When an error message appears, click OK to clear it.**

Figure 11-2

6. **With cell B5 still selected, click the Home tab. In the drop-down list in the Number group, choose Currency, as shown in Figure 11-3.**

   Excel lets you change the cell's formatting.

7. **Click cell B4 (which is unlocked) and on the Home tab, in the drop-down list in the Number group, choose General.**

   Excel lets you change the cell's formatting, too.

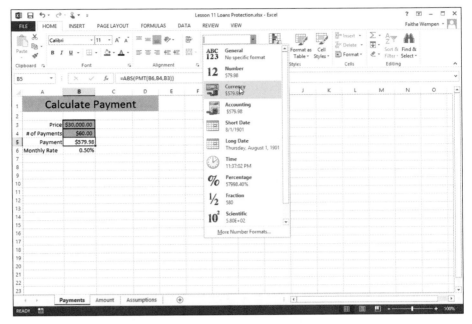

Figure 11-3

8. **In cell B4, type** 45, **replacing the previous value.**

   Excel lets you change the cell's content, as shown in Figure 11-4.

9. **Choose Review⇨ Unprotect Sheet to open the Unprotect Sheet dialog box.**

10. **Type** Unprotect **and click OK; worksheet-level protection is removed.**

11. **Save the workbook.**

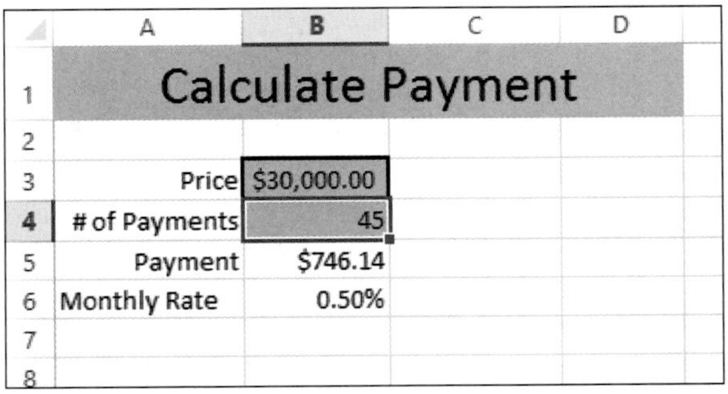

Leave the workbook open for the next exercise.

	A	B	C	D
1		Calculate Payment		
2				
3	Price	$30,000.00		
4	# of Payments	45		
5	Payment	$746.14		
6	Monthly Rate	0.50%		
7				
8				

Figure 11-4

Protecting a workbook

When you protect an entire workbook, you can choose to protect either or both of these aspects:

- ✔ **Structure:** Nobody can add or delete worksheets, rows, columns, or cells.

- ✔ **Windows:** The workbook opens with the worksheet windows arranged in a certain way.

Protecting a workbook doesn't protect any individual cells from having their content altered; that's a function of whether the cells are unlocked and whether the worksheet is protected. (I cover both topics in earlier exercises in this lesson.)

In this exercise, you protect — and then unprotect — a workbook from having structural changes made to it.

Files needed: Lesson 11 Loans Protection.xlsx from the preceding exercise

1. **Choose Review⇨Protect Workbook.**

   The Protect Structure and Windows dialog box opens.

2. **In the Password (Optional) box, type** Unprotect **(see Figure 11-5) and click OK.**

3. **In the Confirm Password dialog box that opens, type** Unprotect **and click OK.**

   The workbook is protected. On the Home tab, the Insert Sheet and Delete sheet commands are unavailable.

4. **Choose Review⇨Protect Workbook.**

   The Unprotect Workbook dialog box opens.

5. **Type** Unprotect **(see Figure 11-6) and click OK.**

   The workbook-level protection is removed.

6. **Save the workbook.**

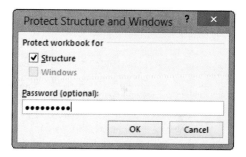

Figure 11-5

Figure 11-6

Leave the workbook open for the next exercise.

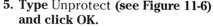

Securing Workbooks

In the preceding section, you learned various techniques for limiting people's ability to change the content of a workbook. Next, you learn about some ways to further safeguard a workbook, such as assigning a password to open a workbook, removing personal details from it, marking it as final, and adding a digital signature that assures others that it hasn't been tampered with.

Encrypting and decrypting a workbook

In this exercise, you encrypt a workbook, open it using the password, and decrypt it.

Files needed: Lesson 11 Loans Protection.xlsx from the preceding exercise

1. **Choose File⇨Info⇨Protect Workbook⇨ Encrypt with Password, as shown in Figure 11-7.**

   The Encrypt Document dialog box opens.

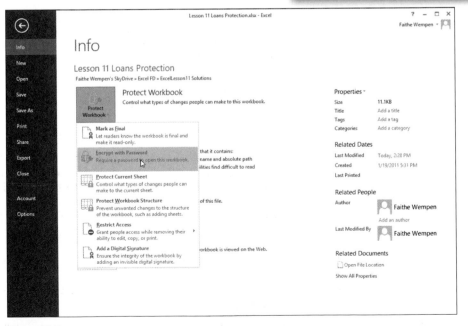

Figure 11-7

2. **Type** Unprotect **(see Figure 11-8)
and click OK.**

The Confirm Password dialog
box opens.

3. **Type** Unprotect **and click OK.**

4. **Close the workbook. If prompted
to save changes, click Save.**

5. **Choose File⇨Recent
Workbooks⇨Lesson 11 Loans
Protection.**

The Password dialog box opens,
as shown in Figure 11-9.

6. **Type** Unprotect **and click OK.**

7. **Choose File⇨Info⇨Protect
Workbook⇨Encrypt with
Password.**

The Encrypt Document dialog
box opens.

8. **Select the password in the
Password box, press the Delete
key to clear it, click OK, and
press the Esc key to exit Backstage view.**

9. **Save the workbook.**

Figure 11-8

Figure 11-9

Leave the workbook open for the next exercise.

Using the Document Inspector

The Document Inspector checks a workbook for types of content that may
cause problems if you decide to share the workbook with others. These
include personal information (such as the author's name), hidden content,
comments, and headers/footers. If Excel finds any such content, it informs you
and allows you to make a decision regarding whether to remove the content.

*In this exercise, you inspect a workbook and remove some of the questionable
content.*

Files needed: Lesson 11 Loans Protection.xlsx from the preceding exercise

1. **Choose File⇨Info⇨Check for Issues⇨Inspect Document, as shown in
Figure 11-10. If prompted to save your document, click Yes.**

The Document Inspector dialog box opens, as shown in Figure 11-11.

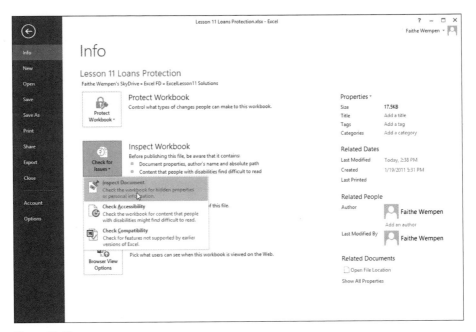

Figure 11-10

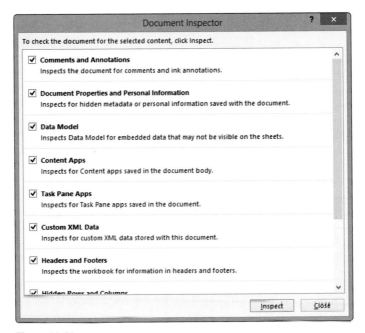

Figure 11-11

2. Click the Inspect button.

The results of the inspection appear, as shown in Figure 11-12.

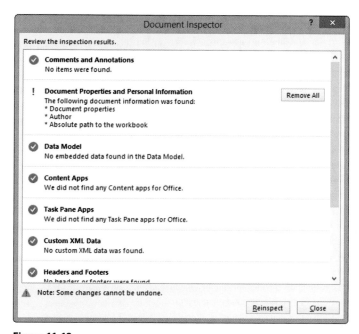

Figure 11-12

3. Click the Remove All button next to Document Properties and Personal Information and then click the Close button.

Later exercises require that document properties and personal information not be blocked, so next you undo that blockage.

4. Choose File⇨Options to open the Excel Options dialog box. Then choose Trust Center⇨Trust Center Settings.

The Trust Center dialog box opens.

5. Click Privacy Options in the list on the left and then deselect the Remove Personal Information from File Properties on Save check box.

The check box is deselected, as shown in Figure 11-13.

Clear this check box.

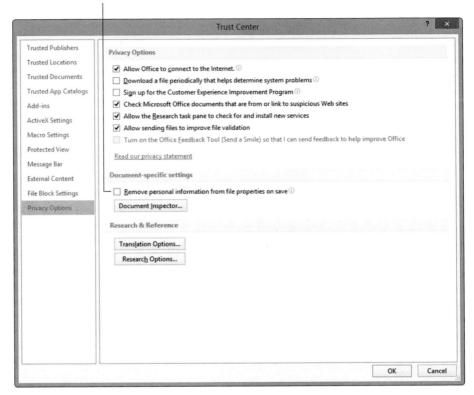

Figure 11-13

6. **Click OK to close the Trust Center and then click OK to close the Excel Options dialog box.**

7. **Save the workbook.**

Leave the workbook open for the next exercise.

Marking a workbook as final

Marking a workbook as final discourages people from editing it; however, doing so isn't a security measure because anyone can easily override it. Instead, marking final is a reminder that the workbook shouldn't be edited casually. You might mark a workbook as final after everyone has approved it, for example. Further changes to it would require another round of approvals, so it shouldn't be done except for an important reason.

In this exercise, you mark a workbook as final and then make additional changes to it, overriding its Final status.

Files needed: Lesson 11 Loans Protection.xlsx from the preceding exercise

1. Choose File⇨Info⇨Protect Workbook⇨Mark as Final (see Figure 11-14); in the confirmation box that appears, click OK.

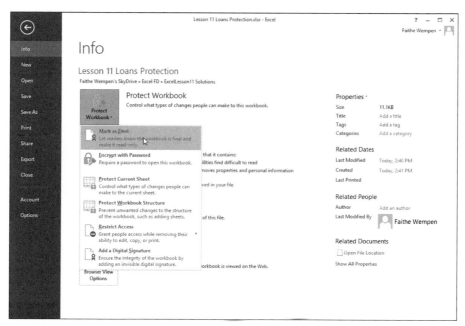

Figure 11-14

A message box appears, explaining what's been done, as shown in Figure 11-15. You might not see this box.

Figure 11-15

TIP

Notice in Figure 11-15 the Don't Show This Message Again check box. If you select this check box, you won't see this message box in the future.

2. **Click OK to close the dialog box if it appears.**

3. **Click the Home tab.**

In Figure 11-16, notice that the information bar at the top of the worksheet indicates the document has been marked as final. Notice also that the Ribbon has disappeared.

Figure 11-16

4. **Click the Edit Anyway button, and the document returns to regular status.**

Leave the workbook open for the next exercise.

Tracking Changes in a Shared Workbook

When multiple people need to edit a workbook, it can be a challenge to manage the various revisions being made, especially with multiple copies circulating, each edited individually. As an alternative to that administrative nightmare, you might prefer to share a workbook on a centrally accessible server. That way everyone can make their changes to a common copy. You can then track the changes that each person makes and merge the changes into a comprehensively reviewed version.

In the following sections, you learn how to share a workbook, how to track changes, how to merge and accept changes, and how to unshare a workbook after the editing process is complete.

Creating a shared workbook

When you share a workbook, you can enable a number of options, including whether to allow multiple users to have simultaneous access, whether to track the changes, and how to deal with conflicting changes. You can also protect the workbook with a password at the same time you share it; if you do so, change tracking can't be disabled unless you know the password.

In this exercise, you share a workbook.

Files needed: Lesson 11 Loans Protection.xlsx from the preceding exercise

1. **Choose Review⇨Share Workbook to open the Share Workbook dialog box.**

2. **Select the Allow Changes by More Than One User at the Same Time check box, as shown in Figure 11-17.**

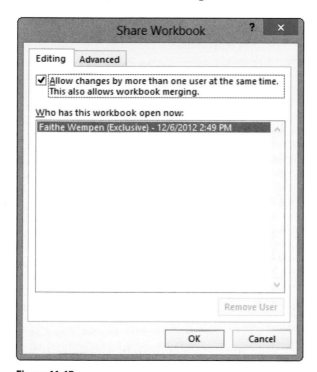

Figure 11-17

3. **Click the Advanced tab and, in the Update Changes section, select the Automatically Every option, as shown in Figure 11-18.**

4. **Click OK, and a confirmation box appears.**

5. **Click OK to confirm that you want to share the workbook, and the workbook becomes shared.**

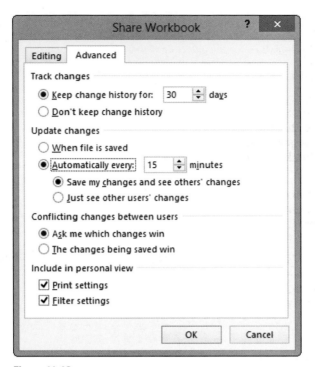

Figure 11-18

Leave the workbook open for the next exercise.

Enabling change tracking

Change tracking enables you to see who has made what changes to a shared workbook. For example, tracking marks such changes as whether rows and columns have been inserted, whether formulas have changed, and whether constant values and text have been altered.

In this exercise, you track some changes to a workbook.

Files needed: Lesson 11 Loans Protection.xlsx from the preceding exercise

1. Choose Review⇨ Track Changes⇨ Highlight Changes, as shown in Figure 11-19.

2. In the Highlight Changes dialog box, make sure that the Track Changes While Editing check box is selected.

3. In the When drop-down list, choose All (see Figure 11-20) and then click OK. Click OK to save your work if prompted.

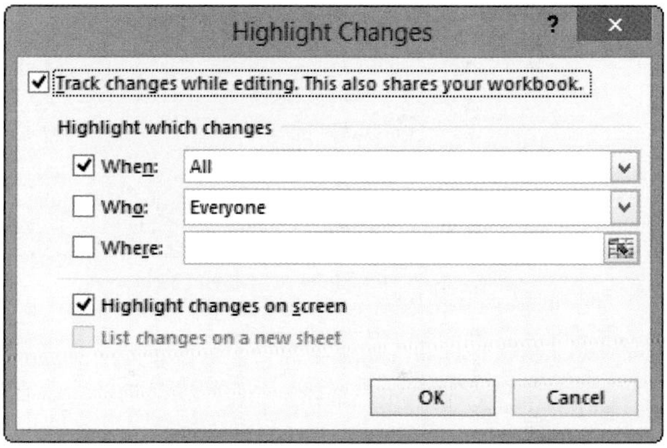

4. On the Payments tab in cell A1, type Present Value, replacing the current entry.

   Notice that a triangle appears in the upper-left corner of the cell, indicating a change.

5. On the Assumptions tab in cell B6, type 5, replacing the current entry.

6. Point to cell B6 with the mouse.

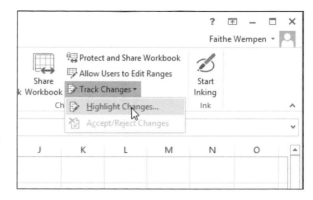

Figure 11-19

Figure 11-20

A comment box opens showing the change that was made, as shown in Figure 11-21.

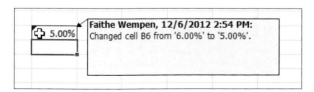

Figure 11-21

7. Save the workbook.

Leave the workbook open for the next exercise.

Accept or reject changes

After everyone makes changes to a shared workbook, you can go through the changes and either accept or reject each one. Excel makes it easy to examine the changes and determine whether each one should stay or go.

In this exercise, you merge the changes in a workbook.

Files needed: Lesson 11 Loans Protection.xlsx from the preceding exercise

1. Choose Review⇨ Track Changes⇨ Accept/Reject Changes. If prompted to save your work, click OK.

The Select Changes to Accept or Reject dialog box appears, as shown in Figure 11-22.

2. Click OK, and the first change is highlighted, as shown in Figure 11-23.

Figure 11-22

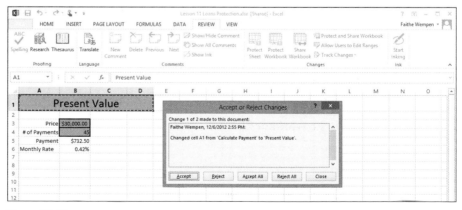

Figure 11-23

3. Click the Reject button.

The text goes back to its previous wording, and the next change appears onscreen (cell B6 on the Assumptions tab). See Figure 11-24.

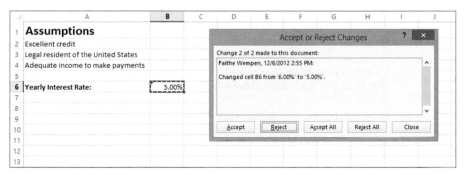

Figure 11-24

4. Click the Accept button.

The dialog box closes because there are no more changes to accept or reject.

5. Click the Payments tab.

Notice that the change indicator from the rejected change is no longer present.

6. Click the Assumptions tab.

Notice that the change indicator from the accepted change is still present.

7. Point at cell B6 to review the change that was made.

8. Choose Review⇨Track Changes⇨Highlight Changes to open the Highlight Changes dialog box.

9. Deselect the Highlight Changes On Screen check box, as shown in Figure 11-25.

10. Click OK.

The change indicator is removed from cell B6.

11. Save the workbook.

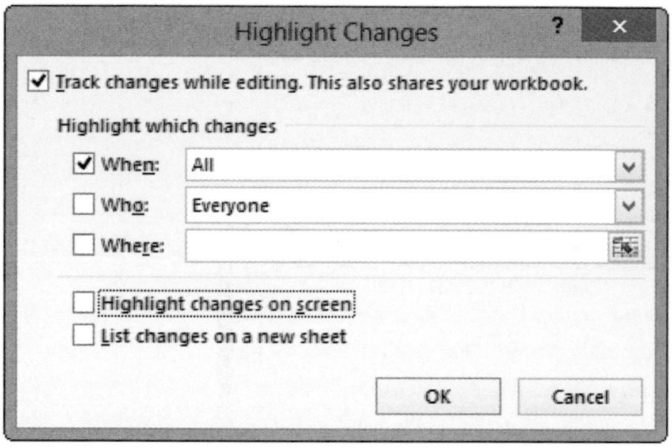

Highlight Changes

☑ Track changes while editing. This also shares your workbook.

Highlight which changes

☑ When: All

☐ Who: Everyone

☐ Where:

☐ Highlight changes on screen

☐ List changes on a new sheet

OK   Cancel

Figure 11-25

Leave the workbook open for the next exercise.

Removing workbook sharing

A shared workbook shows [Shared] in the title bar in Excel to remind you that it's shared.

When you're done sharing the workbook among multiple users, you can remove sharing so the workbook is no longer simultaneously accessible by multiple people.

In this exercise, you stop sharing a workbook.

Files needed: Lesson 11 Loans Protection.xlsx from the preceding exercise

1. **Choose Review⇨Share Workbook.**

   The Share Workbook dialog box opens.

2. **On the Editing tab, deselect the Allow Changes by More Than One User at the Same Time check box, as shown in Figure 11-26.**

3. **Click OK and a message box appears, explaining that the workbook will no longer be shared.**

4. **Click Yes, and the workbook is no longer shared.**

5. **Save the workbook and close it.**

6. **Exit Excel.**

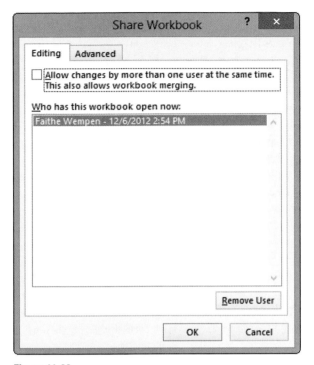

Figure 11-26

 Summing Up

Here are the key points you learned in this lesson:

- ✔ By default, all cells are locked on a worksheet but the worksheet is not protected. Unlock certain cells and then protect the worksheet, and only those unlocked cells will be editable.

- ✔ To unlock a cell, right-click it and choose Format Cells. On the Protection tab, deselect the Locked check box.

- ✔ To protect a worksheet, choose Review⮞Protect Sheet.

- ✔ To protect a whole workbook, choose Review⮞Protect Workbook.

- ✔ To add a password to a workbook, choose File⮞Info⮞Protect Workbook⮞ Encrypt with Password.

✔ The Document Inspector finds and removes unwanted information from a file, such as properties or headers/footers. Choose File➪Info➪Check for Issues➪Inspect Document.

✔ Marking a workbook as final is not a security measure, but it can prevent accidental changes. Choose File➪Info➪Protect Workbook➪Mark as Final.

✔ To share a workbook, choose Review➪Share Workbook, and select the Allow Changes by More Than One User at the Same Time check box. Doing so makes the workbook simultaneously editable by multiple users.

✔ To track changes made, choose Review➪Track Changes➪Highlight Changes.

✔ To accept or reject changes made to a workbook, choose Review➪Track Changes➪Accept/Reject Changes.

Know this tech talk

decrypt: To remove encryption from a workbook.

encrypt: To password-protect a workbook so that nobody can open it except those who know the password.

Appendix
About the CD

To access the content on this CD, just remove the CD and pop it into your Windows computer. This Appendix shows you the ins and outs.

Contents of This CD

The CD contains the companion files that go with this book. As you work through the tutorials in this book, you often need a sample file that goes with the tutorial steps. (Look for the note about Files Needed at the beginning of each tutorial.) In the Data folder that goes with each lesson, you find the Excel workbook or workbooks that you need for each lesson. In the Solutions folder for each lesson, you find the completed worksheets so that you can check your work.

Appendix

System Requirements

This CD is designed to be compatible with the following system requirements. If your system does not meet or exceed these requirements, the CD may not run, or may perform poorly.

Any of these Microsoft operating systems:

- ✔ Windows 8
- ✔ Windows 7
- ✔ Windows Vista
- ✔ Windows XP
- ✔ Windows 2000
- ✔ Windows 2003 Server

Any of the following web browsers:

- ✔ Microsoft Internet Explorer 6.0 or higher
- ✔ Mozilla Firefox 2.x or higher

The following additional hardware/software:

- ✔ A Pentium III, 500 MHz processor (or better)
- ✔ 256MB of RAM (or more)
- ✔ A CD-ROM or DVD-ROM drive

A small amount of hard drive space must be available for tracking data. Typically, less than 1MB will be used.

If you are reading this in an electronic format, please go to `http://book support.wiley.com` for access to the additional content.

Accessing the Excel eCourse

Your purchase of this For Dummies eLearning Kit includes access to the course online at the For Dummies eLearning Center. If you have purchased an electronic version of this book, please visit www.dummies.com/go/get elearningcode to gain your access code to the online course. If you purchased the paperback book, you find your access code behind the CD that comes with this book.

Dummies eCourses require an HTML5-capable browser. If you use the Firefox or Chrome browser, make sure you have the latest version. Internet Explorer 10 is also HTML5-capable.

Using the CD

The interface for this CD is designed to run directly from the CD. Here's how to start it:

1. **Put the CD in the drive.**
2. **Double-click the My Computer icon to view the contents of the My Computer window.**
3. **Double-click the CD-ROM drive icon to view the contents of the Dummies eLearning CD.**
4. **Double-click the `start.bat` file to start the Dummies eLearning CBT.**

   Your computer may warn you about active content. Click Yes to continue starting the CD. The CD may create new tabs in your browser. Click the tab to see the content.

Customer Care

If you have trouble with the CD-ROM, please call Wiley Product Technical Support at 800-762-2974. Outside the United States, call 317-572-3993. You can also contact Wiley Product Technical Support at http://support.wiley.com. John Wiley & Sons, Inc. will provide technical support only for installation and other general quality control items. For technical support on the applications themselves, consult the program's vendor or author.

To place additional orders or to request information about other Wiley products, please call 877-762-2974.

Index

• *G* •

Z

Notes

About the Author

Faithe Wempen, MA, is a Microsoft Office Master Instructor and the author of more than 100 books on computer hardware and software, including the *PowerPoint 2013 Bible* and *Office 2013 eLearning Kit For Dummies*. She is an adjunct instructor of Computer Information Technology at Purdue University, and her corporate training courses online have reached more than one-quarter of a million students for clients such as Hewlett-Packard, Sony, and CNET.

Dedication

To Margaret

Author's Acknowledgments

Thanks to the wonderful editorial staff at John Wiley & Sons, Inc. for another job well done. You guys are top-notch!

Publisher's Acknowledgments

Sr. Acquisitions Editor: Katie Mohr

Sr. Project Editor: Rebecca Huehls

Sr. Copy Editor: Barry Childs-Helton

Technical Editor: Mike Talley

Editorial Assistant: Annie Sullivan

Sr. Editorial Assistant: Cherie Case

Sr. Project Coordinator: Kristie Rees

Project Manager: Rich Graves, Laura Moss

Cover Image: © iStockphoto.com/Mehmet Ali Cida

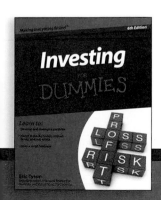
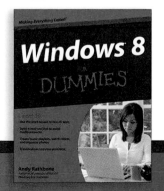

Math & Science

Algebra I For Dummies,
2nd Edition
978-0-470-55964-2

Anatomy and Physiology
For Dummies,
2nd Edition
978-0-470-92326-9

Astronomy For Dummies,
3rd Edition
978-1-118-37697-3

Biology For Dummies,
2nd Edition
978-0-470-59875-7

Chemistry For Dummies,
2nd Edition
978-1-1180-0730-3

Pre-Algebra Essentials
For Dummies
978-0-470-61838-7

Microsoft Office

Excel 2013 For Dummies
978-1-118-51012-4

Office 2013 All-in-One
For Dummies
978-1-118-51636-2

PowerPoint 2013
For Dummies
978-1-118-50253-2

Word 2013 For Dummies
978-1-118-49123-2

Music

Blues Harmonica
For Dummies
978-1-118-25269-7

Guitar For Dummies,
3rd Edition
978-1-118-11554-1

iPod & iTunes
For Dummies,
10th Edition
978-1-118-50864-0

Programming

Android Application
Development For
Dummies, 2nd Edition
978-1-118-38710-8

iOS 6 Application
Development For Dummies
978-1-118-50880-0

Java For Dummies,
5th Edition
978-0-470-37173-2

Religion & Inspiration

The Bible For Dummies
978-0-7645-5296-0

Buddhism For Dummies,
2nd Edition
978-1-118-02379-2

Catholicism For Dummies,
2nd Edition
978-1-118-07778-8

Self-Help & Relationships

Bipolar Disorder
For Dummies,
2nd Edition
978-1-118-33882-7

Meditation For Dummies,
3rd Edition
978-1-118-29144-3

Seniors

Computers For Seniors
For Dummies,
3rd Edition
978-1-118-11553-4

iPad For Seniors
For Dummies,
5th Edition
978-1-118-49708-1

Social Security
For Dummies
978-1-118-20573-0

Smartphones & Tablets

Android Phones
For Dummies
978-1-118-16952-0

Kindle Fire HD
For Dummies
978-1-118-42223-6

NOOK HD For Dummies,
Portable Edition
978-1-118-39498-4

Surface For Dummies
978-1-118-49634-3

Test Prep

ACT For Dummies,
5th Edition
978-1-118-01259-8

ASVAB For Dummies,
3rd Edition
978-0-470-63760-9

GRE For Dummies,
7th Edition
978-0-470-88921-3

Officer Candidate Tests,
For Dummies
978-0-470-59876-4

Physician's Assistant Exa
For Dummies
978-1-118-11556-5

Series 7 Exam
For Dummies
978-0-470-09932-2

Windows 8

Windows 8 For Dummies
978-1-118-13461-0

Windows 8 For Dummies,
Book + DVD Bundle
978-1-118-27167-4

Windows 8 All-in-One
For Dummies
978-1-118-11920-4

Available in print and e-book formats.

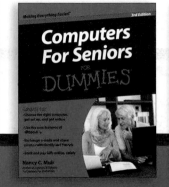
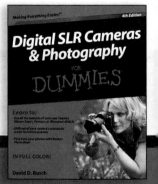

Take Dummies with you everywhere you go!

Whether you're excited about e-books, want more from the web, must have your mobile apps, or swept up in social media, Dummies makes everything easier .

Dummies products make life easier

- DIY
- Consumer Electronics
- Crafts
- Software
- Cookware
- Hobbies
- Videos
- Music
- Games
- and More!

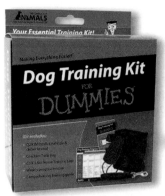

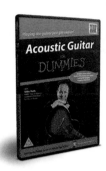

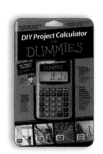

For more information, go to **Dummies.com**® and search the store by category.

DUMMIE

A Wiley Bra

End-User License Agreement

READ THIS. You should carefully read these terms and conditions before opening the software packet(s) included with this book "Book". This is a license agreement "Agreement" between you and John Wiley & Sons, Inc. "WILEY". By opening the accompanying software packet(s), you acknowledge that you have read and accept the following terms and conditions. If you do not agree and do not want to be bound by such terms and conditions, promptly return the Book and the unopened software packet(s) to the place you obtained them for a full refund.

1. **License Grant.** WILEY grants to you (either an individual or entity) a non-exclusive license to use one copy of the enclosed software program(s) (collectively, the "Software") solely for your own personal or business purposes on a single computer (whether a standard computer or a workstation component of a multl-user network). The Software is in use on a computer when it is loaded into temporary memory (RAM) or installed into permanent memory (hard disk, CD-ROM, or other storage device). WILEY reserves all rights not expressly granted herein.

2. **Ownership.** WILEY is the owner of all right, title, and interest, including copyright, in and to the compilation of the Software recorded on the physical packet included with this Book "Software Media". Copyright to the individual programs recorded on the Software Media is owned by the author or other authorized copyright owner of each program. Ownership of the Software and all proprietary rights relating thereto remain with WILEY and its licensers.

3. **Restrictions on Use and Transfer.**

   (a) You may only (i) make one copy of the Software for backup or archival purposes, or (ii) transfer the Software to a single hard disk, provided that you keep the original for backup or archival purposes. You may not (i) rent or lease the Software, (ii) copy or reproduce the Software through a LAN or other network system or through any computer subscriber system or bulletin-board system, or (iii) modify, adapt, or create derivative works based on the Software.

   (b) You may not reverse engineer, decompile, or disassemble the Software. You may transfer the Software and user documentation on a permanent basis, provided that the transferee agrees to accept the terms and conditions of this Agreement and you retain no copies. If the Software is an update or has been updated, any transfer must include the most recent update and all prior versions.

4. **Restrictions on Use of Individual Programs.** You must follow the individual requirements and restrictions detailed for each individual program in the "About the CD" appendix of this Book or on the Software Media. These

limitations are also contained in the individual license agreements recorded on the Software Media. These limitations may include a requirement that after using the program for a specified period of time, the user must pay a registration fee or discontinue use. By opening the Software packet(s), you agree to abide by the licenses and restrictions for these individual programs that are detailed in the "About the CD" appendix and/or on the Software Media. None of the material on this Software Media or listed in this Book may ever be redistributed, in original or modified form, for commercial purposes.

5. **Limited Warranty.**

   (a) WILEY warrants that the Software Media is free from defects in materials and workmanship under normal use for a period of sixty (60) days from the date of purchase of this Book. If WILEY receives notification within the warranty period of defects in materials or workmanship, WILEY will replace the defective Software Media.

   (b) WILEY AND THE AUTHOR(S) OF THE BOOK DISCLAIM ALL OTHER WARRANTIES, EXPRESS OR IMPLIED, INCLUDING WITHOUT LIMITATION IMPLIED WARRANTIES OF MERCHANTABILITY AND FITNESS FOR A PARTICULAR PURPOSE, WITH RESPECT TO THE SOFTWARE, THE PROGRAMS, THE SOURCE CODE CONTAINED THEREIN, AND/OR THE TECHNIQUES DESCRIBED IN THIS BOOK. WILEY DOES NOT WARRANT THAT THE FUNCTIONS CONTAINED IN THE SOFTWARE WILL MEET YOUR REQUIREMENTS OR THAT THE OPERATION OF THE SOFTWARE WILL BE ERROR FREE.

   (c) This limited warranty gives you specific legal rights, and you may have other rights that vary from jurisdiction to jurisdiction.

6. **Remedies.**

   (a) WILEY's entire liability and your exclusive remedy for defects in materials and workmanship shall be limited to replacement of the Software Media, which may be returned to WILEY with a copy of your receipt at the following address: Software Media Fulfillment Department, Attn.: Microsoft Excel 2013 eLearning Kit For Dummies, John Wiley & Sons, Inc., 10475 Crosspoint Blvd., Indianapolis, IN 46256, or call 1-800-762-2974. Please allow four to six weeks for delivery. This Limited Warranty is void if failure of the Software Media has resulted from accident, abuse, or misapplication. Any replacement Software Media will be warranted for the remainder of the original warranty period or thirty (30) days, whichever is longer.

   (b) In no event shall WILEY or the author be liable for any damages whatsoever (including without limitation damages for loss of business profits, business interruption, loss of business information, or any other pecuniary loss) arising from the use of or inability to use the Book or the Software, even if WILEY has been advised of the possibility of such damages.

(c) Because some jurisdictions do not allow the exclusion or limitation of liability for consequential or incidental damages, the above limitation or exclusion may not apply to you.

7. **U.S. Government Restricted Rights.** Use, duplication, or disclosure of the Software for or on behalf of the United States of America, its agencies and/or instrumentalities "U.S. Government" is subject to restrictions as stated in paragraph (c)(1)(ii) of the Rights in Technical Data and Computer Software clause of DFARS 252.227-7013, or subparagraphs (c) (1) and (2) of the Commercial Computer Software - Restricted Rights clause at FAR 52.227-19, and in similar clauses in the NASA FAR supplement, as applicable.

8. **General.** This Agreement constitutes the entire understanding of the parties and revokes and supersedes all prior agreements, oral or written, between them and may not be modified or amended except in a writing signed by both parties hereto that specifically refers to this Agreement. This Agreement shall take precedence over any other documents that may be in conflict herewith. If any one or more provisions contained in this Agreement are held by any court or tribunal to be invalid, illegal, or otherwise unenforceable, each and every other provision shall remain in full force and effect.